Relationship Marketing for Competitive Advantage

The Marketing Series is one of the most comprehensive collections of books in marketing and sales available from the UK today.

Published by Butterworth-Heinemann on behalf of The Chartered Institute of Marketing, the series is divided into three distinct groups: *Student* (fulfilling the needs of those taking the Institute's certificate and diploma qualifications); *Professional Development* (for those on formal or self-study vocational training programmes); and *Practitioner* (presented in a more informal, motivating and highly practical manner for the busy marketer).

Formed in 1911, The Chartered Institute of Marketing is now the largest professional marketing management body in Europe with over 60,000 members located worldwide. Its primary objectives are focused on the development of awareness and understanding of marketing throughout UK industry and commerce and in the raising of standards of professionalism in the education, training and practice of this key business discipline.

Books in the series

Relationship Marketing for Competitive Advantage

Winning and keeping customers

Adrian Payne
Martin Christopher
Moira Clark
Helen Peck

Published on behalf of
The Chartered Institute of Marketing

Butterworth-Heinemann
Linacre House, Jordan Hill, Oxford OX2 8DP
A division of Reed Educational and Professional Publishing Ltd

-ℛ A member of the Reed Elsevier plc group

OXFORD   BOSTON   JOHANNESBURG
MELBOURNE   NEW DELHI   SINGAPORE

First published 1995
Reprinted 1996, 1997

British Library Cataloguing in Publication Data
A catalogue record for this book is available from the British Library

ISBN 0 7506 2020 X

Composition by Genesis Typesetting, Laser Quay, Rochester, Kent
Printed and bound in Great Britain by
Hartnolls Limited, Bodmin, Cornwall

Contents

Levitt T. (1983). After the sale is over . . . *Harvard Business Review*, September/October, 87–93

Bund Jackson, B. (1985). Build customer relationships that last, *Harvard Business Review*, November/December, 120–128.

Campbell, N.C.G. (1990). An Interaction approach to organizational buying behaviour. In Ford, D (ed.), *Understanding Business Markets; Interaction, Relationships and Networks*, Academic Press, originally published in *Journal of Business Research*, **13**, 35–48 (1985).

Berry, L.L. (1983). Relationship marketing. In Berry, L.L., Shostack, G.L. and Upah, G.D. (eds), *Emerging Perspectives on Services Marketing*, American Marketing Association, Chicago, pp. 25–28.

Berry, L.L. and Gresham, L.G. (1986), Relationship retailing: transforming customers into clients, *Business Horizons*, November/December, 43–47.

Grönroos, C. (1990). Relationship approach to marketing in service contexts: the marketing and organizational behaviour interface. *Journal of Business Research*, **20**, 3–11.

Schneider, B. (1980). The service organization: climate is crucial. *Organizational Dynamics*, Autumn, 52–65

Ogbonna, E. and Wilkinson, B. (1990). Corporate strategy and corporate culture: the view from the checkout, *Personnel Review*, **19**, (4), 9–15

Gummesson, E. (1987). Using internal marketing to develop a new culture – the case of Ericsson Quality. *The Journal of Business and Industrial Marketing*, **2**, (3), Summer, 23–28

Introduction

There is a tendency when new ideas in management emerge to embrace them keenly for a while and to see them as the ultimate solution to whatever problems we currently perceive to exist. Equally, there is a tendency to put them aside after the initial novelty has worn off, and they are found to be not quite the panacea that we once thought. Marketing particularly has been prone to this 'flavour of the month' syndrome. The Experience Curve, the Boston Matrix, the Directional Policy Matrix, all useful tools in themselves, are recent examples of ideas that achieved widespread coverage and brief acclaim, only to be quietly dropped by many of their advocates shortly afterwards.

Already, there are some who would claim that 'relationship marketing' is another of these short-lifecycle management phenomena. Indeed, there is always a danger that when something is presented as new and different, it will be oversold and thus be rejected when it fails to deliver everything that was promised.

Relationship marketing, as it is presented here, is not in itself a new concept, rather it is a refocusing of traditional marketing with a greater emphasis being placed upon the creation of 'customer value'. Customer value is the summation of all the positive effects that a supplier has upon the customer's business or, in the case of end users, their personal satisfaction. Creating or enhancing customer value clearly requires a detailed understanding of the customer's value chain and, in particular, whereabouts in that chain the opportunities for value enhancement lie.

The fundamental principle upon which relationship marketing is founded is that the greater the level of customer satisfaction with the *relationship* – not just the product or service – then the greater the likelihood that the customer will stay with us. The importance of retaining customers is that there is strong evidence that customer retention and profitability are directly related. It seems that the longer the customer stays with us, the higher the likelihood that they will place a greater amount of business with us, even to the extent of single sourcing. Further, there is a likelihood that these retained customers will cost less to service and that they will be less likely to be motivated solely by price.

At the heart of the relationship approach to marketing is the integration, company-wide, of hitherto separate customer service and total quality initiatives with the mainstream of marketing strategy. Conventionally, customer service and quality have both been managed separately from marketing. In the relationship marketing paradigm they are intertwined and managed as one. The logic behind this is that it is upon service and quality that relationships are built.

Some of the most significant contrasts between the traditional approach to marketing – which we term the 'transactional' approach – and the emerging concept of relationship marketing are presented in Table 1.

Table 1 *The shift to relationship marketing*

Transactional focus	*Relationship focus*
● Orientation to single sales	● Orientation to customer retention
● Discontinuous customer contact	● Continuous customer contact
● Focus on product features	● Focus on customer value
● Short time scale	● Long time scale
● Little emphasis on customer service	● High customer service emphasis
● Limited commitment to meeting customer expectations	● High commitment to meeting customer expectations
● Quality is the concern of production staff	● Quality is the concern of all staff

Relationship building, by definition, is a long-term process. To develop this notion, we have taken the long-established concept of the 'ladder of loyalty' and added a few rungs to create the 'relationship ladder' (see Figure 1). The idea behind the relationship ladder is that there are a number of identifiable stages in the development of a long-term customer relationship.

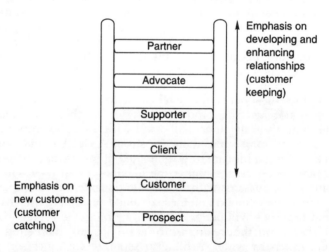

Figure 1 *The relationship marketing ladder of customer loyalty*

At the foot of the ladder is the 'prospect', in other words the target market. Classical marketing has tended to focus on the means by which that individual or organization might be converted into a 'customer'. However, in the relationship marketing model a customer is someone who has only done business with us once or occasionally. The step beyond this is the 'client'. A client is someone who will do business with us on a repeat basis, but may be neutral or even negative about our company. Banks, for example, have clients but those clients might have less than positive views, but stay with the bank out of inertia rather than loyalty.

It is only when we can convert a client into a 'supporter' that the strength of the relationship becomes apparent. These people like being associated with us and they may even be persuaded to become 'advocates' – in other words to actively recommend us to others. The final step on the ladder is where the customer is now a partner and together we seek to identify further ways in which mutual advantage can be gained from the relationship.

In this model, the emphasis in relationship marketing is upon finding appropriate means to move customers up the ladder and to keep them there. Conventional marketing, on the other hand, has tended to focus more upon the winning of customers and building market share without any significant attempt to develop strategies for customer retention.

One further significant difference between the transactional approach to marketing strategy and the relationship model is the wider view of the market that it adopts. Rather than simply focusing on the end user we have suggested that a wider view of 'markets' is appropriate. The idea is that in order to build and sustain real customer value it is important to recognize that relationships must be built with a number of important constituencies. We call this the 'Six Markets' model. These six markets are:

- Internal markets
- Referral markets
- Influence markets
- Employee markets
- Supplier markets
- Customer markets

Internal markets are the individuals and groups within the organization who by their actions and beliefs determine the style and ethos of the business. It is now widely recognized that developing shared values in support of a customer-oriented corporate culture is a critical requirement for sustained success in the marketplace.

Referral markets can be an effective source of new business. Referrals can come from sources of professional advice such as doctors, lawyers, bank managers and accountants as well as from existing satisfied customers. Building relationships with these sources of word-of-mouth recommendation should be an integral part of marketing strategy.

Influence markets comprise entities, organizations and individuals which have the ability positively or negatively to influence the marketing environment within which the company competes. Thus, public relations or public affairs management needs to become an integral part of the relationship marketing process. Successful companies tend to have good relationships with critical sources of influences relevant to their markets.

Employee markets form a focal point for relationship marketing because of the critical need to recruit and retain employees who will further the aims of the company in the marketplace. The aim should be to make the company into an organization that is attractive to people who share the values the company espouses.

Supplier markets, as the name suggests, refer to the network of organizations that provide the materials, products and services to which the marketing company adds further customer value. Surprisingly, it is only recently that many companies have come to recognize the importance of building closer, mutually beneficial relationships with suppliers. Those companies that have done so have found that they have gained significant advantage through such benefits as improved quality, faster time-to-market, more innovative products and lower levels of inventory.

Customer markets represent all the people or organizations that buy goods or services from us. They can be either end users/consumers or intermediaries. A particularly powerful element in the relationship marketing mix as far as this market is concerned is customer service. Indeed, in more and more markets today, customer service provides the only effective means of differentiating the offer from that of competitors.

This book of linked readings has been designed to reinforce the themes that were first developed in *Relationship Marketing* by Christopher, Payne and Ballantyne.[1] The underpinning concept of that book was that marketing, quality and service are not separate elements of strategy but need to be brought together and integrated with the objective of strengthening customer relationships.

Inevitably, in choosing readings to include in a collection such as this there will be a tendency to select contributions that support the views of the editors. Nevertheless, we have tried to include as many of the seminal works in this still underdeveloped area as possible. Thus the reader will find some of the early ground-breaking papers by Berry, Gummesson and Grönroos as well as more recent contributions by Reichheld and Schlesinger and Heskett.

It is only a little over ten years since the first pioneering papers on the topic were published and it is remarkable to note how quickly the principles of relationship marketing have gained acceptance. The twenty-one readings contained within this collection provide, we believe, a solid basis for the further development of relationship marketing as a discipline and as a practical orientation.

Reference

1 Christopher, M., Payne, A. and Ballantyne, D. (1991). *Relationship Marketing*, Butterworth-Heinemann, Oxford.

PART ONE
The Development of
Relationship Marketing

1 RELATIONSHIP MARKETING – KEY CONCEPTS

Introduction

In recent years the traditional approach to marketing has been increasingly questioned. A new perspective is now emerging which recognizes that marketing has two key concerns. The first concern is still the management of the classic marketing mix as a conventional, functional responsibility. The second concern is much broader and company-wide in its scope with a goal of developing a cross-functional, coordinated focus on customers – in other words, to reorient the entire business to face the market. It is probably true to say that most emphasis in the past has been placed upon the first concern with only limited attention being paid to the latter.

Limitations of the traditional marketing paradigm

There is now a growing body of literature which casts doubt on the relevance of traditional marketing theory, especially when applied to international, industrial and services marketing.[1–3] A major concern is that the traditional paradigm – based on the marketing mix, and the concept of exchange[4–6] – was developed using assumptions derived from experiences drawn from the huge US market for consumer goods. Critics point out that this short-term transactional focus is inappropriate for industrial and services marketing, where establishing longer-term relationships with customers is critical to organizational success.[7,8] The concept has also been found wanting when applied to international marketing, as it makes no provision for the fact that trade barriers and politics may deny access to the market altogether.[2] Other writers are more inclined to point to widespread difficulties with implementation as grounds for questioning the validity of the concept.[9]

The relationship marketing paradigm

In response to these criticisms of the marketing concept, Grönroos[10] formulated a relationship-focused definition of marketing: 'The purpose of marketing is to establish, maintain, enhance and commercialise customer relationships (often, but not necessarily always, long term relationships) so that the objectives of the parties involved are met. This is done by the mutual exchange and fulfilment of promises.' The relationship marketing paradigm builds on the concept of relationship marketing as first introduced by Berry[11] but discussed by many others[12-19] when describing a longer-term approach to marketing. Our own view of relationship marketing extends from the work of Christopher, Payne and Ballantyne[16] who suggest a theory of relationship marketing based on a broader perspective than earlier contributions. The key elements of this view are:

● The emphasis in the interaction between suppliers and customers is shifting from a transaction to a relationship focus.
● The relationship marketing approach focuses on maximizing the lifetime value of desirable customers and customer segments.
● Relationship marketing strategies are concerned with the development and enhancement of relationships with a number of key 'markets'. It is concerned with the 'internal' market within the organization as well as building substantial external relationships with customers, suppliers, referral sources, influence markets and recruitment markets.
● Quality, customer service and marketing are closely related. However, frequently they are managed separately. A relationship marketing approach brings these elements into a much closer coherence.

The relationship marketing concept suggests that instead of the narrow, transactional, one-sale-at-a-time view of marketing, marketing should emphasize relationships between the organization and its markets more strongly. However, it is not just the transaction-orientation of the traditional marketing paradigm which hampers the development of customer relationships. In many instances the structure of the organization itself can also limit its ability to satisfy customers.

Structural weaknesses in conventional organizations

Traditional vertical organizations which are hierarchically structured and functionally orientated often optimize individual functions at the expense of the whole business and the customer. The core problem is the lack of coordination across functions, departments and tasks. This functional approach often means that while problems manifest themselves in one part of the organization, their root cause may remain unattended elsewhere. This results in low levels of corporate performance and even lower levels of customer satisfaction, as customers are passed from one functionally focused department to the next, in the quest for a solution to their problems. Unfortunately, performance measurement systems often exacerbate these problems and lead to even further functional emphasis as shown in Figure 1.1.

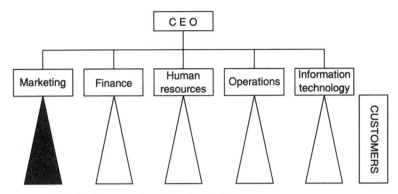

Figure 1.1 *Marketing as a functional activity*

Increasing competition and fast-changing markets have meant that flexibility and coordination within organizations have become as important as functional performance. Companies need to achieve excellence in quality, service levels, cycle times and other performance measures. These challenges require managers to rethink the way companies interact with their suppliers, channels and customers. Hence an approach that organizes the flow of work around company-wide processes that ultimately link with customer needs is necessary. In market-facing organizations, key players are drawn together in multi-disciplinary teams or groups that seek to marshal resources to achieve market-based objectives. The functions will still exist, but they are now seen as 'pools of resources' from which the market-facing teams draw expertise. According to Ostroff and Smith[20] 'there is real performance leverage in moving toward a flatter, more horizontal mode of organization, in which cross functional, end-to-end work flows link internal processes with the needs and capabilities of both suppliers and customers'. This market-facing focus is illustrated in Figure 1.2.

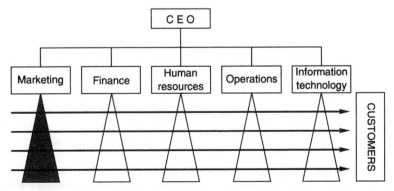

Figure 1.2 *Marketing as a cross-functional activity*

The relationship chain

The notion of the relationship chain builds upon the ideas of Gluck[21] and Porter[22] who recognized the importance of business processes as a sequence of events whereby value is created and costs incurred. This simple idea has many implications, not the least for pointing the ways in which added-value could be enhanced at less cost through process re-engineering. There is now a widely held view that marketing should be viewed as a business-wide process – a process that has the goal of creating superior *customer-value*. To achieve this goal will often require the integration of elements that were previously dispersed across different functions of the business. These elements include research and development, value engineering, in-bound logistics, order fulfilment and customer service (including after-sales service). The successful management of these interrelated processes requires a fundamentally different approach to their planning and execution. It is through the continuing delivery of superior customer value that enduring customer relationships are built.

To maximize customer value at the least cost to the business will frequently require a rearrangement of the sequence in which tasks are performed. In some cases these tasks will be eliminated or combined with other tasks, or performed in parallel. The basis for this re-engineered sequence of events is what we term the *relationship chain*. It is so described because it begins with the basic proposition that the purpose of all business processes is to create and sustain mutually advantageous relationships *throughout the chain*, culminating in enhanced customer value. Under this scheme of things it is just as important, for example, to have strong supplier relationships as it is to have strong relationships with customers.

To construct an effective relationship chain within the organization will require a focus upon a number of critical issues which have a logical sequence (Figure 1.3):

1 Defining the value proposition
2 Identifying appropriate customer value segments
3 Designing value delivery systems
4 Managing and maintaining delivered satisfaction

Defining the value proposition

Value, in the sense most widely used in marketing, is customer-specific and essentially subjective to the customer. At its most fundamental it represents the perceived benefits that customers believe they receive from ownership or consumption of a product or service. The perceived value of an offer can be translated into the maximum price (in total life cost terms) that a customer will pay. Customer value can best be defined in terms of the impact that the supplier's offer has on the customer's own value chain. If the offer delivers enhanced performance, increased

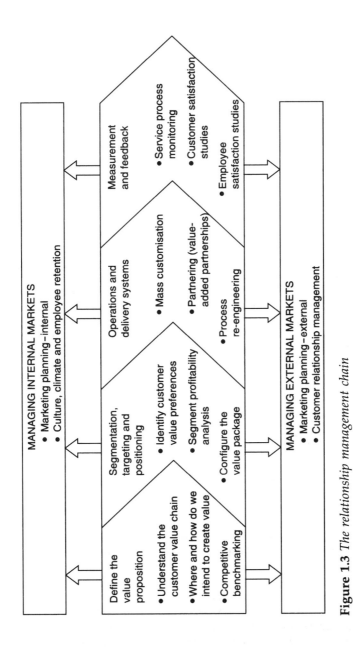

MANAGING INTERNAL MARKETS
- Marketing planning–internal
- Culture, climate and employee retention

Define the value proposition
- Understand the customer value chain
- Where and how do we intend to create value
- Competitive benchmarking

Segmentation, targeting and positioning
- Identify customer value preferences
- Segment profitability analysis
- Configure the value package

Operations and delivery systems
- Mass customisation
- Partnering (value-added partnerships)
- Process re-engineering

Measurement and feedback
- Service process monitoring
- Customer satisfaction studies
- Employee satisfaction studies

MANAGING EXTERNAL MARKETS
- Marketing planning–external
- Customer relationship management

Figure 1.3 *The relationship management chain*

perceived benefits or lower customer costs, then there is a clear added-value from the customer's perspective.

The starting point therefore of any relationship marketing programme should be the clear definition and specification of the precise nature of the value to be delivered, market segment by market segment – or even customer by customer. This we term the value proposition.

Identifying appropriate customer value segments

Because customer value requirements and perceptions will differ between customers, this provides the marketer with a powerful means of market segmentation. In-depth customer research will help reveal the salient dimensions of value and through the use of techniques such as 'trade-off analysis'[23] we can identify groups of customers who share common value preferences. In other words, markets can be segmented on the basis of groupings of customers sharing common value preferences. It is quite possible that the resulting segments might cut across the more traditional bases for segmentation such as demographic or socio-economic variables, but the likelihood is that the construction of marketing strategies based around enhancing relevant customer values are more likely to achieve success.

Quite likely not all identified value segments will be equally attractive to the organization. There will obviously be differences in the profitability of different types of customer and certain types of customer may also display greater or lesser 'promiscuity' in their choice of brands or suppliers. Successful value-based marketing strategies will be focused upon carefully selected segments with highly tailored, 'micromarketing' offers.

Designing value delivery systems

The means by which value is 'delivered' to customers is in itself a potential contributor to relationship building. When we talk of delivery systems we refer not only to the physical delivery of products or the presentation of services but also to the marketing channels employed, the flexibility of response, the linking of buyer/supplier logistics and information systems and so on. In other words, we view the design of the value delivery system as a critical means of engineering stronger linkages between the customer's value chain and our own. Because of the increasing fragmentation of the marketplace in many industries, which has led to a demand by customers for a greater variety in the format of products or services, there is a consequent need to engineer more flexibility into our delivery systems.

Flexibility in this context refers to the organization's ability to tailor products and services to the precise needs of individual customers or segments. It frequently will involve a radical review of conventional wisdom on manufacturing and distribution – for example, focusing upon reducing batch quantities in production and in distribution, moving to a just-in-time delivery environment and delaying the final configuration of the finished product. The phrase 'mass customization' has been coined[24] to signify the philosophy of individualizing the delivered offer while still seeking to achieve cost optimization in the chain.

Focusing on how the business actually delivers customer value will frequently lead to the recognition of the need to re-engineer processes and in some cases, to consider outsourcing certain activities to partners who may be able to enhance the cost-effectiveness of the value delivery process.

Managing and maintaining delivered satisfaction

Because the quality and strength of customer relationships is so critical to the survival and profitability of any business it is essential that the processes that deliver satisfaction, as well as the customers' perceptions of performance, are regularly monitored. In the same way that it is now widely accepted that the quality of physical products is dependent upon the control of the process that manufactures them, so too the quality of customer service is determined by the extent to which the delivery process is under control. Service process monitoring should be continuous and, in particular, all potential 'fail points' should be identified and if they cannot be made fail-safe, should be carefully controlled. Managing the 'moments of truth' makes the difference between customer satisfaction and customer disappointment in any service process.

Employee satisfaction studies as well as customer satisfaction studies should form an integral part of the management of the service delivery process. Many companies already conduct such studies but only on an *ad hoc* basis. Paradoxically, those same companies might monitor brand awareness or attitudes and usage every month, but fail to pay equal attention to such vital performance indicators as employee and customer satisfaction.

Organizationally there is an issue of how the process of delivered satisfaction should be managed. Traditionally, it has been managed as a series of fragmented, functionally based tasks. Under the new model, in which relationship building is seen as a cross-functional process, then it is essential that these previously dispersed activities should be brought together and managed as a unified system.

We suggested earlier that one of the distinguishing features of the relationship marketing paradigm was its concern with the definition of 'markets'. In particular, it was suggested that there are *internal* as well as *external* markets. Internal markets comprise the people who work within the organization and whose attitudes and motivation will have a direct or indirect impact upon customer relationships. External markets include not only the final customer market but also suppliers, referral sources, influencers and the recruitment market.

Figure 1.3 suggests that the management of internal and external markets must parallel the relationship management chain and that they should be managed on an integrative basis, rather than as independent processes. The success of a relationship marketing strategy will ultimately hinge upon the way in which the external and internal marketing programmes are aligned.

Managing external markets

Traditionally, marketing plans have focused upon customers or consumers. They have not generally recognized the importance of, for example, supplier development, recruitment markets, referral sources and 'influencers'. However, each of these 'external' markets can have considerable impact upon our performance in the customer/consumer marketplace.

Supplier development

Working more closely with suppliers as partners, rather than adversaries, typically brings many advantages. Where there is long-term commitment to a supplier, based upon a mutually profitable relationship, the result will often be: enhanced product and service quality and a focus on continuous improvement; a greater likelihood of supplier-driven product and process innovation; lower total costs through supply chain integration and a higher level of responsiveness. Companies like the UK's Rover Group now talk of the 'extended enterprise' in which very close relationships are developed with a much-reduced supplier base – the result of which is greater competitiveness in the marketplace.

Recruitment markets

A number of research studies[25] have highlighted the importance that recruitment practices can have upon company performance. This is particularly important if we seek to develop a certain culture and style within the company. The aim should be to become an organization that attracts the type and calibre of person that matches the profile that the company seeks to sustain in the eyes of the customer. More and more companies are now identifying the psychometric profile of the type of person most likely to be successful in achieving customer-driven goals. Organizations such as Disney and SouthWest Airlines in the USA are examples of companies whose success, in part, is due to the care with which they undertake their recruitment.

Referral sources

The power of word-of-mouth is widely accepted, even if inadequately researched.[26] Satisfied customers can be powerful advocates of a company's products or services and may be encouraged through incentives to recruit further customers for us. Similarly, non-customers may sometimes act as referral sources – for example, a solicitor referring a client to an investment adviser. While the potential importance of referral is widely recognized, it is only rarely formally built into the marketing plan.

There are analogies between the way that referral can work and the diffusion of innovation. Given a high enough level of the number of referral sources, there will exist the possibility of a greatly leveraged response in terms of new customers. Many leading business schools, for example, know that the major source of applications for their MBA programmes are referrals from past graduates.

Influencer markets

There has been a tendency of late to view the management of public relations – or public affairs, as it is sometimes called – as a separate activity from mainstream marketing. Under the relationship marketing paradigm the 'influencer' market is seen as an integral component of the customer relationship-building process.

Influencers come in many forms. Government ministries or agencies, senior civil servants, the media, consultants and advisers, the stock market – the list of potential sources of influence is endless. Every business can benefit, and lose, from the influence that may be exerted from these sources.

A massive industry has grown up worldwide in the management of public relations, public affairs and corporate communications and its impact has been considerable. As a component of a relationship marketing strategy, the management of influencers is of vital importance.

Managing internal markets

The role and importance of internal marketing has only recently gained a wider recognition.[27] While definitions of internal marketing vary, the generally accepted view is that it is concerned with the creation of an internal culture and orientation which assists and supports the organization in the achievement of its goals.

The development and sustenance of a customer-orientated culture within the organization is a critical determinant of long-term success in relationship marketing. It is an organization's culture – its deep-seated, unwritten system of shared values and norms – which has the greatest impact on employees, behaviour and attitudes. The culture of an organization in turn dictates its climate – the policies and practices which characterize the organization and reflect its cultural beliefs.[28]

A study of the retail banking industry in the USA found that customers' perceptions of an organization's climate were linked to customer retention.[29] A later study (also in retail banking) identified a direct relationship between well-designed service encounters, enhanced customer satisfaction and employee satisfaction.[30] A satisfied employee is likely to be a retained employee. Employee retention becomes an important part of the equation when we consider that relationships are built and maintained by individuals, and customers are often more loyal to the employee who deals with them than to the wider organization. Sales-people, hairdressers and professional service workers are notoriously good at taking favoured clients with them when they leave to work for rival businesses.

In most industries the connection between customer retention and employee retention is less obvious. The inadequacies of accounting systems mean that the costs of high employee turnover – such as increased costs of recruitment and training, and the inefficiency of inexperienced workers – are rarely monitored. The impact of high staff turnover on customers' perceptions of service quality, customer satisfaction and retention, are also unlikely to be recognized.

An integrated approach to marketing and human resource management is therefore needed, one that recognizes employees as a valuable and finite resource, and a potential source of competitive advantage. Because – despite the best technology, and the most carefully planned procedures – in the final analysis relationship marketing stands or falls on the quality and willingness of the people who implement it.

The relationship marketing plan

Because of the need to ensure that all the dimensions of both external and internal markets are addressed in an integrated and cohesive way and to achieve a sharper focus on the goal of building long-term customer relationships, we advocate the development of a *relationship marketing plan*. The purpose of this plan is to ensure the highest degree of integration and focus across the six critical markets that form the platform for successful customer relationships. Figure 1.4 summarizes this idea.

Ideally, the relationship marketing plan will begin with a clearly expressed definition of the customer-retention goals of the organization. In other words, what are the target levels of retention across which customer types and what are the profit growth targets that are sought from these customers? These are radically different goals from those more commonly encountered in conventional marketing plans which tend to focus more upon broader, aggregate targets for sales growth and market penetration.

In this revised approach to marketing planning, the objective becomes one of holding on to and developing today's (and tomorrow's) 'Gold Card' customers. These 'Gold Card' customers are, in effect, the 20 per cent of the total customer base who provide 80 per cent of the profit. Understanding who they are, their characterizations and their motivations, is critical to the success of a relationship marketing strategy.

Because the management of relationships in each of the six markets is critical to the achievement of the overall customer-retention objectives, there must be a clear linkage between these objectives and the six market

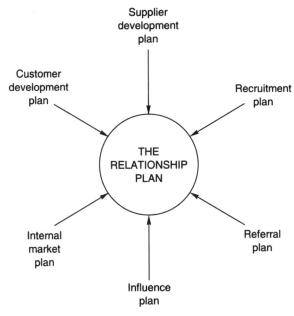

Figure 1.4 *The relationship marketing plan*

plans. Thus in developing, for example, the recruitment plan, the aim should be to articulate a strategy whereby the profile of recruits to the organization is appropriate to the customer needs and characteristics (whether these customers be external or internal). Similarly, in writing the influence plan, a linkage must be established between the stated retention objectives and the various 'publics' whose influence can assist in the achievement of those objectives.

A further distinguishing feature of the relationship marketing plan is that it is cross-functional and process-oriented. What this means is that once the overall customer-retention goals and the subsidiary six market goals have been defined, the next step is to identify the requisite strategies for those processes that must be managed to achieve those goals.

Hence marketing planning under this new paradigm is about establishing 'game plans' for the processes that impact upon the achievement of customer retention goals. This, it must be admitted, is a rather different view of marketing planning from the traditional model more often encountered.

Managing customer relationships

More and more organizations are now seeking to formalize the management of customer relations. Many banks, for example, have appointed 'relationship managers' whose responsibility it is to act as the interface between a corporate client and the various services provided by the bank. Other companies use the concept of 'key account management' in the same way.

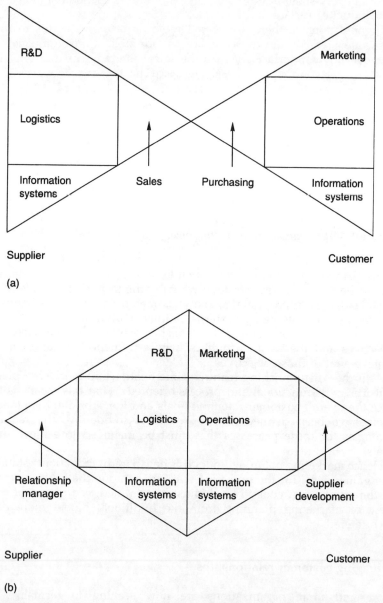

Figure 1.5 *The transition from selling to relationship management*

For this approach to be meaningful and not just cosmetic, it is essential that the relationship manager is given the authority to actually *manage* the relationship. Customer relationship management should be more than progress chasing and customer care. Its primary concern must be to plan and manage the 'moments of truth' or the encounters with customers that occur at every stage from the placement of orders to the final delivery of the product or service and beyond.

Organizationally, there are considerable implications if this relationship management approach is to be adopted. Conventionally, the supplier/buyer interface tends to be fairly limited with the only real contact on a continuous basis being between the salesperson and the person responsible for purchasing within the customer's business. It is an interface where both parties seek to maximize the outcome in their own favour, and rarely results in a 'win – win' outcome. This type of relationship can be represented (see Figure 1.5(a)) as two triangles that only connect at a single point. It is a relationship that is easy for competitors to break because it tends to be one based on cost rather than business development. The alternative approach is that typified by Figure 1.5(b), where there are multiple points of contact between corresponding functions and processes within the selling and the buying companies. The role of the relationship manager is to coordinate those multiple contacts and to seek new ways in which further customer value can be created.

Relationship marketing is emerging as an actionable framework for developing enduring, longer-term (and hence more profitable) relationships with customers. In the few years since the idea was first formulated, it has gained widespread recognition as a concept with considerable potential. The challenge now is to take the theory and convert it into action.

References

1 de Ferrer, R.J. (1986). A case for European management. *International Management Development Review*, **2**, 275–281.
2 Gummesson, E. (1987). The new marketing – developing long-term interactive relationships. *Long Range Planning*, **20**, No. 4, August, 10–20.
3 Grönroos, C. (1990). Marketing redefined. *Management Decision*, **28**, No. 8, 5–9.
4 Borden, N.H. (1965). The concept of the marketing mix, in Schwartz, G. (ed.), *Science in Marketing*, John Wiley, New York, pp. 386–397.
5 Bagozzi, R.P. (1975). Marketing as exchange. *Journal of Marketing*, October, 32–39.
6 Kotler, P. (1984). *Marketing Management*, Prentice Hall, Englewood Cliffs, NJ.
7 Hakansson, H. (ed.) (1982). *International Marketing and Purchasing of Industrial Goods*, John Wiley, New York.

8 Grönroos, C. (1990). The marketing strategy continuum, toward a marketing concept for the 1990s. Meddelanden Fran Svenska Handelshogskolan, Working Paper, 201.

9 Brownlie, B. and Saren, M. (1992). The four Ps of the marketing concept: prescriptive, polemical, permanent and problematical. *European Journal of Marketing*, **26**, No. 4, 34–47.

10 Grönroos, C. (1990). Relationship approach to marketing in service contexts: the marketing and organisational behaviour interface. *Journal of Business Research*, **20**, No. 1, 3–11.

11 Berry, L.L. (1983). Relationship marketing. In Berry, L.L., Shostack, G.L. and Upah, G.D. (eds), *Emerging Perspectives on Services Marketing*, American Marketing Association, Chicago, pp. 25–28.

12 Levitt, T. (1983). After the sale is over, *Harvard Business Review*, September-October, 87–93.

13 Rosenberg, L.J. and Czepiel, J.A. (1984). A marketing approach for customer retention. *The Journal of Consumer Marketing*.

14 Jackson, B. (1985). Build customer relationships that last. *Harvard Business Review*, November-December, 120–128.

15 Crosby, L.A. and Stephens N. (1987). Effects of relationship marketing on satisfaction, retention and prices in the life insurance industry. *Journal of Marketing Research*, **24**, November, 404–11.

16 Christopher, M., Payne, A.F.T. and Ballantyne, D. (1991). *Relationship Marketing*, Butterworth-Heinemann, Oxford.

17 McKenna, R. (1991) *Relationship Marketing*, Century Business. London.

18 Gummesson, E. (1981). Marketing costs concepts in service firms. *Industrial Marketing Management*, No. 3.

19 Grönroos, C. (1978). A service-orientated approach to marketing of services. *European Journal of Marketing*, **12**, 588–601.

20 Ostroff, F. and Smith, D. (1992). The horizontal organisation. *McKinsey Quarterly*, Winter, 148–167.

21 Gluck, F.W. (1980). Strategic choice and resource allocation. *The McKinsey Quarterly*, Winter, 22–23.

22 Porter, M. (1985). *Competitive Advantage: Creating and Sustaining Superior Performance*, Free Press, New York.

23 Christopher, M.G. (1992). *The Customer Service Planner*, Butterworth-Heinemann, Oxford.

24 Pine, B.J. (1993). *Mass Customization: The New Frontier in Business Competition*, Harvard Business School Press, Harvard, MA.

25 Schlesinger, L.A. and Heskett, J.L. (1991). Breaking the cycle of failure in service. *Sloan Management Review*, **32**, No. 3, Spring, 17–28.

26 Reingen, P.H. and Kernan, J.B. (1986). Analysis of referral networks in marketing methods and illustration. *Journal of Marketing Research*, November, 370–378.

27 Collins, B. and Payne, A. (1991). Internal services marketing. *European Management Journal*, **9**, No. 3, September, 216–270.

28 Webster, C. (1990). Towards the measurement of the marketing culture of a service firm. *Journal of Business Research*, **21**, 345–362.

29 Schneider, B. (1973). The perception of organisational culture: the customer's view. *Journal of Applied Psychology,* **57**, No. 3, 248–256.
30 Schneider, B. and Bowen, D. (1991). New services design, development and implementation and the employee. In George, W.R. and Marshall, C.E., (eds), *Developing New Services*, American Marketing Association, Chicago, pp. 82–101.

2 RELATIONSHIP MARKETING – INDUSTRIAL PERSPECTIVES

In the 1990s, relationship marketing has become a topic of central importance within many companies. While organizations from virtually all sectors are now embracing relationship marketing, it is probably within the service sector where it has received the greatest attention. However, relationship marketing has been practised for many years by leading industrial companies and it is in industrial markets that the subject has its origins. In the section that follows, we include three articles which emphasize industrial aspects of relationship marketing. These three articles – by Levitt, Jackson and Campbell – reflect the development of relationship marketing, in an industrial context, over the past decade.

The readings in this chapter illustrate two different perspectives of industrial relationship marketing. The first two articles emphasize the need to understand different types of relationships and the extent to which relationship or transaction-oriented approaches are appropriate. These articles by Theodore Levitt and Barbara Bund Jackson have influenced many in their thinking. The tradition of relationships in industrial marketing has been furthered by many academics within the USA, including the case study-oriented approach of Thomas Bonoma at Harvard and the work of David Wilson[1] at the Institute for the Study of Business Markets at the Pennsylvania State University, to mention but two.

Theodore Levitt's article points out how the real value of a relationship between customer and supplier is added *after* the sale is made. He argues that the seller's focus needs to move from closing a sale to delivering a high level of customer satisfaction over the lifetime of the relationship.

His article draws attention to the need to understand what the customer is buying – an augmented product – and it is this which the customer values. He emphasizes how misplaced the notion is that the salesperson needs charisma because it is the charisma of the salesperson, rather than the quality of the product, which makes the sale. In many ways this article marks the start of an increased recognition that being 'a good salesperson' is not sufficient and that the development of an on-going relationship represents one of the company's most important assets.

Barbara Bund Jackson's work is among the earliest that characterizes 'relationship marketing' and 'transaction marketing' and the distinction between them.[2] Drawing on examples of different industrial buying situations, including computer systems and shipping services, Jackson emphasizes the alternative approaches that are needed in different buying situations. She introduces a spectrum of buyer behaviours based on what she calls 'always-a-share' which assumes a customer can easily switch all or part of its business from one supplier to another, and 'lost-for-good' which emphasizes a customer highly committed to one vendor. The implications for both ends of this spectrum are discussed as well as the role the sellers can play, in part, by undertaking action to position themselves at a given point of this spectrum.

This article contains a good discussion of switching costs and how seller-induced changes can result in a more favourable positioning. She concludes by emphasizing how different situations require different degrees of closeness and that marketers should seek to clarify how close a relationship is feasible.

The third article draws upon the IMP Group's work within Europe. The IMP (Industrial Marketing and Purchasing or International Marketing and Purchasing – depending on the audience) group of researchers have become well known in Europe for their research on industrial markets. The IMP body of work shares a strong qualitatively-driven approach which Ford[3] has described as much more about listening to managers and developing ideas rather than assembling a large amount of quantitative analysis. The IMP Group, originally consisting of some twelve researchers from France, Germany, Italy, Sweden and the United Kingdom, undertook research which led to a considerable contribution to the literature on industrial marketing. Those unfamiliar with and interested in this research should see Turnbull and Cunningham,[4] Håkansson,[5] Ford[3] and Axelsson and Eastern.[6]

Given the vast amount of material that has been written by members of the IMP Group, a choice of one representative article is clearly impossible. Nigel Campbell's article entitled 'An interaction approach to organisational buyer behaviour' is based on an intensive two-year research study which builds on earlier research carried out by the IMP Group. In contrast to the original IMP research project which focused on fifteen different industries within five countries, this study examines 167 product relationships in one specific industry, the packaging industry, thus keeping the product technology variable in the relationship constant. This article is chosen as it places an emphasis on the managerial implications of relationships, from a perspective of both marketing and purchasing managers, and provides some clear guidelines for marketing strategies in different contexts.

The IMP approach is particularly worth noting as, unlike some of the better-known and more dominant models of buyer behaviour emphasized in the USA, it places equal emphasis on both buyer and seller characteristics. This is in contrast to other models which tend to concentrate on the buyer's side of the transaction. Campbell's work goes beyond the earlier work of the IMP, by introducing the concept of interaction strategies, whose interplay affects both the interaction mechanism, as well as the interaction atmosphere, in a two-way relationship.

These three articles help us to understand the development of relationship marketing from an industrial perspective. Undoubtedly much of the thinking in relationship marketing in services industries, discussed in the next chapter, is derived from insights gained in industrial markets. These three contributions characterize both the 'industrial relationship marketing' movement at Harvard Business School in the 1980s and the 'network-interaction' approach developed in Europe by the IMP Group over the same period. They capture the essence of relationships, the importance of understanding both the buyer and the seller perspectives and the need to develop appropriate managerial actions according to the specific circumstances of the relationship.

References

1 Wilson, D. (1993). Commentary on 'The Markets-as-Networks Tradition in Sweden'. In Laurent, G., Liliea, G.L. and Pras, B. (eds), *Research Traditions in Marketing*, Kluwer Publishers, New York.
2 Jackson, B.B. (1985). *Winning and Keeping Industrial Customers: The Dynamics of Customer Relationships*, D.C. Heath, Lexington, MA.
3 Ford, D. (ed.) (1990). *Understanding Business Markets: Interaction, Relationships, Networks*, Academic Press, New York.
4 Turnbull, P.W. and Cunningham, M.T. (1981). *International Marketing and Purchasing*, Macmillan, London.
5 Håkansson, H. (ed.) (1982). *International Marketing and Purchasing of Industrial Goods*, John Wiley, New York.
6 Axelsson, B. and Easton, G. (1992). *Industrial Networks; A New View of Reality*, Routledge, London.

AFTER THE SALE IS OVER
Theodore Levitt

Theodore Levitt is one of the best-known authors in marketing. He is the Edward W. Carter Professor of Business Administration, Emeritus, at the Harvard Business School. He is a former editor of the *Harvard Business Review*.

This article is a landmark piece in the area of relationship marketing. In the article, Levitt points out the shift in the dynamics of the sales process and how it is changing as the economy becomes more service and technology oriented, and how, as a consequence, the emphasis needs to shift from making sales to ensuring on-going satisfaction after the sale. Levitt's practical advice is 'peppered' with practical examples from organizations using this approach. The article concludes by identifying four specific requirements managers need to adopt to manage customer relationships effectively.

The relationship between a seller and a buyer seldom ends when a sale is made. Increasingly, the relationship intensifies after the sale and helps determine the buyer's choice the next time around. Such dynamics are found particularly with services and products dealt in a stream of transactions between seller and buyer – financial services, consulting, general contracting, military and space equipment, and capital goods.

The sale, then, merely consummates the courtship, at which point the marriage begins. How good the marriage is depends on how well the seller manages the relationship. The quality of the marriage determines whether there will be continued or expanded business, or troubles and divorce. In some cases divorce is impossible, as when a major construction or installation project is underway. If the marriage that remains is burdened, it tarnishes the seller's reputation.

Companies can avoid such troubles by recognizing at the outset the necessity of managing their relationships with customers. This takes special attention to an often ignored aspect of relationships: time.

The theory of supply and demand presumes that the work of the economic system is time-discrete and bare of human interaction – that an instantaneous, disembodied sales transaction clears the market at the intersection of supply and demand. This was never completely accurate and has become less so as product complexity and interdependencies have intensified. Buyers of automated machinery do not, like buyers at a flea market, walk home with their purchases and take their chances. They expect installation services, application aids, parts, postpurchase repair and maintenance, retrofitted enhancements, and vendor R&D to keep the products effective and up to date for as long as possible and to help the company stay competitive.

The buyer of a continuous stream of transactions, like a frozen-food manufacturer that buys its cartons from a packaging company and its cash-management services from a bank, is concerned not only with completing transactions but also with maintaining the process. Due to the growing complexity of military equipment, even the Department of Defense makes most of its purchases in units of less than a hundred and therefore has to repeat transactions often.

Because the purchase cycles of products and major components are increasingly stretched, the needs that must be tended to have changed. Consider the purchase cycles and the changing assurances backing purchases (see Table 1). Under these conditions, a purchase decision is not a decision to buy an item (to have a casual affair) but a decision to enter a bonded relationship (to get married). This requires of the would-be seller a new orientation and a new strategy.

Selling by itself is no longer enough. Consider the compelling differences between the old and the new selling arrangements in Table 2. In the selling scheme the seller is located at a distance from buyers and reaches out with a sales department to unload products on them. This is the basis for the notion that a salesperson needs charisma, because it is charisma rather than the product's qualities that makes the sale.

Table 1 *Purchase cycles and assurances*

Item	Purchase cycle in years	
Oil field installation	15 to 20	
Chemical plant	10 to 15	
EDP system	5 to 10	
Weapons system	20 to 30	
Major components of steel plant	5 to 10	
Paper supply contract	5	
Item	*Previous assurance*	*Present assurance*
Tankers	Spot	Charter
Apartments	Rental	Cooperative
Auto warranties	10,000 miles	10,000 miles
Technology	Buy	Lease
Labor	Hire	Contracts
Supplies	Shopping	Contracting
Equipment	Repair	Maintenance

Table 2 *The change from selling to marketing*

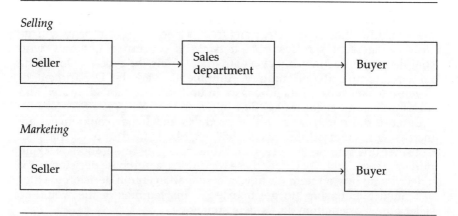

Consider, by contrast, marketing. Here the seller, being physically close to buyers, penetrates their domain to learn about their needs, desires, and fears and then designs and supplies the product with those considerations in mind. Instead of trying to get buyers to want what the seller has, the seller tries to have what they want. The 'product' is no longer merely an item but a whole bundle of values that satisfy buyers – an 'augmented' product.*

Thanks to increasing interdependence, more and more of the world's economic work gets done through long-term relationships between sellers and buyers. It is not a matter of just getting and then holding on to customers. It is more a matter of giving the buyers what they want. Buyers want vendors who keep promises, who'll keep supplying and standing behind what they promised. The era of the one-night stand is gone. Marriage is both necessary and more convenient. Products are too complicated, repeat negotiations too much of a hassle and too costly. Under these conditions, success in marketing is transformed into the inescapability of a relationship. Interface becomes interdependence.

Under these circumstances, being a good marketer in the conventional sense is not enough. When it takes five years of intensive work between seller and buyer to 'deliver' an operating chemical plant or a telecommunications system, much more is required than the kind of marketing that simply lands the contract. The buyer needs assurance at the outset that the two parties can work well together during the long period in which the purchase gets transformed into delivery.

The seller and the buyer have different capital structures, competitive conditions, costs, and incentives driving the commitments they make to each other. The seller has made a sale that is expected to yield a profit. The buyer has bought a tool with which to produce things to yield a profit. For the seller it is the end of the process; for the buyer, only the beginning. Yet their interdependence is inescapable and profound. To make these differently motivated dependencies work, the selling company must understand the relationship and plan its management in advance of the wedding. It can't get out the marriage manual only after trouble has begun.

The product's changing nature

The future will be marked by intense business relationships in all areas of marketing, including frequently purchased consumer goods. Procter & Gamble, copying General Mills's Betty Crocker advisory service, has found that the installation of a consumer hot line to give advice on its products and their uses has cemented customer brand loyalty.

In the industrial setting we have only to review changing perceptions of various aspects of product characteristics to appreciate the new emphasis on relationships (see Table 3). The common characteristic of the terms in the 'future' column of this table is time. What is labeled 'item' in the first column was in the past simply a product, something that was

---

* See my article 'Marketing success through differentiation – of anything' *Harvard Business Review*, January-February 1980, 83.

Table 3 *Perceptions of product values*

Category	Past	Present	Future
Item	Product	Augmented product	System contracts
Sale	Unit	System	System over time
Value	Feature advantages	Technology advantages	System advantages
Leadtime	Short	Long	Lengthy
Service	Modest	Important	Vital
Delivery place	Local	National	Global
Delivery phase	Once	Often	Continually
Strategy	Sales	Marketing	Relationship

bought for its own value. More recently that simple product has not been enough. Instead, buyers have bought augmented products.

During the era we are entering the emphasis will be on systems contracts, and buyer–seller relationships will be characterized by continuous contact and evolving relationships to effect the systems. The 'sale' will be not just a system but a system over time. The value at stake will be the advantages of that total system over time. As the customer gains experience, the technology will decline in importance relative to the system that enables the buyer to realize the benefits of the technology. Services, delivery, reliability, responsiveness, and the quality of the human and organizational interactions between seller and buyer will be more important than the technology itself.

The more complex the system and the more 'software' (including operating procedures and protocols, management routines, service components) it requires, the greater the customer's anxieties and expectations. People buy expectations, not things. They buy the expectations of benefits promised by the vendor. When it takes a long time to fulfill the promise (to deliver a new custom-made automated work station, for example) or when fulfillment is continual over a long period (as it is in banking services, fuel deliveries, or shipments of components for assembly operations), the buyer's anxieties build up after the purchase decision is made. Will the delivery be prompt? Will it be smooth and regular? Did we select the best vendor?

Differing expectations

When downstream realities loom larger than up-front promises, what do you do before, during, and after the sale? Who should be responsible for what?

To answer these questions it helps to understand how the promises and behavior of the vendor before the sale is made shape the customer's expectations. It is reasonable for a customer who has been promised the moon to expect it to be delivered. But if those who make the promises are paid commissions before the customer gets everything he bargained for, they're not likely to feel compelled to ensure that the customer gets fully satisfied later. After the sale, they'll rush off to pursue other prey. If marketing plans the sale, sales makes it, manufacturing fulfills it, and service services it, who's in charge and who takes responsibility for the whole process?

Problems arise not only because those who do the selling, the marketing, the manufacturing, and the servicing have varying incentives and views of the customer but also because organizations are one-dimensional. People, with the exception of those who work in sales or marketing, seldom see beyond their company's walls. For those inside those walls, inside is where the work gets done, where the penalties and incentives are doled out, where the budgets and plans get made, where engineering and manufacturing are done, where performance is measured, where one's friends and associates gather, where things are managed and manageable. Outside 'has nothing to do with me' and is where 'you can't change things.'

Many disjunctions exist between seller and buyer at various stages of the sales process. These may be simply illustrated, as in Table 4.

Table 4 *Varying reactions and perceptions before and during sale process*

When the sale is first made	
Seller	*Buyer*
Objective achieved	Judgment postponed; applies test of time.
Selling stops	Shopping continues
Focus goes elsewhere	Focus on purchase; wants affirmation that expectations have been met
Tension released	Tension increased
Relationship reduced or ended	Commitment made; relationship intensified

Throughout the process		
Stage of sale	*Seller*	*Buyer*
1 Before	Real hope	Vague need
2 Romance	Hot & heavy	Testing & hopeful
3 Sale	Fantasy:bed	Fantasy:board
4 After	Looks elsewhere for next sale	'You don't care'
5 Long after	Indifferent	'Can't this be made better?'
6 Next sale	'How about a new one?'	'Really?'

After the fact

The fact of buying changes the dynamics of the relationship. The buyer expects the seller to remember the purchase as having been a favor bestowed, not as something earned by the seller. Hence it is wrong to assume that getting an account gives you an advantage because you've got a foot in the door. The opposite is more often the case. The buyer that views the sale as a favor conferred on the seller in effect debits the seller's account. The seller owes the buyer one. He is in the position of having to rebuild the relationship from a deficit stance.

In the absence of good management, the relationship deteriorates because both organizations tend naturally to face inward rather than outward toward each other. The natural tendency of relationships, whether in marriage or in business, is toward erosion of sensitivity and attentiveness. Inward orientation by the selling organization leads to insensitivity and unresponsiveness in customer relations. At best the company substitutes bureaucratic formalities for authentic interaction.

A healthy relationship maintains, and preferably expands, the equity and the possibilities that were created during courtship. A healthy relationship requires a conscious and constant fight against the forces of decline. It becomes important for the seller regularly and seriously to consider whether the relationship is improving or deteriorating, whether the promises are being completely fulfilled, whether he is neglecting anything, and how he stands *vis-à-vis* his competitors. Table 5 compares actions that affect – for better or worse – relationships with buyers.

Table 5 *Actions that affect relationships*

Positive actions	Negative actions
Initiate positive phone calls	Make only call backs
Make recommendations	Make justifications
Use candid language	Use accommodative language
Use phone	Use correspondence
Show appreciation	Wait for misunderstandings
Make service suggestions	Wait for service requests
Use 'we' problem-solving language	Use 'owe us' legal language
Get to problems	Respond only to problems
Use jargon or shorthand	Use long-winded communications
Air personality problems	Hide personality problems
Talk of 'our future together'	Talk about making good on the past
Routinize responses	Fire drill/emergency responsiveness
Accept responsibility	Shift blame
Plan the future	Rehash the past

Building dependencies

One of the surest signs of a bad or declining relationship is the absence of complaints from the customer. Nobody is ever *that* satisfied, especially not over an extended period of time. The customer is either not being candid or not being contacted. Probably both. The absence of candor reflects the decline of trust and the deterioration of the relationship. Bad things accumulate. Impaired communication is both a symptom and a cause of trouble. Things fester inside. When they finally erupt, it's usually too late or too costly to correct the situation.

We can invest in relationships and we can borrow from them. We all do both, but we seldom account for our actions and almost never manage them. Yet a company's most precious asset is its relationships with its customers. What matters is not whom you know but how you are known to them.

Not all relationships can or need be of the same duration or at the same level of intimacy. These factors depend on the extent of the actual or felt dependency between the buyer and the seller. And of course those dependencies can be extended or contracted through various direct links that can be established between the two parties. Thus, when Bergen Brunswig, the booming drug and health care products distributor, puts computer terminals in its customers' offices to enable them to order directly and get instant feedback regarding their sales and inventory, it creates a new link that helps tie the customer to the vendor.

At the same time, however, the seller can become dependent on the buyer in important ways. Most obvious is vendor reliance on the buyer for a certain percentage of its sales. More subtle is reliance on the buyer for important information, including how the buyer's business will change, how changes will affect future purchases, and what competitors are offering in the way of substitute products or materials, at what prices and including which services. The buyer can also answer questions like these for the vendor: How well is the vendor fulfilling the customer's needs? Is performance up to promises from headquarters? To what new uses is the customer putting the product?

The seller's ability to forecast the buyer's intentions rests on the quality of the overall relationship. In a good relationship the buyer shares plans and expectations with the vendor, or at least makes available relevant information. With that information the vendor can better serve the buyer. Surprises and bad forecasts are symptoms of bad relationships. In such instances, everybody – even the buyer – loses.

Thus, a system of reciprocal dependencies develops. It is up to the seller to nurture the relationship beyond its simple dollar value. In a proper relationship both the buyer and the seller will benefit or the relationship will not last.

Moreover, both parties should understand that the seller's expenses rarely end with acquisition costs. This means that the vendor should work at convincing the customer of the importance of maintaining the vendor's long-term profitability at a comfortable level instead of squeezing to get rock-bottom delivered prices. Unless the costs of the expected post-purchase services are reflected in the price, the buyer will end up paying extra in money, in delays, and in aggravation. The smart relationship manager in the selling company will help the buyer do long-term life-cycle costing to assess the vendor's offering.

Bonds that last

Professional partnerships in law, medicine, architecture, consulting, investment banking, and advertising rate and reward associates by their client relationships. Like any other assets, these relationships can appreciate or depreciate. Their maintenance and enhancement depend not so much on good manners, public relations, tact, charm, window dressing, or manipulation as they do on management. Relationship management requires companywide maintenance, investment, improvement, and even replacement programs. The results can be spectacular.

Examine the case of the North Sea oil and gas fields. Norway and Britain urged and facilitated exploration and development of those resources. They were eager and even generous hosts to the oil companies. The companies, though they spent hundreds of millions of dollars to do the work, didn't fully nurture their relationships. When oil and gas suddenly started to flow, the host countries levied taxes exceeding 90% of the market prices. No one was more surprised than the companies. Why should they have been surprised? Had they built sound relationships with the governments, the politicians, and the voters – by whatever means – so as to have created a sense of mutuality and partnership, they might have moderated the size of the taxes. What would it have been worth?

This is not an isolated occurrence. The same problem crops up in similar circumstances where vendors are required to make heavy expenditures to get accounts and develop products. Table 6 depicts cash flows to a vendor of this type during the life of the account. During the customer-getting and development period, cash flows are negative and the customer eagerly encourages the expenditures. When the product is delivered or the joint venture becomes operative, cumulative cash flows turn up and finally become positive. In the case of the North Sea, the surprising new high taxes represent the difference between what revenues to the oil companies might have been (the upper level of potential revenue) and what they actually became. With worse relationships they might, of course, have fallen to an even lower level of potential revenue.

Consider also the case of Gillette North America. It has four separate sales forces and special programs for major accounts to ensure Gillette's rapid and smooth response to customers' requirements. Gillette also has a vice president of business relations who has among his major duties cultivation of relationships with major retailers and distributors. He carries out that responsibility via a vast array of ceremonial activities

Table 6 *Cumulative cash flow history of an account*

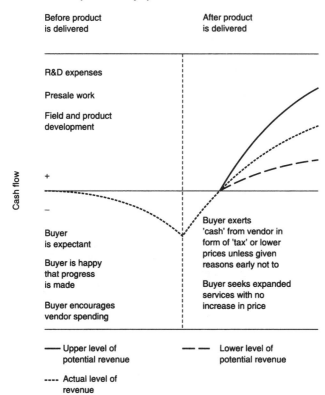

ranging from entertainment at trade association conventions to organization of special events for major accounts in connection with the annual All-Star baseball game, the World Series, the Superbowl, and the NCAA playoffs. These activities establish bonds and affirm reciprocal obligations and benefits.

Some companies now require engineering and manufacturing people to spend time with customers and users in the field – not just to get product and design ideas or feedback regarding present products but also to get to know and to respond to customers in deep and abiding ways so as to build relationships and bonds that last. The Sperry Corporation's much-advertised 'listening' campaign has included training employees to listen and communicate effectively with each other and with customers.

All too often company officials take action instead of spending time. It is all too easy to act first and later try to fix the relationship, instead of the other way around. It is all too simple to say, 'We'll look into it and call you back' or 'Let's get together for lunch sometime.' These are tactics of diversion and delay, not of relationship building.

When a purchase cycle is long – as when a beer-making plant contracts with a can-making vendor to build a factory next door or when the US Air Force commits itself to buying a jet engine with a life of 20 to 30 years – the people in the vendor organization who did the selling and those in the customer organization who did the buying will be replaced over the course of those relationships. So, in all likelihood, will the entire upper levels of management on both sides. What must the seller do to ensure continuity of good relations? What is expected of the customer when people who did the buying are changed and gone? Clearly the idea is to build bonds that last no matter who comes and goes.

Making it happen

To effectively manage relationships, managers must meet four requirements:

1 *Awareness*. Understand both the problem and the opportunity areas.
2 *Assessment*. Determine where the company now stands, especially in terms of what's necessary to get the desired results.
3 *Accountability*. Establish regular reporting on individual relationships, and then on group relationships, so that these can be weighed against other measures of performance.
4 *Actions*. Make decisions and allocations and establish routines and communications on the basis of their impact on the targeted relationships. Constantly reinforce awareness and actions.

Relationship management can be institutionalized, but in the process it must also be humanized. One company has regular sensitivity sessions and role-playing seminars in which sales officials assume the buyer role. It also conducts debriefings on meetings with customers. And it requires its customer-contact people (including those who make deliveries and handle receivables) to regularly ask of various accounts the seminal questions: How are we doing in the relationship? Is it going up or down? Are we talking with the right people about the right issues? What have we *not* done lately?

The emphasis on 'lately' is not incidental. It reflects the recognition that relationships naturally degrade and have to be reinvigorated. If I owe you a favor, I forget – but you don't. And when I've done you a favor, you feel obligated – but not for long. You ask, 'What have you done for me lately?' A relationship credit must be cashed in or it expires, and it must be used soon or it depreciates.

Another way companies can institutionalize relationship management is by establishing routines that ensure the right kinds of customer contacts. A well-known Wall Street investment firm requires its security analysts and salespeople to make regular 'constructive' contacts with their institutional customers. *Constructive* is defined as conveying useful information to them. The firm has set up a regular Monday-morning investment strategy 'commentary' that analysts and salespeople can convey by telephone to their customers. In addition, each analyst must develop periodic industry commentaries and updates, to be mailed or telephoned to customers. Analysts and salespeople are required to keep logs of these contacts, which are compiled, counted, and communicated to all in a weekly companywide report. Those salespeople and analysts making the fewest contacts have to explain their inaction to supervisors.

The firm allocates end-of-year bonuses on the basis of not only commissions earned from the various institutions but also the number and types of contacts initiated and maintained. Meanwhile, the firm conducts regular sensitivity-training sessions to enhance the contacts and the quality of the relationships. The results, which show that the efforts have been highly successful, are analyzed and made known to all, thus reinforcing the importance of the process.

Relationship contracts

Although our relationships change and develop over time, we tend to develop a set of assumptions and expectations in each of them about what our behavior and that of the other 'should' be like. Most of these assumptions are not in our awareness, but nonetheless they provide important expectations about how we should 'be' in the relationship. It is almost as if an unstated contract develops between us and the other, which we are often not aware of until one of us breaks it. The feelings of surprise or hurt that we sometimes experience over another's behavior when he or she does something or behaves in ways we did not expect is often a signal that some part of an unarticulated contract has been violated. The existence of these contracts does not have to be in our awareness to influence our behavior . . . .

The fact that people do change and develop over time has important implications for developing awareness about relationships that we value and want to last. First is a need for awareness that the other person may be changing in ways that mean that our assumptions about them and about the relationship are out of date. Second, we ourselves may be undergoing changes of which the other person is not aware, so that our present behavior is inconsistent with the other's expectations and creates problems for him or her in the relationship . . . .

. . . Greater mutual awareness of how each person has changed holds the promise that some conscious accommodation or change might take place that could strengthen or reestablish the relationship. This seems far better than perpetuating a precarious relationship that can only offer the possibility that things could become worse, for reasons that are not understood. The passive acceptance of such a situation can promise only continued anger, frustration, and the anxiety accompanying the realization that what is wrong is either unknown or must be denied. In most cases, efforts to be open will result in making relationships more adaptive, vital, and fulfilling to the people involved, and will allow for the growth of the relationship as well as that of the people in the relationship.

From Anthony G. Athos and John J. Gabarro, *Interpersonal Behavior: Communication and Understanding in Relationships* (Englewood Cliffs, NJ: Prentice-Hall, 1978). © Prentice-Hall.

Relationship management is a special field all its own and is as important to preserving and enhancing the intangible asset commonly known as 'goodwill' as is the management of hard assets. The fact that it is probably more difficult makes hard work at it that much more important.

Author's note

This article profited immensely from work done by James L. Crimmins, president of Business Times, Inc., the morning business news show on ESPN Cable, and his colleagues at Playback Associates.

BUILD CUSTOMER RELATIONSHIPS THAT LAST
Barbara Bund Jackson

Barbara Bund Jackson is a leading expert in industrial marketing. At the time of writing, she was Vice President of Index Systems, a consulting firm based in Cambridge, Massachusetts. Dr Jackson spent eleven years on the Harvard Business School Faculty where she conducted much of the field research for the book on which this article is based – *Winning and Keeping Industrial Customers*.

Based on her research, this article outlines the importance of relationships and how the context of the industrial sale sets the scene for the type of relationship that is feasible. She argues that building and maintaining lasting customer relationships involves concentrating on a number of things which must be executed in a consistent manner over long periods. She also points to the coordination tasks on the part of the seller in managing the needs of the customer over the length of the relationship. Her work is based on organizations operating in communications, shipping and computer industries.

Scene 1: The executive committee meeting ends at 5:30 p.m. and the committee members adjourn, pleased with what they have accomplished. Their company, Superior Shipping Services, provides trucking to large industrial users, giving customers reliable scheduling and careful handling.*

In response to decreased regulation in trucking and related industries, Superior's executives believe their company needs a stronger marketing orientation. They want to build and maintain lasting – and profitable – relationships with their customers. That, they believe, is what getting 'close to the customer' means.

At an earlier meeting, the executive committee had decided to recruit a sales-marketing manager from a renowned marketer in the computer industry. Superior's president argued that such a person was likely to have attitudes and values that would fit well with the company's reputation for especially high quality and service.

The president and administrative vice president then identified possible candidates. The leading choice was Dale Spencer, a senior salesperson with an impressive record. At this meeting, the committee has outlined an offer that Superior's president believes would be attractive to Spencer.

Scene 2 (one month later): Dale Spencer assumes the job of vice president – sales for Superior Shipping. The negotiations have been smooth and Spencer is pleased. Spencer and Superior's president have agreed completely on what Spencer ought to do.

In the past, Spencer had been a patient and successful builder of customer relationships. On occasion, sales efforts became protracted as Spencer and other support people devoted long hours to wooing prospects. They eventually won most of the orders – and the resulting relationships proved close and highly satisfactory to both parties.

Superior's managers want similar customer ties. They plan to invest time and effort in studying their customers' shipping needs. They will help customers plan. They will also maintain the high quality of Superior's service. As a result, they expect to maintain – indeed, strengthen – Superior's relationships with its existing customers. They also expect to win important new customers.

Spencer will have responsibility for instilling the new attitude and approach in Superior's sales force. Spencer will also personally handle sales efforts at some of the key new accounts. Spencer is excited about the challenge.

Scene 3 (two years later): Several of Superior Shipping's important executives are discussing Dale Spencer's future with the company. Spencer has been severely disappointed with the results to date. The executives, knowing that Spencer may leave, are thinking about whether to encourage or discourage the change. They wonder what has happened at Superior – and why.

* The Superior Shipping Services example is hypothetical but built around elements of several actual field situations. The individuals described are fictitious.

Spencer has been a respected manager. The salespeople have indeed learned better ways of analyzing customers' long-term shipping requirements and of identifying opportunities for improving them. Superior's other managers have kept more in touch with customers as part of the overall sales effort; they have heard numerous compliments about their salespeople – and especially about Dale Spencer.

Yet all these efforts have not produced more sales. True, many prospects have responded to Superior's attention by awarding the company some business. But many of those new customers – as well as many of Superior's old accounts – have also experimented with other shippers.

One competitor, Efficiency Truckers, has proven especially irksome, competing on the basis of price and doing so increasingly effectively. Many of Superior's established customers have given Efficiency their largest and most regular shipments in exchange for price concessions. Three of the company's most desired new customers have done the same thing even after Superior salespeople had helped them create their shipment patterns through consolidation and more careful planning.

Virtually all those customers have also continued to do some business with Superior, giving the company their last-minute smaller shipments, severely testing Superior's ability to provide quality service. Superior's revenue has slipped, its sales force expenses have increased, and all of Superior's managers are deeply concerned by the developments. Dale Spencer is especially upset by them.

What happened?

Close relationships

Superior's managers did not adequately consider the differences between the market for computers and the market for shipping services, from the customers' point of view. They wanted to be close to the customer, but close to the customer means different things in the two marketplaces. The Superior example is especially instructive because a surprising number of marketers don't probe deeply enough into the nature of their relationships with customers. They want very much to believe that they're building lasting ties with buyers – but they're not. They want very much to do what I call 'relationship marketing' – but their customers think more in terms of 'transaction marketing.'

Also, surprisingly, the distinctions between relationship marketing and transaction marketing are not clear, partly because successful relationship marketing is so complex and also because so many complicated and hard (or impossible) to measure factors determine what is appropriate to a situation, whether relationship marketing, transaction marketing, or something in between.

Because marketing practice and the marketing literature have devoted more attention to transaction marketing, this article and the research project on which it is based (see the insert) instead emphasize lasting relationship marketing between industrial companies and their customers. Accordingly, I first contrast customer behavior in the markets for computers and for shipping services, and then I consider a wider variety of customer behavior.

Customer commitments

A customer for medium-size or large computer systems generally commits strongly to the vendor that provides the important parts of the system and that thereby defines the technical parameters of the installation. When a company chooses such a lead vendor, it generally expects to continue with that supplier for an extended period. In short, it expects a relationship.

The costs and pain of changing computer suppliers have led to this pattern. Most users are well aware of the expense and tumult involved in transferring programs from one computer to another; many have first-hand experience with the trauma. Further, leading computer vendors facilitate software conversions from one to another of their own machines, thus making it much easier for customers to remain with current suppliers than to switch.

Because commitments from their customers usually last a long time, mainframe computer vendors have been able to take a long view of their customers' relationships. They have sensibly invested up-front resources to win commitments, helped customers with long-term planning for computers, and generally acted as if their customer relationships would continue. For them, relationship marketing has been a sound choice.

By contrast, customers for shipping services can easily share their business among multiple suppliers. A customer can award a small initial order to a new supplier. If all goes well, the customer can award more business to the supplier; if not, the damage from using the new supplier has been contained. In turn, a successful new vendor may find that yet another competitor will win away some of its business from the same customer.

The seller of shipping services cannot necessarily justify up-front investments to win accounts. The seller cannot assume that by helping customers plan for their longer run needs it will gain a principal role in executing the long-term plan. Customers may gratefully accept the planning help today but, if switching costs are low, they may accept concessions from another source tomorrow.

Transaction marketing is appropriate here; relationship marketing can be dangerous. Perhaps Dale Spencer failed because he never understood transaction marketing.

Spectrum of behavior

In many situations, sellers will benefit from an examination of the commitments they enjoy from customers, including consideration of the closeness of their ties with them and the time horizon their customers use in their commitments. Some sellers will identify strong ties that they expect to last – like those in the computer example. Others will find weaker, more transient affiliations – like those in shipping. Others may identify intermediate or even more extreme patterns.

The foregoing leads us into two simplified pictures or models of accounts' possible behavior that can be considered as the end points of a spectrum. Accounts in real situations will generally occupy less radical positions along the spectrum.

Always-a-share model

One extreme is what I call the 'always-a-share model,' which assumes that a customer making purchases of some product category repeatedly can easily switch part or all of its patronage from one vendor to another. The customer can therefore share its patronage among multiple suppliers. Though extreme, this model suggests the actual behavior of some buyers of commodity chemicals, some apartment building owners who purchase major appliances, some buyers of computer terminals, and some mailing services and shipping services customers.

Because the always-a-share customer faces low switching costs, a vendor can sensibly assume that it has a chance of winning business from such an account – provided that the seller offers an immediate attractive combination of product, price, support, and/or other benefits. The seller is not locked into an account from which it currently enjoys patronage, nor is it locked out of one to which it does not now sell.

In some situations suggesting always-a-share behavior, a customer may make a series of purchases each from a single supplier but sharing its patronage among vendors over time (e.g., a purchaser of simple machine tools). In other situations suggesting the always-a-share model, the product is more divisible and the customer shares its business among multiple vendors at one time (e.g., a purchaser of carbon steel).

Implications of always-a-share

The always-a-share buyer is likely to have a short time horizon in its ties with suppliers. Even vendors who make consistent sales to that customer are obliged to give good immediate reasons for continuing the relationship with each purchase.

Transaction marketing is apt for the always-a-share customer.

Lost-for-good model

The opposite end of the behavior spectrum also assumes a series of purchases over time, but it presumes that at any one time the account is committed to only one vendor. The account faces high costs of switching vendors and therefore changes only reluctantly. As a result, it is likely to remain committed to its current supplier.

If the account does leave a vendor, it is at least as hard to win back as it was to win in the first place. I call such behavior the 'lost-for-good model,' emphasizing the pain of losing such a customer. The flip side is more cheerful; once won this type of customer is likely to be won for a long time.

The behavior picture in this lost-for-good model is indeed extreme. It is also a reasonable simplification for actual situations in which switching vendors involves considerable cost and disruption. The model suggests the behavior of some but not all purchasers of, for example, computers, communications equipment, office automation systems, heavy construction equipment, magazine fulfillment services, and aircraft engines.

Implications of lost-for-good

The essence of this model is that since the account cannot easily switch its patronage, it will therefore view its commitment to a vendor as permanent and use a long time horizon in the relationship. In choosing a supplier, it will consider the seller's likely future abilities to satisfy its needs and it will not focus exclusively on the seller's immediate capabilities and inducements.

Because the customer takes a long time horizon, an industrial marketer can also sensibly take a long-term view of the relationship. Often the seller can justify heavy up-front investment in trying to win new (or significantly increased) commitments from such customers.

Relationship marketing is apt for the buyer who might be lost-for-good.

Research design

This article is based on a research project that explored long-term relationships between industrial customers and their vendors. In my fieldwork, which included companies dealing with a variety of products, I compared the findings with existing marketing research that focuses on individual sales and short-term relationships

I carried out extensive (multihour) interviews with managers about their organizations' histories of purchases and usage of communications equipment (PBXs and related products) and of computers. The sample included 11 customers of communication equipment and 16 computer purchasers. In half the organizations, I held interviews with at least 2 managers; in 2 companies, I conducted 3 separate interviews. In interviews with 6 potential customers, I explored office automation and local area networks; 3 customer interviews concerned purchases of supplies for offset platemakers.

I talked with approximately 35 industry experts and vendors' representatives, covering each product area. (I did not include vendor representatives, however, if legal and regulatory concerns made them reluctant to talk about how their organizations built and maintained strong ties with customers.) In numerous briefer and less formal discussions, I explored the application of the ideas presented here in other product marketplaces.

Intermediate types

Real customers are likely to approximate various spectrum points between lost-for-good and always-a-share. The position of a certain customer will depend in part on characteristics of the product category, on the customer's usage system for the product, and on actions both the vendor and the customer take. Examples of such customers are fleet purchasers of cars or trucks, buyers of carbon steel, and users of banking services.

At first glance, a fleet purchaser is appropriately placed near the always-a-share end of the behavior spectrum: the buyer could use products from several vendors and could switch its patronage easily. Other factors, however, might move fleet buyers somewhat closer to the lost-for-good model. A customer's in-house maintenance staff might be skilled in working on a particular vendor's products; mixing vendors might require retraining. Similarly, if a vendor designed its products to use a common set of parts, the customer who uses one vendor could save on spare parts inventory (and/or could reduce the time required to obtain needed parts). Thus while some fleet purchasers would be close to the always-a-share model, vendor actions and buyer invest-ments would move others to the middle of the behavior spectrum – or even beyond.

In a similar way, a purchaser of carbon steel might appear to be the prototypical always-a-share buyer, able to mix and match suppliers even within a single time period. Many purchasers would indeed approximate that model. Consider, however, a steel user that is adopting a just-in-time system for its materials and component inventories. Just-in-time requires extremely close cooperation and scheduling between buyer and seller; it will usually work much more smoothly with a single supplier per time period. Moreover, once a supplier and buyer have learned to work well together, the buyer will be reluctant to change and have to orient a new vendor. Hence even for a commodity such as carbon steel, the customer's usage pattern and the vendor's investment in adapting to the buyer's procedures can create behavior more like lost-for-good.

Finally, look at a customer for banking services. Again, it would appear that a company (or individual) could conduct business simultaneously with several banks – perhaps using checking accounts in multiple banks. While some banking customers do so, other corporate financial managers save time and money by using integrated financial packages from their banks. Along with the savings they gain, they establish closer ties to the bank – and end up in the middle of the behavior spectrum.

It is important to note that positions are determined in part by vendor actions. Marketers can consequently benefit from understanding their own customers' positions – for two reasons.

First, diagnosis with regard to the spectrum can help sellers under-stand their customers' concerns and interests. It can, for example, help them identify the issues that will determine purchase decisions. An always-a-share customer will almost certainly emphasize shorter term, more immediate concerns. A lost-for-good account will place considerable emphasis on longer term issues, like the seller's ability to provide an ongoing stream of suitable products and to facilitate graceful upgrades from one product to another as appropriate over time. Such a customer will not ignore more immediate concerns, but it will not emphasize those considerations exclusively.

Second, the behavior spectrum can help vendors evaluate possible marketing strategies. Obviously, marketing actions that are well suited to customers toward one side of the spectrum will not necessarily be at all appropriate for customers toward the opposite end. In addition, the spectrum can help marketers evaluate the potential impact of marketing actions on moving customers closer to one end of the spectrum or the other.

Costs of change

An important point about switching costs is that customers face such costs in making many types of changes, regardless of whether a vendor change is involved. For example, a computer user faces some switching costs to modify existing programs even in changing from one operating system to another with the same vendor. In a similar way, a customer often faces switching costs when its vendor institutes new procedures – even if those procedures eventually improve service to the customer. For example, a supplier of manufactured parts may install an efficient new system for entering orders and for tracing previous orders. While the intended result is better service, the change will require an adjustment on the part of the customer.

In considering possible changes from one selling company to another, a customer will consider the relative switching costs (or savings) of the available choices. Therefore, marketers should consider both the absolute and the relative levels of disruption that changes will mean for the customer. The seller may find it useful to design its products and services so as to reduce switching costs that customers will face if they stay with that seller. To put it another way, the marketer should try to get the costs of intra-vendor switches considerably lower than the costs of inter-vendor changes.

Investment actions

The first, most obvious types of switching costs are the investments of time and money that customers must make to adapt to new products, services, or systems. Customers invest in their relationships with vendors in a variety of ways. They invest *money*; they invest in *people*, as in training employees to run new equipment; they invest in *lasting assets*, such as the equipment itself; and they invest in changing basic business *procedures* like inventory handling.

Naturally, the larger and more disruptive the investment actions required, the greater customer reluctance to change commitments and incur switching costs. Reluctance is especially high to abandoning previous investments in dollars, people, lasting assets, or procedures.

The amounts spent on products, being the only type of switching costs that can usually be determined precisely, are often emphasized in procurement evaluations. Other types of investments, however, can be more disruptive for the customer – and therefore can be more important switching costs. My field investigation suggests that past investments in procedures are particularly likely to create inertia against change.

For example, in adopting a comprehensive office automation system, many organizations must undergo thorough revisions in their procedures. The effects of change will reach widely throughout their organizations. As a result, many managers are wary of making mistakes; they want to move slowly into office automation. They especially want to avoid errors that would require yet another round of investments in procedures.

In the same way, because of past investments, buyers may be reluctant to incur the switching costs of modifying or replacing lasting assets. Computer software programs act as lasting assets. So do pieces of industrial equipment adapted to raw materials from a particular vendor.

Risk or exposure

The second major category of switching costs concerns risk or exposure – that is, the danger to customers of making bad choices. While obviously not as immediately tangible or quantifiable as investments in time and money, the risks involved in switching can be just as important in determining customer behavior.

The immediate risks involved in changes frequently concern performance – that is, whether a purchase will work as intended and for the intended cost. Fear of immediate disruption and unsatisfactory performance can make a customer reluctant to change. Customers will feel more exposed when they buy products important to their own operations, when they buy from less well-known and less-established vendors, and when they buy complex and difficult-to-understand products. For the short run, a manager or an organization may feel considerably safer with the status quo – with not fixing something that is not demonstrably broken.

For the long run, however, customers often face risks in not changing. Fear of exposure can interfere with an organization's willingness and ability to adapt to external changes and to take advantage of strategic opportunities. It can also give competitors time to make successful preemptive moves.

Today some advanced users of computers are experiencing the pain of large conversions to new systems and vendors with which they can grow.

Such customers are willing to undergo the immediate switching costs because of the benefits they will gain from being up-to-date in a product area that is growing in strategic importance.

Marketplace dynamics

A customer's position on the behavior spectrum does not remain constant over time, of course, especially in dynamic marketplaces. Changes occur because of environmental fluctuations, competitors' actions, other customer changes, sellers' actions, or simply because of the passage of time.

The computer marketplace provides an example of behavior change in process. One important force has been the movement toward what is called 'network architecture' in large computer systems, with explicit rules for interfacing different parts of a system, facilitating the use within a single network of individual parts of different types, often from different vendors. In comparable fashion, conventions for interfacing can facilitate the use of software packages from different sources. It is becoming easier to mix and match components from different vendors or different components from the same vendor.

My field investigation shows that large computer system users are well aware of these networking effects. They have welcomed the change, sensing that it gives them bargaining power with suppliers and access to the innovations of more than one marketer.

Customers are making strong lost-for-good commitments to the technology of the lead vendor that determines the backbone or underlying network design. At the same time, however, customers are beginning to show always-a-share behavior in their purchases of individual hardware and software items.

A computer seller in the 1980s cannot assume that a customer is either totally committed or totally lost for the future, though such an assumption would have been reasonable in the 1960s. In the 1980s, customers' choices of their lead vendors and basic technology have been made with long time horizons and have emphasized long-term concerns and capabilities. At the same time, however, even marketers that won commitments as lead vendors have had to compete on short-term issues to win customers' patronage for components of the newer computer networks. Customers can view those individual purchases as separate transactions.

Vendor-induced changes

Other changes along the behavior spectrum can be induced by actions of customers and/or vendors, such as the use of formal procedures to create buying systems for customers and suppliers. Such systems provide efficiencies and improved service for the customer. They also create stronger links between the two organizations and raise the costs of switching suppliers.

American Hospital Supply's ASAP system demonstrates a strong bond between a vendor and its customers. The ASAP system allows customers to place orders for supplies and equipment easily and efficiently. For example, customers can order via a computer terminal, use standing or repetitive order files (to avoid retyping regularly ordered lists of products), and obtain order confirmations on their own tailored forms. The most advanced ASAP systems provide computer-to-computer links between the vendor and the hospital's materials management computer program; the customer's computer can automatically order needed items from the vendor without any human intervention.

While one might expect hospitals to show always-a-share behavior in purchasing such items as syringes and hospital gowns, the ASAP system has moved its customers close to the lost-for-good end of the spectrum. Customers buy groups of products as a system; they lose efficiency and convenience when they mix and match.*

In the example at the beginning of this article, Superior Shipping's sales force was trying to help customers plan their logistics. Superior might be able to help customers set up procedures that link them more closely to the seller, using information exchanged between buyer and seller that will facilitate efficient service. Superior might in this way offer improved service if customers involve Superior more closely in their scheduling procedures. If Superior's customers could be induced to make such investments in procedures, their behavior would move toward the lost-for-good end of the spectrum and Superior might then find it worthwhile to invest in helping customers plan and improve. (If Dale Spencer had done some of these things, perhaps he might have succeeded at Superior.)

In other cases, vendors can raise customer switching costs and move accounts closer to the lost-for-good model by offering system benefits – additional real benefits that customers can obtain if they source more (or all) of their purchases from a single vendor. For example, a chemical company offers auto body shops access to a computer program for matching colors; the program translates information about a car's original color, age, condition, and other factors into instructions for using the vendor's pigments to match the car's current color for touch-ups and repairs. The program uses only the vendor's set of pigments; customers cannot easily mix and match.

Likewise, potential customers for private branch communication exchanges are urged to buy whole PBX systems from one vendor to obtain full software compatibility among individual products. For example, some procedures for reducing costs of long-distance calls and future electronic mail systems will depend on such compatibility.

---

* For other such uses of information technology, see F. Warren McFarlan and James L. McKenney, *Corporate Information Systems Management: The Issues Facing Senior Executives* (Homewood, Ill.: Richard D. Irwin, 1983); see also James I. Cash and Benn R. Konsynski, 'IS Redraws Competitive Boundaries,' *Harvard Business Review*, March-April 1985, p. 134.

In other situations, actions by one vendor can move another supplier's accounts closer to the always-a-share end of the spectrum, thus allowing the new vendor to enter the accounts. Product designs compatible with those of an established vendor can serve this purpose. Many suppliers of computer peripherals and software, for example, offer products that are compatible with IBM products; customers, therefore, can buy individual items that fit into an existing IBM system. Customers can experiment with new vendors in a limited way. In the process, they show behavior a little closer to the always-a-share model.

Vendors sometimes commit themselves to make their products work with those of other vendors. Lanier Business Products, for example, a supplier of individual devices for office automation, has advertised that its products will plug into (or work with) any of the emerging standards for networking such products together. Such accommodations allow customers to make purchase decisions without fear of locking themselves into a prescribed choice for their office networks.

Using the spectrum

Effective use of the behavior spectrum in marketing thus first involves analyzing patterns of customer behavior. It then calls for exploring possible actions by the vendor (or by the vendor's competitors) that can affect customers' positions along the spectrum. Here are some points to remember:

1 *To diagnose customers' behavior, analyze switching costs.*
   What are the investments in dollars, people, lasting assets, or procedures required for the buyer to change? As noted, the larger and more disruptive the required investments, the closer the account will be to the lost-for-good end of the spectrum; the smaller the investments, the closer it will be to always-a-share.

   What is the risk or exposure involved in changing? Will a difficult or unsuccessful change seriously hurt the customer's operations or the career of one of its managers? Such exposure will make the buyer more conservative, more reluctant to change.

   What is the nature of the customer's usage system? Is it modular so that the buyer can try a new product in a reasonably isolated experiment? If so, the account can behave more like the always-a-share model. On the other hand, a closely integrated usage system that allows only substantial changes will produce behavior more like lost-for-good.

2 *To select a marketing approach, consider the position along the behavior spectrum*
   Use relationship marketing for buyers near the lost-for-good end of the spectrum. Purchasers of office automation systems or aircraft engines are apt examples.

Use transaction marketing for buyers near the always-a-share end of the spectrum, for example, purchasers of many commodity chemicals.

For customers in intermediate positions on the spectrum, use intermediate approaches. Such buyers will look beyond the immediate transaction but they will not have the long-term orientations of lost-for-good buyers.

3 *To analyze additional possible marketing actions, consider changes along the behavior spectrum.*
To move accounts closer to the lost-for-good end, build switching costs. Create systems that link the customers more closely to the vendor, for example, either through ordering systems or through procedures for delivery and inventory. Make it easier for the customer to do business with one supplier than with many. Or choose product designs that give customers substantial benefits from using a system of products from the same vendor.

To move accounts closer to always-a-share, give the buyers painless ways to mix and match. Sell products that fit into the customer's existing system built from other suppliers' products. Provide easy interfaces; give the customer assistance in making mixed usage systems work. Promise and deliver compatibility.

4 *To use the concept of the spectrum successfully, consider the dimension of time.*
Select a time horizon for evaluating marketing actions in light of the time horizons customers use in making commitments to suppliers. Obviously, don't make substantial up-front investments to win commitments that won't last. In addition, plan for and/or guard against preemptive moves that will affect customers' behavior along the spectrum. Successful competitive actions that move customers closer to the lost-for-good end can be extremely difficult to counter. Try to get there first.

Marketing challenge

The picture of long-term commitments from customers in the lost-for-good end of the behavior spectrum seems to be attractive in many ways. Close to the customer is good isn't it? The answer to this question appears to be 'yes, but.' First, different degrees of closeness are possible in different situations; marketers should assess how much closeness is feasible. Also, my research indicates that building and maintaining strong, lasting customer ties (even where feasible) is a difficult marketing challenge.

Customers who are making strong commitments with long time horizons are concerned both with marketers' long-run capabilities and also with their immediate performance. Because the customers feel

---

Bargaining by pantomime

The blue town, Tartary, is noted for its great trade in camels. The camel market is a large square in the center of the town. The animals are ranged here in long rows, their front feet raised upon a mud elevation constructed for that purpose, the object being to show off the size and height of the creatures. The uproar and confusion of this market are tremendous, with the incessant bawling of the buyers and sellers as they dispute, their chattering after they have agreed, and the horrible shrieking of the animals at having their noses pulled, for the purpose of making them show their agility in kneeling and rising. . . .

The trade in camels is entirely by proxy – the seller and the buyer never settle the matter between themselves. They select indifferent persons to sell their goods, who propose, discuss, and fix the price; the one looking to the interest of the seller, the other to those of the purchaser. These 'sale speakers' exercise no other trade; they go from market to market, to promote business, as they say. They have generally a great knowledge of cattle, have much fluency of tongue, and are, above all, endowed with a knavery beyond all shame. They dispute by turns, furiously and argumentatively, as to the merits and defects of the animal; but as soon as it comes to a question of price, the tongue is laid aside as a medium, and the conversation proceeds altogether in signs. They seize each other by the wrist, and beneath the long, wide sleeves of their jackets indicate with their fingers the progress of the bargain. After the affair is concluded, they partake of the dinner, which is always given by the purchaser, and then receive a certain number of sapeks, according to the custom of the different places.

From 'Bargaining by Pantomime – Trade in Camels' in Frazar Kirkland (pseudonym for Richard Miller Devens) *Cyclopaedia of Commercial and Business Anecdotes*, D. Appleton and Company, New York, 1865, vol. 2, p. 603.

---

exposure, they especially demand vendor competence and commitment. They are likely to be frightened by even minor signs of supplier inadequacy.

As a result, successful relationship marketing involves doing a large number of things right, consistently, over time. It takes coordination on the part of the seller of resources and tools to meet the customer's future as well as its immediate needs.

The good news, therefore, is that (where feasible) strong, long-lasting relationships toward the lost-for-good end of the spectrum can be extremely attractive for marketers, whose actions can sometimes effectively encourage such behavior. The bad news – but also the opportunity – is that relationship marketing can be a difficult challenge for the marketer, often requiring up-front investment and consistently good performance on a variety of tasks.

AN INTERACTION APPROACH TO ORGANIZATIONAL BUYING BEHAVIOUR
Nigel Campbell

Nigel Campbell is a senior lecturer in Strategic Management and Director of Japanese Studies at the Manchester Business School. He is an active researcher working in the area of industrial marketing and is a contributor to the IMP body of research.

This article is based on research which follows earlier work carried out by the IMP Group. It develops a classification of buyer–seller relationships and identifies common strategies which buyers and sellers use in their interactions. It provides some management guidelines for marketing strategies appropriate to different types of relationships.

Although interest in and research on organizational buying have increased over the past two decades, few empirical generalizations have emerged to provide specific guidelines for management action. This conclusion by Wind and Thomas[28] reinforces the view expressed by Wind[27] in the first edition of *Review of Marketing*. This paper attempts to fill this gap by developing the interaction approach associated with the International Marketing and Purchasing (IMP) Group.

The lack of empirical generalizations may be due to the complexity of available models.[17,22,23] The popular Webster and Wind model placed great emphasis on analysis of the buying center, the buying decision process, and the buying situation. In practice, this tripartite analysis has proved difficult to perform because the interpersonal processes at work in a buying center are hard to unravel, the stages of the buying decision process are hard to distinguish, and even the distinction between 'new buy' and 'modified rebuy' is not always clear. Industrial marketing managers are well aware that their jobs are complex.

In order to guide marketing managers and resolve the research problems, attention has focused on discrete buying decisions. In consequence, research has concentrated on new buy situations in which discrete decisions are easy to identify. Routine response behavior, which Möller[17] claims is more common, has been neglected. In other words, the emphasis has been on the process of discrete purchase decisions rather than on the development of strategies for the management of a pattern of relationships over long periods of time.

In contrast, this paper stems from research in areas where long-term stable relationships are important, as attested to by many authorities.[2,9,11,26] In such situations, the study of discrete purchase decisions is less relevant than the study of the patterns of interaction between buyers and their supply markets.

This paper results from an intensive two-year research study designed to complement previous work carried out by the IMP Group. The original IMP research project[12] was an international, cross-sectional study aimed at understanding the nature of buyer–seller relationships. Some 300 companies covering 15 different industries in 5 countries were involved. The IMP researchers placed great emphasis on a comparative analysis of how suppliers and customers in various product technologies and end-use industries handled their relationships with counterpart companies in domestic and foreign markets. In contrast, the research study on which this paper is based focused on 167 trading relationships in the packaging industry in Europe. Both sides of the buyer–seller relationships were researched, and by examining one industry, the product technology variable in the relationships was held constant.

To understand the trading relationships, this paper classifies buyer–seller relationships and identifies the common strategies which buyers and sellers use in their interactions. This classification enables attention to focus on the critical variables which give rise to the different strategies. In addition, useful managerial guidelines are developed which assist sellers in choosing a strategy in response to the strategy being used by their counterpart.

Classification of buyer–seller relationships

The classification adopted is based on the three types of governance structure proposed by Williamson[25] for commercial transactions. Campbell and Cunningham[4] provide an extensive review of other approaches to the classification of buyer–seller relationships. Williamson's approach arises from his work on markets and hierarchies[24] and is linked to Ouchi's[18,19] concern with ensuring equity in relationships.

Equity is assured in many exchanges by the market mechanism. A fair price is established by competitive market forces, and the price itself contains most of the information needed by the parties. Such relationships are independent. However, where the exchange is contingent on uncertain future events, assessment of price is very difficult. Nevertheless, the requirement for equity remains and, for this reason, a bureaucratic, or hierarchical, relationship is preferred. The perception of equity depends on a social agreement that the bureaucratic system has the legitimate authority to decide what is fair. In these relationships, one party is dependent on the other.

Intermediate between the market and bureaucratic mechanisms is the clan mechanism, which Ouchi claims can also ensure equity. Equity based on clan control involves a long process of socialization, which develops common values and beliefs. The evidence for long-term relationships and source loyalty suggests that the clan form, an interdependent relationship, is common in buyer–seller relationships.

Independent, dependent, and interdependent relationships arise in different situations. For example, independence arises when the buyer plays the market and the seller has plenty of potential customers. Marketing and purchasing strategies in these commodity-type markets are competitive. Independence also arises in a buyer's market, in which there are many competitive sellers, and in a seller's market, where there are many buyers. On the other hand, interdependence arises when both parties approach the relationship with a strategy of cooperation. They are both willing to establish a long-term relationship, to exchange information openly, and to trust each other. Finally, a dependent relationship results from the dominance one party exerts over the other.

Marketing or purchasing strategies which result when one party has a dominant position of strength are called *command* strategies. Thus, the independent, interdependent, and dependent types of relationships result from the interplay of interaction strategies, classified here as competitive, cooperative, and command. Campbell and Cunningham have described similar classifications developed by other researchers.[1,6,7,10,12] The interplay of these strategies leads directly to the nine-cell matrix in Figure 1.

Marketing strategies

		Competitive	Cooperative	Command
Purchasing strategies	Competitive	1 Independent Perfect market	2 Mismatch	3 Independent Seller's market
	Cooperative	4 Mismatch	5 Interdependent Domesticated market	6 Dependent Captive market
	Command	7 Independent Buyer's market	8 Dependent Subcontract market	9 Mismatch

Figure 1 *Classification of buyer–seller relationships.*

In Figure 1 there are three cells with independent relationships, one with interdependent relationships, two with dependent relationships, and three labeled 'Mismatch.' The typical strategies and responses which apply to these different situations are discussed in the final section of this paper.

Thus, in place of the Webster and Wind classification of buying situations into new buy, modified rebuy, and straight rebuy, Figure 1 proposes a new typology of buyer–seller relationships. In this typology, the buying situation is determined by the interplay of marketing and purchasing strategies, which are themselves determined by a variety of other factors. Therefore, a model is required which incorporates the interplay of marketing and purchasing strategies and identifies the conditions which determine their choice.

Interaction model

Neither the Sheth[22] model nor the Webster and Wind[23] model fulfills the above stated need to incorporate the interplay of marketing and purchasing strategies and their determinants. The Sheth model is mainly concerned with the psychological aspects of individual buyer behavior. However, in addition to individual factors, Sheth introduces product-specific and company-specific factors, as well as the outcome of previous decisions and situational factors, which he says are too varied and broad to analyze in detail. These factors converge in a 'black box' called the *industrial buying process*.

Although it is more comprehensive and considers four sets of variables – environmental, organizational, interpersonal, and individual – the Webster and Wind model also poses problems. The desire for comprehensiveness leads to the inclusion of every possible influence, which makes the model difficult to use. Laczniak and Murphy[15] have cautioned against a 'laundry list of possible influences.'

Another disadvantage of both models is that they concentrate on the buyer's side. Scant attention is paid to the seller's influence on buyer behavior. By contrast, the interaction model developed by the IMP Group[12] stresses the interaction between two active parties, and the model proposed here (see Figure 2) gives equal weight to buyer and seller characteristics.

This model goes beyond the work of the IMP Group by introducing the concept of *interaction strategies*, whose interplay affects the interaction mechanisms and interaction atmosphere in a two-way exchange. Figure 2 also emphasizes a different set of variables from those in the IMP model.

Three groups of variables are shown – the characteristics of the buyer, the supplier, and the product. The characteristics of the buyer and the supplier are divided into three sets representing the industry, the company, and the individuals or buying center members. One could argue that the characteristics of the two industries should be separated from those of the two companies and the two groups of individuals. However, the strong interconnection between company strategy and industry structure suggests the need to keep them together.[20] The impact of general environmental factors is presumed to take place through changes in the characteristics of the buyer's and/or supplier's industry. This has the advantage that the environments of both buyer and seller are explicitly considered, and it avoids the weakness of the IMP model, which includes only an aggregated environment.

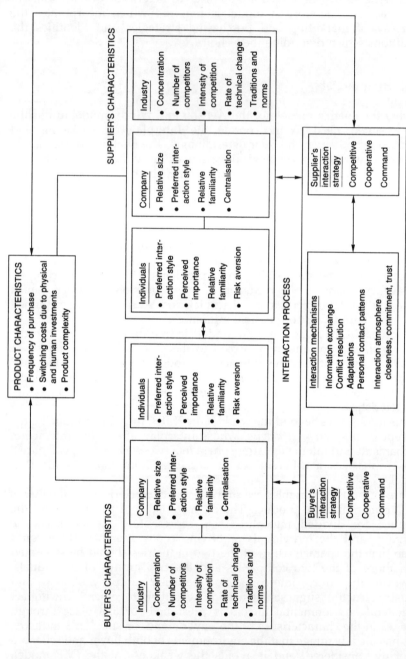

Figure 2 *Buyer–seller interaction model*

Table 1 *Interaction variables*

Buyer's side	Interaction variables	Supplier's side
Product	Frequency of purchase Switching costs due to physical and human investments Product complexity	Product
Industry characteristics	Concentration Number of alternative partners Intensity of competition Rate of technical change Traditions and norms	Industry characteristics
Company characteristics	Relative size Preferred interaction style Relative familiarity Centralization of purchasing	Company characteristics
Individual characteristics	Relative familiarity Preferred interaction style Perceived importance of the purchase (sale) Risk aversion	Individual characteristics

A full list of the variables considered in the model is given in Table 1. There is no attempt to be comprehensive. Rather, variables are included which research indicates cause a particular buyer or seller to choose a strategy.

Product characteristics

Different writers have used different attributes in their attempts to classify products. Robinson, Faris, and Wind[21] proposed the three buy classes. Cardozo[5] suggests a classification by product use, degree of standardization, and the product's importance to the buyer. Other writers have also used characteristics of the product's importance to the buyer.[17,20] Homse[13] classifies products according to their complexity, and Williamson[25] concentrates on the three key dimensions of frequency of transaction, switching costs, and uncertainty.

Frequency of transaction distinguishes between the purchase of capital goods required infrequently and components and raw materials delivered more regularly. Where the transaction occurs frequently, the relationships are likely to be more interdependent. At the other extreme, the infrequent purchase of standard capital equipment is often dealt with by competitive tenders.

Switching costs are the costs incurred in changing suppliers. This dimension incorporates the ideal of standardization because standard products will normally have lower switching costs than customized products. The higher the switching costs, the greater the specific investments which each party has made in the relationship. Switching costs can result from human as well as physical investments. Salesmen and buyers invest in getting to know each other's business. Table 2 summarizes the main sources of switching costs between industrial buyers and marketers.

While switching costs are a function of the product in the sense that some products must be more closely adapted to the customer's needs than others, they also reflect the type of relationship that exists. In an independent relationship, a buyer pursuing a competitive strategy in a particular supply market will try to minimize switching costs to avoid being tied to one supplier. The aim is to standardize purchases, and the buyer tends to have a technical staff to solve problems. On the other hand, a buyer pursuing a cooperative strategy is more ready to pay switching costs in return for joint efforts to find the best solution to his or her problem. Such a buyer has a relatively smaller technical staff, and is

Table 2 *Source of switching costs in buyer–seller relationships*

Activity	Source of switching costs	
	Supplier	*Customer*
Product introduction	Supplying prototype and test data	Testing a new product
	Training customer's staff	Training own staff
Production	Changing materials, design, processing, or production equipment to meet customer's needs	Changing product, design, or production methods to accommodate the supplier
	Special quality control	Special quality control
	Especially rapid production	
Logistics	Special stock-holding and delivery requirements	Special warehousing and handling
Product development and technical service	Time needed to get to know customer's problems and technical staff	Time needed to understand supplier's technical resources and staff
Buying, selling, and administration	Time required to get to know the customer, his or her staff, and ways of doing business; special documentation and procedures	Time required to get to know supplier, his or her staff, and ways of doing business; special documentation and procedures

willing to cooperate on development work and to accept special products. In general, the higher the switching costs, the greater the tendency for cooperative or command strategies to be used.

The third dimension, product complexity, is preferred by Williamson's uncertainty. Homse[13] has identified six types of product complexity. A product has *functional complexity* when it consists of numerous parts and subassemblies. *Manufacturing complexity* is straightforward, but *specification complexity* refers to products which require extensive trial periods.[13] Products have a high *application complexity* due either to the extensive training required before the buyer knows how to use them or to the uncertainty inherent in the customer's pattern of demand. *Commercial complexity* refers to transactions involving complicated commercial arrangements, such as stage payments, penalty clauses, and performance bonds. Finally, *political complexity* applies to purchases which Lehmann and O'Shaughnessey[16] call 'political problem products' – purchases for which different factions will be for and against. In general, the more complex the product, the more interdependent the buyer/seller relationships.

Industry characteristics

The variables proposed in Figure 2 are concentration, number of competitors, intensity of competition, rate of technical change, and traditions and norms. These variables are similar to those proposed by Robinson, Faris, and Wind[21] in their discussion of the key characteristics of the supplying industry which influence buyer behavior. Their variables are the number of potential suppliers, the type of competition (whether price or nonprice), the threat of material or parts shortages, the traditional ways of doing business, social-political-economic conditions, and significant events such as technological breakthroughs.

The importance of concentration and the number of alternative partners was recognized by the IMP Group in their original formulation of the interaction model. They also included 'dynamism' as a variable, referring to the heterogeneity of the supply market. Buyers in dynamic markets or buyers purchasing from dynamic markets, in which there is a high rate of technical change, tend to use competitive buying strategies to protect themselves from being tied to a partner who cannot keep pace. Most writers recognize that the traditions and norms of each industry have an important influence on buyer behavior, and these represent the final variable. Some industries, such as automobile manufacturing, have a reputation for using competitive buying approaches, which they are only now beginning to change.[3]

Company characteristics

The interplay of marketing and purchasing strategies and the mechanisms and atmosphere of the relationship depend on the characteristics of the parties involved. The IMP researchers proposed that the technology, size, structure, and strategy of the company be considered.[12] Some of these variables are included in Figure 2.

The relative size of the two companies is obviously important; command buying is more likely to occur when the buyer is larger than the supplier. *Relative familiarity* refers to how well the two companies know each other relative to their knowledge of other partners. Familiarity resulting from many years of trading together, as found in mature markets, favors cooperative purchasing.

Familiarity is also important with respect to technology and the costs and ways of doing business. The buyer who is familiar with the technology of the supplier and knows the supplier's costs is in a powerful position. This buyer can either use a command strategy or, where several alternatives exist, adopt a competitive purchasing approach.

The interviews on which this paper is based also revealed that companies tend to have a preferred interaction style. One well-known U.S. consumer company operating in Europe invariably uses a competitive purchasing strategy. In contrast, another U.S. company has a policy of preferring interdependent relationships with one or two key suppliers for each class of purchase.

The last interaction variable covers organization. Möller[17] distinguishes between departmental and company organization, recognizing that the structure, managerial style, and organizational climate of individual departments, as well as those of the company as a whole, must be taken into account. Möller identifies many variables but does not indicate which ones he considers most important. Research in the packing industry suggests that the extent of centralization in the buying department is a key variable. For simplicity, this is the only variable included in the model.

Individual characteristics

A relationship must ultimately depend on the interaction of the individuals who participate. In complex interactions, several members of a buying center interact with their opposite numbers in the supplying company.

Understanding of the patterns of behavior between members of a buying center is still rudimentary[14] and only recently has work been done on the interaction between the buying center and the sales team.[8,13] Cunningham and Turnbull[8] point out that interpersonal contacts fulfill different roles in different circumstances and that they vary widely in intensity and style. Indeed, individuals in some companies have preferred interaction styles. An individual's preference depends on his or her psychology. The IMP Group emphasizes motivation and experience. Möller includes all of these factors. In addition, he includes buying-related knowledge and interindividual behavior. Again, there are too many variables. In the interests of simplicity, only four variables are included in Figure 2: preferred interaction style, perceived importance of the sale or purchase, relative familiarity, and risk aversion.

Table 3 *Conditions favoring different buying strategies*

	Competitive buying	Cooperative buying	Command buying
Product characteristics	Low or high frequency of purchase Low switching costs (standardized product) Product performance can be precisely specified	High frequency of purchase High switching costs (customized product) Product performance difficult to specify	High frequency of purchase High switching costs Product can be specified but is customized
Industry characteristics	Supplier's industry fragmented Intense price competition among suppliers High rate of technical change Tradition of competitive buying	Both industries are concentrated Stable competitive situation in each industry Low rate of technical change Tradition of cooperative buying	Buyer's industry concentrated but supplier's industry fragmented Average level of competition Low rate of technical change Tradition of command buying
Company characteristics	Buying company is larger than supplier Buying company prefers competitive buying Buying company lacks familiarity with the product (new buy) Centralized buying organization	Both companies are similar in size Both companies seek a cooperative relationship Both companies are familiar with each other and respect each other's technical knowledge Organizational structures are similar	Buying company much larger than supplier Buying company prefers to dominate supplier's costs and technology Buying company is familiar with suppliers Buyer has more professional organization than supplier
Individual characteristics	Product perceived as important by buyer Buyer is not risk averse for this purchase Individuals who interact do not know each other well Buyer prefers competitive buying approach	Product is perceived as important by both parties Buyer is risk averse for this purchase Individuals who interact know each other Both buyer and seller prefer a cooperative relationship	Product is important to buyer Buyer is risk averse for this purchase Individuals know each other personally Buyer prefers a command strategy and supplier accepts cooperative role

If the buyer has a number of alternatives and the product is perceived as important, then a competitive buying approach is more likely to prevail. High relative familiarity indicates the close, cooperative relationship of the buying center members with suppliers' sale teams.

Summary

Figure 2 develops the IMP Group's interaction model by introducing the interaction strategies of the buyer and seller. It identifies the main variables which determine the choice of strategy of the buyer or seller. Three groups of variables are discussed: the product and, for both buyer and seller, the characteristics of their industry, their company, and the individuals involved in the interaction. Table 1 identified 16 variables of prime importance. Table 3 summarizes the above discussion and identifies the conditions favoring competitive, cooperative, and command purchasing strategies.

Management implications

Figure 1 identified six common types of relationships. Marketing and purchasing managers can readily identify the type of situation they are facing. Table 4 indicates the typical strategies and responses used in these

Table 4 *Marketing and purchasing strategies and responses in different types of markets*

Type of market	Typical strategies and responses	
	Marketing	Purchasing
Perfect market	Take it or leave it Try to obtain lowest cost Try to differentiate	Play the market Standardize requirements
Seller's market	Take it or leave it Form a cartel Legitimize, placate Standardize the product	Accept gracefully Buy jointly Exchange information with other buyers Complain, agitate Encourage competitors
Buyer's market	Competitive bidding Try to obtain lowest cost	Put out tenders Play the market
Domesticated market	Customize, specialize, differentiate, innovate	Adapt, cooperate, work together
Captive market	Educate the buyer	Learn from the supplier
Subcontract market	Learn from the buyer	Educate the supplier

situations. In a buyer's market, there are normally many suppliers and only a few powerful buyers. The buyers request quotations or put out competitive tenders; their approach is to 'play the market.' Suppliers must submit quotes and try to gain a competitive advantage by obtaining cost leadership or by differentiating.

In a seller's market, there are a few large suppliers and many small buyers. The sellers may see the advantage of forming a cartel to maintain prices. In this event, buyers may collaborate with other buyers and try to break the cartel, or at least exchange information to improve their bargaining position. Monopoly suppliers have different problems. Their marketing strategies are frequently directed at legitimizing their position and placating customers with elaborate complaint procedures and information campaigns. Thus, at this general level, some management insights are possible. More specific guidelines for marketing and purchasing management now follow.

Marketing management

First, the marketer must remember that buyers use more than one approach in a given supply market. Nevertheless, one approach usually predominates, and the marketer's own sales force can help to collect some simple data, such as those in Table 5, which will help to distinguish between competitive and cooperative buying strategies. Once the buying approach or strategy has been identified, clear guidelines for marketing strategies are available, as detailed in Table 6.

Marketing strategies for cooperative customers

Cooperative customers require a lot of attention. They need reassurance that their decision to concentrate their purchases and put their faith in one or two suppliers is correct. To give this reassurance,

Table 5 *Buying characteristics and buying strategies*

	Buying strategy	
Buying characteristic	Competitive	Cooperative
Number of suppliers	Many	Few
Proportion of purchases held by main suppliers	Low	High
Number of new suppliers taken on recently	Several	Few
Proportion of business given to new suppliers	Moderate	Low
Willingness to accept special adaptations	Unwilling	Willing
Desire for standardization of the product	High	Average
Technical dependence on suppliers	Low	High
Emphasis in buying	Price	Service, quality

Table 6 Marketing strategies to match different buying approaches

	Cooperative	Competitive	Command
Existing customers			
Pricing	Don't overcharge	Match market price	Negotiate prices
Customer service	Nothing is too much trouble	Competitive but no frills	At your service
Personal contacts	Frequent, including courtesy visits from senior managers	Regular visits	Ensure that personal relationships are maintained
Product development	Grasp all opportunities to work with the customer Stay ahead technically	Do what is required Beware of stealing of ideas	Work as required by the customer
New customers	Where competition is established, offer a major advantage, e.g., by innovation, or wait until there is a lapse by current competitors Beware of being exploited by a customer who has no intention of changing	Offer comparable price, service, and quality, and stress benefits of multiple sourcing	Offer facilities to make whatever is required; propose trial order

senior management from the supplying company must visit these customers and take every opportunity to develop social changes. The service which cooperative customers receive needs to be excellent, and the supplier must stay ahead technically to justify this privileged position. Pricing is one of the most difficult areas with cooperative customers, since the marketer must recover operating costs but avoid overcharging lest this provide an opportunity for competitors to penetrate the account. The objective should be to use customers' cooperation to find ways to meet their needs, preferably over time. This could lead to reduced costs, and enable a marketer to supply at a competitive price and make a good margin. Marketers who take advantage of a cooperative customer's loyalty and charge an elevated price run the risk of permanently ruining the relationship if the customer realizes that he or she has been overcharged. Such an occurrence breaks the feeling of mutual dependence and shared objectives on which this type of relationship depends. Deprived of reassurance of equity in the relationship, the customer is likely to react sharply.

Knowledge of a customer's purchasing approach is very helpful when deciding which companies are the best prospects for future business. In mature markets, customers with cooperative purchasing strategies have, by definition, developed long-term relationships. These are difficult to penetrate unless the marketer can offer a significant price reduction or innovation which the existing supplier cannot match.

Marketers should be cautious about spending large sums in an effort to obtain business from such customers, who normally favor existing suppliers and are likely to give them an opportunity to match any new offers they receive. If the marketer has no significant advantage to offer, the only option is to wait until the customer is dissatisfied with the existing supplier or until there is a structural change such as a merger or takeover, which may sever existing links between personnel. The bonds with existing customers are also broken when there is a change in the customer's own market position. Such events provide good opportunities for the astute marketer.

Marketing strategies for competitive customers

Customers with competitive purchasing strategies require different handling. Marketing costs and contracts with competitive customers must be kept to a minimum because their prime concern is price. Many suppliers know the frustration of losing an order to a lower-priced competitor. A careful balance has to be struck between the advantages of differentiating the product by providing additional services and the disadvantage of a price which is out of step with the market price. Resources may be better deployed in searching for production economies which will lower the price.

Companies with competitive purchasing strategies may be the easiest to obtain as new customers. Their interest can often be gained by offering a comparable, or preferably better, price, quality, and service. The marketer should stress the benefits of multiple sourcing.

Marketing strategies for companies with command purchasing

The company subject to a command purchasing strategy should also keep its marketing costs to a minimum. The supplier's role is to do the buyer's bidding, and the keys to success are flexibility, personal attention to the buying company's needs, and efficient production facilities. These are the points to stress in the search for new customers.

Conclusions

This paper sets out to overcome the problem that research on organizational buying behavior has yielded few guidelines for management action.

Marketing and purchasing behaviors are classified into three interaction strategies. The buying decision process is modeled as resulting from the interplay of these strategies, which in turn are influenced by the characteristics of the product, the buyer, and the seller. A multitude of variables influence buyer and seller behavior. Sixteen variables relevant to both buyers and sellers are incorporated in the model because they seem to be the most important in influencing the choice of interaction strategy. Although useful guidelines have been developed, research has been conducted only in the packaging industry, and additional research in other industries is now required.

References

1 Blois, K.J. Vertical quasi-integration. *Journal of Industrial Economics* 20:253–272 (1972).
2 Bubb, P.L., Van Rest, D.J. Loyalty as a component of the industrial buying decision. *Industrial Marketing Management* 3:25–32 (1973).
3 *Business Week*, 1982, pp. 62–63.
4 Campbell, N.C.G., Cunningham, M.T. Interaction strategies for the management of buyer/seller relationships. *Journal of Marketing*. In Review.
5 Cardozo, R.N. Situational segmentation of industrial markets. *European Journal of Marketing* 14:22–238 (April-May 1981).
6 Corey, E.R. *Procurement Management: Strategy, Organization and Decision Making*. Boston: CBI Publishing (1978).
7 Cunningham, M.T. An interaction approach to purchasing strategy, in H. Håkasson, ed., *International Marketing and Purchasing of Industrial Goods: An Interaction Approach*. Chichester: Wiley (1982).

8 Cunningham, M.T., Turnbull, P.W. Inter-organizational personal contact patterns, in H. Håkansson, ed., *International Marketing and Purchasing of Industrial Goods: An Interaction Approach*. Chichester: Wiley (1982).

9 Cunningham, M.T., Kettlewood, K. Source loyalty in the freight transport market. *European Journal of Marketing* 10:66–79 (January 1976).

10 Farmer, D.H. Developing purchasing strategies. *Journal of Purchasing and Materials Management* 6–11 (Fall 1978).

11 Ford, D. The development of buyer–seller relationships in industrial markets, in H. Håkansson, ed., *International Marketing and Purchasing of Industrial Goods: An Interaction Approach*. Chichester: Wiley (1982).

12 Håkasson, ed. *International Marketing and Purchasing of Industrial Goods: An Interaction Approach*. Chichester: Wiley (1982).

13 Homse. E. An interaction approach to marketing and purchasing strategy. Unpublished Ph.D. dissertation, University of Manchester, Institute of Science and Technology (1981).

14 Johnston, W.J., Spekman, R.E. Industrial buying behavior: A need for an integrative approach. *Journal of Business Research* 10:135–146 (June 1982).

15 Laczniak, G.R., Murphy, P.E. Fine tuning organizational buying models, in C.W. Lamb and P.M. Dunne, eds., *Theoretical Development in Marketing*. Chicago: American Marketing Association (1982).

16 Lehmann. D.R., O'Shaughnessy. J. Difference in attribute importance for different industrial products. *Journal of Marketing* 38:36–42 (April 1974).

17 Möller. K. *Industrial Buying Behaviour of Production Materials: A Conceptual Model and Analysis*. Helsinki: School of Economics Publications. Series B-54 (1981).

18 Ouchi, W.G. A conceptual framework for the design of organizational control mechanisms. *Management Science* 25:833–848 (1979).

19 Ouchi, W.G. Markets, bureaucracies and clans. *Administrative Science Quarterly* 25:129–139 (March 1980).

20 Porter, M.E. *Competitive Strategy*. New York: Free Press (1980).

21 Robinson, P.J., Faris. C.W., Wind, Y. *Industrial Buying and Creative Marketing*. Boston: Allyn and Bacon (1967).

22 Sheth, J.N. A model of industrial buyer behaviour. *Journal of Marketing* 37:50–56 (1973).

23 Webster, F.E., Wind, Y. *Organizational Buying Behaviour*. Englewood Cliffs, N.J.: Prentice-Hall (1972).

24 Williamson, Oliver E. *Markets and Hierarchies*. New York: Free Press (1975).

25 Williamson, O.E. Transaction cost economics: The governance of contractual relations. *Journal of Law and Economics* 22:223–261 (October 1979).

26 Wind, Y. Industrial source loyalty. *Journal of Marketing Research* 7:450–457 (November 1970).

27 Wind, Y. Organizational buying behaviour, in G. Zaltman and T. Bonoma, eds., *Review of Marketing*. Chicago: American Marketing Association (1978).
28 Wind, Y., Thomas, R.J. Conceptual and methodological issues in organizational buying behaviour. *European Journal of Marketing* 14:239–261 (May-June 1981).

3 RELATIONSHIP MARKETING – SERVICES PERSPECTIVE

Relationship marketing has been receiving increasing attention in recent years as more and more organizations focus their attention on retaining existing customers rather than attracting new ones. Although the origins of relationship marketing are to be found in an industrial context, it is with the increasing importance of the services sector during the last decade that relationship marketing has emerged as an important topic in helping marketers focus on maintaining and enhancing customer relationships.

Berry first introduced the concept of relationship marketing, in a service context, to describe a longer-term approach to marketing. A similar idea emerged in what has been called 'The Nordic School of Services', which emphasizes interactive marketing and building interactive relationships in industrial and services markets.[1-6] Research undertaken in the Nordic School over the past decade, in the area of industrial and services marketing, has concluded that 'the most important issue in marketing is to establish, strengthen and develop customer relationships: – where this can be done at a profit, and – where individual and organisational objectives are met'.[4]

The three articles chosen for this chapter address some key issues relating to relationship marketing from a services perspective. The article by Berry defines the relationship marketing concept and considers the conditions under which the practice of relationship marketing is most applicable. Berry goes on to outline five specific relationship marketing strategies available to service organizations which should be considered when developing a relationship marketing plan. These are: core service marketing; relationship customization; service augmentation; relationship pricing; and internal marketing. Each of these strategies are illustrated with examples of companies that have successfully used relationship marketing strategies in the development of their businesses.

The article by Berry and Gresham discusses developing relationship marketing strategies and implementation guidelines in a retailing context. The central theme of this article is the need to transform customers into clients. Berry and Gresham argue that by treating the customer as a client rather than 'a face in the crowd', and by individualizing service and tailoring it to customers' specific requirements, clients are more likely to be loyal to particular retailers. This is particularly important in today's competitive environment, where retailers are frequently offering the same merchandise and where the only key differentiator is in the way retailers treat their customers.

In order to transform the customers into clients Berry and Gresham provide a series of useful implementation guidelines. They refer to these guidelines as 'the quality loop' and briefly discuss each of the sections in the loop, namely: establish standards; hire helpful personnel; train staff; monitor staff performance; and reward staff competence.

Although the issues presented in this article are industry-specific, they are nevertheless relevant to many other business sectors and the implementation section provides a very useful framework for companies embarking on a relationship marketing programme.

Grönroos's article is a valuable contribution. First, it builds on Berry's relationship marketing concept and further develops the relationship marketing definition. Second, it highlights two crucial interfaces between marketing and organizational behaviour, namely, the need for a service culture and internal marketing. Grönroos argues that because the service production cannot be standardized and because customers and their behaviour cannot be standardized, a service-oriented culture is needed which tells employees how to respond to unusual and unforeseen circumstances. He also sees internal marketing as a means of developing and maintaining a service culture. The focus here is how to get and retain customer-conscious employees. These two critical topics will be discussed as a means of establishing a customer-oriented culture for relationship marketing in the following chapters.

These three articles were chosen because they highlight the key issues relating to relationship marketing in a service context. The first two discuss key relationship strategies, whilst introducing the importance of internal marketing and having the 'right' staff. The third article examines in more detail the critical interface between marketing and organizational behaviour and challenges academics and practitioners from both disciplines to work together and break down the traditional functional barriers which so often prevent business success.

References

1 Gummesson, E. (1981). Marketing cost concepts in service firms. *Industrial Marketing Management*, No. 3.
2 Gummesson, E. (1987). The new marketing – developing long-term interactive relationships. *Long Range Planning*, **20**, No. 4, 10–20.
3 Grönroos, C. (1978). A service-oriented approach to marketing of services. *European Journal of Marketing*, **12**, 588–601.
4 Grönroos, C. (1990a). Marketing redefined, *Management Decision*, **28**, No. 8, 5–9.

5 Grönroos, C. (1990b). The marketing strategy continuum, toward a marketing concept for the 1990's, *Meddelanden Fran Svenska Handel-shogskolan*, Working Paper, 201.
6 Hakansson, H. (ed.) (1982). *International Marketing and Purchasing of Industrial Goods*, John Wiley, New York.

RELATIONSHIP MARKETING
Leonard L. Berry

Leonard Berry is Foley's/Federated Professor of Retailing and Marketing Studies and director of the Center for Retailing Studies in the College of Business Administration at Texas A&M University. He is president of the American Marketing Association and writes a marketing column for *American Banker*. His most recent books are *Marketing Financial Services: A Strategic Vision* and *Bankers Who Sell*.

This article, like the Levitt article in the previous chapter, is a landmark piece in the area of relationship marketing with a services perspective. In the paper Berry introduces the concept of relationship marketing and defines it as '... attracting, maintaining and – in multi-service organizations – enhancing customer relationships'. He argues that it is a useful approach for many service organizations and discusses some of the main relationship marketing strategies available to such organizations. In his paper, Berry provides many examples of organizations using such approaches.

Introduction

When it comes to marketing, many service firms devote most of their resources to attracting new customers. Efforts to retain existing customers are minimal, at least insofar as formal marketing programming is concerned. This view of marketing is needlessly restrictive and potentially wasteful.

It is needlessly restrictive because firms benefit by keeping valued customers as well as by attracting new customers. Assuming equality in customer attractiveness, the firm that attracts 100 new customers and loses 20 existing customers for a net gain of 80 customers is better off than the firm attracting 130 new customers but losing 60 for a net gain of 70 customers.

The 'new customer only' approach to marketing can also be wasteful since it conceivably may cost more to acquire new customers than retain or build up existing ones. For example, a firm spending $1 million in advertising to attract new customers may experience less of a gain in net business than if it were to spend $750,000 divided among new customer advertising, direct mail to existing customers promoting additional services, and staff training to improve service quality.

Thinking of marketing in terms of *having customers*, not merely *acquiring customers*, is crucial for service firms. The combined impact of low growth rates in many service industries and deregulation – which has centered on service industries – is resulting in 'everyone getting into everyone else's business.' Securities brokerage companies have attracted billions of deposit dollars from banking and thrift institutions through money market mutual funds. Sears, which announced the acquisition of the nation's largest real estate company (Coldwell-Banker) and fifth-largest securities firm (Dean Witter) within the span of one month in 1981, is gearing up to become the United States' largest department store of financial services. The discount brokerage sector of the securities industry is emerging as a significant competitive influence and will become a major factor now that banks are entering this business. The Airline Deregulation Act has resulted in intense competition – and price cutting – on popular routes. Consumers can now select from among multiple suppliers of long-distance telephone service. Clearly, marketing to *protect the customer base* is becoming exceedingly important in a wide variety of service industries.

This paper introduces the concept of 'Relationship Marketing' and discusses some of the principal relationship marketing strategies available to service organizations. The theme is that relationship marketing is an appropriate and useful approach for many service firms.

What is relationship marketing?

Relationship marketing is attracting, maintaining and – in multi-service organizations – enhancing customer relationships. Servicing and selling existing customers is viewed to be just as important to long-term marketing success as acquiring new customers. Good service is necessary to retain the relationship. Good selling is necessary to enhance it. The marketing mind-set is that the attraction of new customers is merely *the first step* in the marketing process. Cementing the relationship, transforming indifferent customers into loyal ones, serving customers as clients – this is marketing too.

For such a basic idea, there has been relatively little attention paid it in the services marketing literature. As Schneider (1980, p. 54) writes:

> What is surprising is that (1) researchers and businessmen have concentrated far more on how to attract consumers to products and services than on how to retain those customers, (2) there is almost no published research on the retention of service consumers, and (3) consumer evaluation of products or services has rarely been used as a criterion or index of organizational effectiveness.

Although smaller than one would expect, a body of literature relating to the idea of relationship marketing is developing. Levitt (1981) emphasizes the need for firms marketing intangible products to engage in constant reselling efforts. Ryans and Wittink (1977) have categorized services based on the degree of differentiation of competing service offerings and the ability of consumers to change suppliers and have suggested that many service firms pay inadequate attention to encouraging customer loyalty. Grönroos (1981), Berry (1980, 1981), George (1977) and others have stressed improving the performance of service personnel as a means of retaining customers. Berry and Thompson (1982) have applied relationship marketing to the banking industry, claiming the concept 'will dominate retail bank marketing practice and thought throughout the 1980s.'

The practice of relationship marketing is most applicable to a service firm when each of the following conditions exists:

1 There is an ongoing or periodic desire for the service on the part of the service customer, e.g., telephone or janitorial service versus funeral home service.
2 The service customer controls selection of the service supplier, e.g., selecting a dry cleaner or dentist versus entering the first taxi in the airport waiting line.
3 There are alternative service suppliers and customer switching from one to another is common, e.g., patronizing various restaurants or airlines versus buying electricity from the one electric utility serving a community.

These conditions are actually quite prevalent. Relatively few service firms sell 'one-time' services and in most service situations the customer both controls the choice process and has alternatives from which to choose. When these conditions do exist, the opportunity to not just attract customers but to build relationships with them is present. Required are specific strategies that differentiate the service from competitive offerings on dimensions that are meaningful to customers and difficult for competitors to duplicate (Ryans and Wittink, p. 314).

Relationship marketing strategies

There are a number of possible relationship marketing strategies to be considered in the development of a relationship marketing plan. Discussed in this paper are five such strategies:

1 Core Service Strategy
2 Relationship Customization
3 Service Augmentation
4 Relationship Pricing
5 Internal Marketing

These strategies are not totally independent of one another and can be used in combination. A firm might use all five simultaneously.

Core service

A key strategy in relationship marketing is the design and marketing of a 'core service' around which a customer relationship can be established. The ideal core service is one that attracts new customers through its need-meeting character, cements the business through its quality, multiple parts, and long-term nature, and provides a base for the selling of additional services over time (Berry and Thompson). Core services are directed toward central rather than peripheral target market needs.

An example of a core service is the 'Individual Financial Services' program offered through the trust department of Wachovia Bank and Trust headquartered in Winston-Salem, North Carolina. In this program customers select those specific services they wish from a package of services including tax preparation, cash flow analysis, budget assistance, insurance analysis, investment analysis, purchase and safekeeping of securities, financial record keeping, bill paying, asset management, and estate planning. Customers pay only for those services they select. The Individual Financial Services program addresses affluent consumer needs that many banks fail to address, has multiple parts, is long-term in nature, and offers a platform from which other financial services can be sold.

Merrill-Lynch's Cash Management Account also illustrates the concept of a core service. Introduced in 1977, the Cash Management Account is a $20,000 minimum balance margin account that automatically sweeps money from stock or bond sales into a money market fund. Consumers can access the dollars in their money fund account by writing a check or using a Visa debit card. If the balance in the money fund account is insufficient to cover such transactions, credit collateralized by securities is automatically extended.

By the fall of 1982, Merrill-Lynch had more than 750,000 Cash Management Account customers with an average account balance of about $67,000. The appeal of this service to upscale consumers has recently prompted other securities firms and, increasingly, commercial banks to develop their own versions of the service. However, the lag time of several years between when Merrill-Lynch launched the service and when similar services began appearing from competitors allowed Merrill-Lynch to attract many thousands of new clients who then became prospects for the firm's other service lines.

Customizing the relationship

The nature of services affords many service firms the opportunity to customize the relationship. By learning about the specific characteristics and requirements of individual customers, and then capturing these data for use as needed, service firms can more precisely tailor service to the situation at hand. In so doing, they provide their customers with an incentive to remain as customers rather than 'starting over' with other suppliers.

The possibilities for relationship customization are considerable, especially when personal service capabilities are combined with electronic data processing capabilities. For example, Xerox has introduced a service system called 'Field Work Support System' that involves keeping the history of a customer's equipment in a computerized data bank. When assistance is required, the customer calls a 'work support representative' on a toll-free number. The representative can instantly access data concerning the customer's location, equipment, and its service record. If the problem cannot be worked out over the telephone using a computer checklist, a field service representative is sent to the customer's site.

American Express has recently run a print advertisement for the American Express Card with the headline: 'When you have a question on a bill, you'll get some human understanding.' The small copy then reads:

> This is not a recording. American Express Card customer service telephones are answered by real live people. Sure, the service centers are equipped with some amazing computers, but we count on our people to be equipped with brains of their own, as well. So they're expected and authorized to use their judgment and initiative to solve billing problems, and to explain the many services that go along with the Cardmembership.

Free Spirit Travel, a Colorado-based travel agency with several outlets, assigns frequent traveler commercial clients a specific travel agent to coordinate all travel arrangements. The travel consultant develops a personal profile card on each business traveler in a company and records such information as preferred form of payment, secretary's name, and seating preferences in computerized reservation system client files. Clients receive personalized baggage tags with the travel consultant's business card on one side (in case of emergency) and the traveler's own business card on the other side.

Automotive Systems, a foreign car repair firm near Atlanta, provides explicit notes on customer service bills specifying the work that still needs to be done on the car and the time frame within which it should be done.

Whereas goods are manufactured, services are performed. Frequently they are performed by people who are in the position to custom-fit the service to the customer's particular requirements. If the customer receives custom service from company A but not from company B – and if receiving custom service is valued by the customer – then the customer is less likely to leave company A for B than would otherwise be the case.

Service augmentation

Another relationship marketing strategy is service augmentation. Service augmentation involves building 'extras' into the service to differentiate it from competitive offerings. For meaningful service differentiation to occur, the extras must be genuine extras – that is, not readily available from competitors – that are valued by customers. When this is the case, customer loyalty is encouraged. As Levitt writes (1974, pp. 9–10): 'Having been offered these extras, the customer finds them beneficial and therefore prefers doing business with the company that supplies them.'

One practitioner of service augmentation is the Fairfax Hotel in Washington, D.C. The Fairfax attempts to differentiate itself with its upscale target market by providing concierge service, night butler and 24-hour room service, a multi-lingual staff, a morning newspaper delivered to all guest rooms, a mint and cognac with the evening turn-down service, and room amenities including terry-cloth robe, linen laundry bag and bathroom telephone. More than 60% of the Fairfax Hotel guests have stayed there previously (Gates 1982).

A totally different application of service augmentation in the same industry is Holiday Inn's 'No Excuses' room guarantee program. Holiday Inn places the following written guarantee in each room:

● Your room will be right. It will be clean, everything will work properly, and you'll have enough of everything you need.
● Or we will make it right.
● Or we will refund the cost of your room for that night.

One form of service augmentation becoming more prominent is the 'preferred customer club.' By inviting priority customers to join a company-sponsored club, the service company augments the offer with special services and added prestige while establishing a vehicle to stay in touch with these customers through promotional mailings, newsletters and the like. Marriott's Club Marquis provides still another example from the hotel industry. There is no membership fee to belong to Club Marquis. To qualify for membership, an individual must stay at Marriott hotels on five separate occasions and have their visits validated. Members receive the following services:

● Express reservation service through a toll-free number.
● Reservations automatically guaranteed for late arrival.
● Pre-registration.
● Most deluxe accommodations in the rate category requested.
● Check-cashing privileges.
● Complimentary *Wall Street Journal* delivered to the room each morning.
● Express check-out.
● Semi-annual newsletter.

Members also receive an identification card and personalized luggage tags. Club Marquis memberships are honored at all Marriott properties.

The three hotel examples used demonstrate the inherent flexibility of service augmentation. The 'extras' can be anything so long as they are valued by the target market and not easily matched by competitors. The use of hotel examples does not mean, however, the concept is applicable only to hotels. The real estate company that spends a portion of an anticipated listing commission to cosmetically upgrade a home prior to marketing it is using service augmentation. So is the car rental company that provides time-saving services to members of a preferred membership club and the bank that conducts business management seminars for its small business clients.

Relationship pricing

An old marketing idea – a better price for better customers – forms the basis of relationship pricing, another strategy option available to service companies pursuing customer loyalty. Relationship pricing means pricing services to encourage relationships. In effect, customers are given a price incentive to consolidate much or all of their business with one supplier.

Although the concept of quantity discounts is not new, some service companies are applying the concept in innovative ways. The 'frequent flyer' programs of various airlines, which offer travelers upgrades to first class seating and free trips if they fly a certain number of miles on a given carrier, are an attempt to build brand loyalty in what many regard as a commodity business. An April 1982 poll of more than 6,000 frequent flyers indicated that 77% of the respondents were participating in an airline frequent flyer incentive program (*Frequent Flyer* 1982).

Transamerica Corporation sponsored a program during 1982 in which passengers on its airline could receive first day car rental free when renting from Budget Rent a Car for three or more days. Citibank was one of the first banks to offer consumers reduced installment and mortgage loan rates in return for their checking and savings account business.

As with the other relationship marketing strategies presented, relationship pricing can be implemented in various ways in various service industries. For example, a sports team could package a third or one half its home games for a reduced per game price to encourage fans who cannot afford or do not want season tickets to attend more games. A university could offer reduced tuition for each additional family member enrolling. A movie theater could sponsor a 'Tuesday Night at the Movies Club' with participants buying a ticket packet including five regularly priced tickets, five reduced priced tickets, and two free tickets. Regardless of the form relationship pricing takes, the objective remains the same: to encourage customer loyalty by rewarding it.

Internal marketing

A pivotal relationship marketing strategy for many service firms is internal marketing. There are several forms of internal marketing. What all forms have in common is the 'customer' is inside the organization. The usage in this paper is the employee as the customer and the job as the product.

The people who buy goods and services in the role of consumer are the same people who buy jobs. What is known in marketing about selling and reselling them goods and services can also be used in selling and reselling them jobs. The stress placed on customer satisfaction in external marketing is just as appropriate, just as necessary, in internal marketing.

Internal marketing is relevant to virtually all organizations. It is especially important, however, for labor-intensive service organizations. In these organizations, the quality of services sold is determined in large measure by the skills and work attitudes of the personnel producing the services. To the extent that labor-intensive service firms can use marketing to attract, keep, and motivate quality personnel, they improve their capability to offer quality services. Offering services that consistently meet the quality requirements of target markets is clearly an important factor in building strong customer relationships in many service industries.

The processes one thinks of as marketing – for example, marketing research, market segmentation, product modification, and communications programming – are just as relevant to internal marketing as to external marketing. Just as marketing research procedures can be used to identify needs, wants and attitudes in the external marketplace, so can they be used for the same purposes in the internal marketplace. Marriott Corporation, for instance, annually surveys employees at each of its hotels about their jobs. Survey results are discussed with the management of the hotel property and shared with upper management at Marriott headquarters. Minnesota Power and Light and GEICO are among the service companies that have regularly used small group meetings between senior management and employees to encourage dialogue and feedback (*Business Week* 1979). If employee needs and wants are to be satisfied, they must first be identified. The tools and techniques of marketing research can help.

To combat high turnover rates for bank tellers, which averaged 40% in 1979 (Zweig 1980), a growing number of banks are implementing teller accreditation/career advancement programs. Generally, these programs are designed to raise the stature of the teller position while allowing promotion and personal growth opportunities *within* it. In-bank and non-bank courses, examinations, time-in-grade, and favorable job performance evaluations are typical requirements for becoming certified. First Interstate Bank of Arizona lowered its teller turnover rate from 42% in 1979 to 35% in 1980 after instituting a teller certification program (*American Banker* 1981). In effect, banks developing such programs are modifying the teller job-product for a market segment willing to take on extra assignments and tasks to move forward in their jobs.

The growing number of service companies instituting 'flexible work hour' or 'cafeteria benefit' programs are also responding to the heterogeneity of the work force by segmenting the market and modifying the job-product to better fit the requirements of different segments.

Formal communications programming designed to shape work attitudes and behavior can also be an important element of an internal marketing strategy. For example, a service company's advertising directed to the external customer can often be designed in such a way that it motivates and/or educates employees as well. Indeed, employees are an important 'second audience' for a company's advertising (George and Berry 1981). Recent Delta Airline advertising making repeated references to Delta employees as 'professionals' and including pictures of actual employees is an example of advertising to external and internal audiences simultaneously.

In essence, internal marketing involves creating an organizational climate in general, and job-products in particular, that lead to the right service personnel performing the service in the right way. In consumption circumstances in which the performance of people is what is being sold, the marketing task is not only that of encouraging external customers to buy but also that of encouraging internal customers to perform. When internal customers perform, the likelihood of external customers *continuing* to buy is increased.

Conclusion

Relationship marketing concerns attracting, maintaining and – in multiservice firms – building customer relationships. The relationship marketing firm invests in formal marketing programming not only to attract new customers but also to keep and improve existing customers. Attracting new customers is viewed as an *intermediate* objective.

Relationship marketing is applicable when there is an ongoing or periodic desire for the service and when the customer controls the selection of a service supplier and has alternatives from which to choose. The concept is critical for those service firms vulnerable to customer loss due to intensifying intratype and/or intertype competition.

Discussed in this paper were the five relationship marketing strategies of core service marketing, relationship customization, service augmentation, relationship pricing, and internal marketing. These strategies can be used in combination and in fact a service firm might use all five simultaneously. The common element in all relationship marketing strategies is the *incentive* the customer is given to remain a customer. The incentive may be extra service (service augmentation) or a price break (relationship pricing) or something else but in each case the customer is given one or more reasons not to change suppliers.

References

American Banker (1981), 'Incentives Lower Teller Turnover in Arizona,' (March 6), 2.

Berry, Leonard L. (1980), 'Services Marketing Is Different,' *Business*, (May-June), 25–26.

—— (1981), 'The Employee as Customer,' *Journal of Retail Banking*, (March), 33–40.

—— and Thomas W. Thompson (1982), 'Relationship Banking: The Art of Turning Customers into Clients,' *Journal of Retail Banking*, (June), 64–73.

Business Week (1979). 'Deep Sensing: A Pipeline to Employee Morale,' (January 28), 124–128.

Frequent Flyer (1982), 'The Frequent Flyer Poll,' (September), 13.

Gates, Anita (1982), 'Roots,' *Frequent Flyer*, (July), 43.

George, William R. (1977), 'The Retailing of Services: A Challenging Future,' *Journal of Retailing*, (Fall), 85–98.

—— and Leonard L. Berry (1981), 'Guidelines for Advertising Services,' *Business Horizons*, (July-August), 52–56.

Grönroos, Christian (1981), 'Internal Marketing – An Integral Part of Marketing Theory,' in *Marketing of Services*, James H. Donnelly and William R. George, eds., Chicago: American Marketing Association.

Levitt, Theodore (1974), *Marketing For Business Growth*, New York: McGraw-Hill Book Company, 9–10.

—— (1981), 'Marketing Intangible Products and Product Intangibles,' *Harvard Business Review*, (May-June) 94–102.

Ryans, Adrian B. and Dick R. Wittink (1977), 'The Marketing of Services: Categorization with Implications for Strategy,' in *Contemporary Marketing Thought*, Barnett Greenberg and Danny Bellenger, eds., Chicago: American Marketing Association, 312–314.

Schneider, Benjamin (1980), 'The Service Organization: Climate Is Crucial,' *Organizational Dynamics*, (Autumn), 54.

Zweig, Phillip L. (1980), 'Role of Tellers Reassessed; Banks Opening Career Paths,' *American Banker*, (December 10), 17.

RELATIONSHIP RETAILING: TRANSFORMING CUSTOMERS INTO CLIENTS
Leonard L. Berry and Larry G. Gresham

Leonard Berry is Foley's/Federated Professor of Retailing and Marketing Studies and director of the Center for Retailing Studies in the College of Business Administration at Texas A&M University. He is president of the American Marketing Association and writes a marketing column for *American Banker*. His most recent books are *Marketing Financial Services: A Strategic Vision* and *Bankers Who Sell*. Larry Gresham is assistant professor of marketing at Texas A&M, where he is a member of the Center for Retailing Studies Faculty Committee.

This paper focuses on marketing to existing clients in a retailing context. It makes the distinction between customers and clients and argues that when specific personnel handle an account, customers become clients. Like the previous paper, it also introduces and defines relationship marketing. However, it goes on to discuss strategy approaches and presents implementation guidelines in a retailing context.

Retailers can build sales volume in three ways. One way is to attract new customers. Another way is to do more business with existing customers. A third way is to reduce the loss of customers. Retailers who direct formalized marketing to *existing* customers address two of the three possibilities; they increase the opportunity to sell more products to present customers while reducing the chances of customers straying to the competition.

Moreover, marketing costs per unit of sales are typically lower for existing customers than for customer prospects. As one retailer states: 'It is easier to expand sales from an already loyal customer base than to convert non-shoppers to shoppers.'[1]

Thinking of marketing in terms of *having* customers, not merely *acquiring* customers, is crucial as fierce competition reshapes the retailing environment. This article focuses on marketing to existing customers. It introduces and defines the concept of 'relationship retailing,' which can be a potent response to competitive turbulence. It discusses strategy approaches and presents implementation guidelines.

What is relationship retailing?

Relationship retailing means attracting, retaining, and enhancing client relationships. Service and sales to existing clients are considered just as important to long-term marketing success as the acquisition of new clients. Good service is necessary to retain the relationship. Good selling is necessary to enhance it. The marketing mind-set is that attracting new customers is an *intermediate* step in the marketing process. Building the relationship, transforming indifferent customers into loyal clients – this, too, is considered marketing.

The practice of relationship retailing is most appropriate when:

- The consumer periodically rebuys in the product classifications sold by the retailer (for example, buying fashion apparel rather than a cemetery plot);
- The consumer has alternatives from which to choose (for example, buying housewares rather than electricity);
- The consumer is ego-involved (for example, buying home furnishings rather than frozen foods);
- The consumer requires personal service and/or selling (for example, buying an automobile rather than a light bulb).

The first two conditions apply to the vast majority of retailers. The last two conditions apply largely to service-intensive specialty and department store companies. Relationship retailing's potential is greatest when all four conditions exist. A related concept – 'retention retailing' – is more appropriate when only the first two conditions exist, such as with most self-service retail outlets.

The key factor in assessing the potential for relationship retailing is the degree of personal interaction, service, and selling involved in the retailer/customer encounter. Labor-intensive encounters – especially for ego-intensive products – present the opportunity to transform customers into clients. The distinction between 'customer' and 'client' is important. Clients are served by specific personnel who 'handle' their accounts. Personalized marketing, tailored to individual personalities and requirements, is emphasized.

Strategies in relationship retailing

Relationship retailing requires specific strategies that differentiate a retailer's offer in ways that are important to the target market and difficult for competitors to duplicate.[2] Two strategies that potentially meet these criteria are *relationship customization* and *offer augmentation*. The most powerful relationship programs incorporate both strategies.

Relationship customization

Relationship customization involves learning the preferences of individual clients, capturing this information so that it can be readily accessed, and then using it to best advantage in merchandising and serving client requirements. Relationship customization can be powerful:

- The telephone call to the client who is partial to the color red about the striking red dress that just arrived in the store;

- The invitation to a select group of clients to attend a special fashion seminar;
- The handwritten card to thank a client for a purchase.

Facing a growing array of discount, off-price, and no-frills competitors, many department and specialty store retailers are finding that their best marketing opportunities lie in *adding* rather than *reducing* service. Adding value by 'custom-fitting' client personalities (as well as their bodies), by contacting clients with ideas rather than waiting for them to initiate contact, by standing ready to serve *after* the sale, not just before the sale – in these ways relationship customizing institutions earn their higher margins.

The most effective relationship customizers specialize in individual clients, not just lines of merchandise. Relationship customizers give clients an incentive to remain loyal rather than starting over as 'customers' with other companies.

Personal shopper services, such as Macy's 'Buy Appointment,' Carson Pirie Scott's 'Executive Delivery Service,' Neiman-Marcus' 'Silver Key Club,' and Broadway's 'TIME,' illustrate the relationship customization approach. These programs generally require clients to provide demographic, size, and life-style information as well as color, style, and fabric preferences. This information is then used by personal consultants, who assemble suitable merchandise for clients to consider during a scheduled appointment.

Macy's 'Buy Appointment' service works as follows: The client and consultant confer by telephone about the client's need for several outfits. An appointment to meet in the store is made. When the client arrives at the store, various outfits to consider and try on are waiting. If the size, color, or styling is wrong or accessories are needed, the consultant searches the store for additional merchandise. The client remains in the dressing room area, being spared the inconvenience of dressing to find other outfits in the store to try on. The consultant – likely one of the most knowledgeable and polished salespeople in the entire store – keeps on file all of the gathered client information. The next time the client needs a special gift for an uncle's seventy-fifth birthday or a wedding present for a business associate, the client can ask the consultant to pull together some gift ideas or even to select a gift to be discussed on the telephone. If acceptable, the consultant then arranges for the card to be prepared and the gift to be wrapped and delivered.

The 'Buy Appointment' service appeals to client prospects who:

- Need to shop but don't like to;
- Perhaps like to shop but don't have the time; and
- Are responsive to specialized, personalized attention.

The possibilities for relationship customization are especially impressive when personal service capabilities are combined with electronic data processing capabilities. A Ritz-Carlton hotel in California stores all information from guest registration cards in a computerized system. This information is immediately displayed on terminals used by front-desk personnel when a repeat guest visits the hotel. The marketing implications of such a system are considerable. For example, the guest's assigned room may be prestocked with the whiskey brand and hairdryer that were requested on a previous visit.

If a consumer receives personalized, customized service from retailer A but not from retailer B – and if this service is valued – then the consumer will be less likely to leave retailer A for B. Simply put, clients are more likely to be loyal than are customers.

Offer augmentation

A related strategy is offer augmentation. Offer augmentation involves building 'extras' into the retail offer to differentiate it from competitive offerings. For meaningful augmentation to occur, the extras must be genuine extras which are not readily available from competitors and are valued by clients.

An example of offer augmentation is Sears' 'Mature Outlook' program for consumers 50 years of age or older. Meant to strengthen ties with a growing, increasingly affluent market segment, the program includes such extras as a magazine and newsletter targeted for this market, discounts on Sears' products and on the products of other companies, travel accident insurance, and financial reviews and seminars. A nominal annual membership fee is charged.

The extras in offer augmentation need not be expensive to be effective. Curtis Mathes' service personnel complete each television installation by placing a rose atop the newly purchased set. This program adds far more value to Curtis Mathes' client relationship than the cost of each rose.

Intangibles may also be used to augment the retail offer. Macy's and Bloomingdale's, among others, have combined merchandise fashion, store fashion, and special event programming with such zeal and effectiveness that they in effect augment the basic retail offer with prestige and entertainment. These retailers are sensory retailers; their chief tool is the stunning visual effect.[3] The store is a stage, and the idea is to make good theater to keep consumers coming back for more.

A special kind of offer augmentation is reward augmentation, where clients earn extras based on purchasing performance. Palais Royal's VIP credit card and Neiman-Marcus' InCircle program illustrate this approach. Palais Royal, a Houston-based apparel chain, mails the VIP card to consumers who charge more than $1,000 in a given year. The card entitles its holder to free gift wrapping, free monogramming on sweaters, use of a 24-hour toll-free message service, birthday reminders, and other services.

Neiman-Marcus' InCircle program offers free gift selections to clients based on cumulative charge purchases during a 12-month period. One recognition point is awarded for every dollar spent on a Neiman-Marcus charge account. Clients are notified of accumulated InCircle points on billing statements. Eligibility for gift redemption starts at 3,000 recognition points. Program participants may accumulate points toward a higher recognition level. InCircle participants also receive a quarterly newsletter, important date reminders, special charge cards with the InCircle logo, a toll-free number to call for special assistance, and other services.

Offer augmentation is a flexible concept. The possibilities include *blanket* augmentation for everyone (Macy's sensory strategies), *selective* augmentation for a market segment (Sears' Mature Outlook program), or *reward* augmentation for core clients (Neiman-Marcus' InCircle program). In each case the idea is to offer extras not available from competitors to encourage more loyalty and patronage.

Implementing relationship retailing

Competing retailers frequently offer the same merchandise, acquired from the same vendors. They typically mimic each other's price promotions. Stores often look more alike than different, a row of storefronts in a mall. The potential for sameness in retailing is ever present. Accordingly, retail companies can benefit by achieving distinctiveness in ways important to their target markets.

For service-intensive retailers, a key opportunity for differentiation lies in *how they treat customers*. The foundation of relationship retailing is quality of service. No consumer wants a relationship with a retail company that is unreliable, unresponsive, incompetent, or otherwise deficient on quality-of-service dimensions.[4] The heart and soul of relationship retailing is personal attention: treating the customers as a client rather than as a face in the crowd, individualizing service, tailoring it, adding a touch of grace, making the client feel special.

Service-intensive retailers may *look* alike to customers, but they don't *feel* alike. Whereas many retailers are service-intensive in form but not in substance, the great relationship retailers are service-intensive in substance, not just in form. Becoming service intensive in substance is not accomplished easily or quickly. Any retail firm that is serious about transforming customers into clients must be prepared to invest in behalf of personalized service quality.

It is best to think of personalized service in terms of a quality loop. The loop has five sections: setting standards for service, hiring helpful personnel, training the staff to meet the standards, monitoring staff performance, and rewarding excellence.

1 Establish standards

First, precise standards for various facets of the service encounter must be established. What is the maximum acceptable waiting time in a dressing room before another article of clothing is brought? What level of product knowledge should staff have about new merchandise?

A service program without standards is a program that is ill-defined. The staff won't have benchmarks; they won't know what quality means. Quality-of-service standards help a retail company build an achievement culture.

2 Hire helpful personnel

Second, personnel with the capacity to meet the standards must be employed. It is essential to identify the optimum mix of skills, knowledge, and personal traits that contact personnel need in order to implement a relationship strategy. It is not enough that personnel be willing to perform client retailing; they must be *able* to perform it as well. Relationship retailing requires that the staff have *credibility*, which in turn requires the right blend of competence, attitude, and appearance for the target market. Thinking through who should be the salesperson is as important as thinking through who should be the client.

Identifying the best candidates for sales positions is one challenge; actually *hiring* these people is another. Few retail companies take full advantage of opportunities to attract the most qualified candidates available. Help-wanted advertising, for example, is typically buried in the classified sections of newspapers. The ads rarely make any statement about the company's philosophy, business concept, or quality of work life.

A successful relationship retailing program takes a marketing point of view towards the staffing of the sales function by

● Placing more emphasis on positioning and selling the institution; and
● Exploring nontraditional media and methods for doing so.

After all, the people a retail company hires to be on the sales floor *are* the retail company to the customer.

3 Train staff

Third, the staff must be prepared both in terms of knowledge and skills to meet the quality standards. Ongoing product knowledge development is especially important if the retailer expects to earn loyalty by helping clients make wiser purchase decisions than they might make at competing stores. The sales skills component is important for the staff to be able to convey product knowledge effectively. Formal training in listening skills is recommended. The most client-driven salespeople 'hear needs' and then find just the right merchandise to satisfy those needs.

4 Monitor staff performance

Fourth, staff performance must be monitored against the standards. Contact personnel need to know that management will know how they are performing. One approach to quality performance measurement is an ongoing 'shopping' program. Researchers pose as customers and then rate the quality of their encounter. Shopping research can be a plus in the eyes of the staff if properly executed. One example is same-day bonuses given by the store manager to sales staff receiving high shopper scores.

Another measurement approach is to sample recent purchasers systematically and to ask them several Yes/No questions concerning their experience. Was the salesperson courteous and friendly? Did the salesperson seem interested in helping you make a good selection? Was the salesperson knowledgeable about the merchandise?

This method necessitates identifying the customer, salesperson, and merchandise involved in each transaction. The output is a periodic printout showing the percentage of 'yes' answers for each question for each salesperson. The salesperson who receives a quarterly average of 85 percent 'yes' answers on 'courteous and friendly' but only 65 percent on 'knowledgeable about the merchandise' is given excellent direction in terms of future development. The salesperson's manager is also helped. Counseling may be indicated if the relatively low product knowledge score is specific to the one salesperson. If, however, a number of salespeople score low in product knowledge, a more systematic solution probably is indicated.

5 Reward staff competence

Fifth, staff who perform well against the standards must be rewarded. The staff knows management is serious about quality of service if management is willing to pay for it.

Consultant George Rieder proposes a 'layer cake' approach to reward systems.[5] The first layer is salary and benefits. The next layer is a bonus for *all* employees in department or store units that rank highest in sales and quality-of-service performance. (This layer can foster teamwork and fuel peer pressure, a powerful motivator.) The next layer is bonus or commission payments to the top individual performers. The next layer is nonmonetary recognition for the top individual performers – membership in the 'president's top twenty' club, for example.

A quality-of-service program is in jeopardy to the extent that any one of the five elements reviewed is missing. If a program has standards but not the staff to meet them, the standards will be unmet. A program that measures performance but does not prepare staff to deliver these performances will result in suboptimal performance. A program without measurement and rewards will lack credibility. A quality loop exists, and the loop must be closed!

Relationship retailing means attracting, maintaining, and building client relationships. It means converting customers to clients. Attracting new customers is an intermediate objective.

Implementing a relationship retailing program is easier said than done. Client loyalty cannot be assumed; it cannot even be bought. It can only be earned. In relationship retailing, performance is what counts.

References

1 Paul Leblang, as quoted in *Hear, There and Everywhere,* a newsletter published by Harrison Services, Inc., September 1981.
2 Adrian B. Ryans and Dick R. Wittink. 'The Marketing of Services: Categorization with Implications for Strategy,' *Contemporary Marketing Thought,* ed. Barnett A. Greenberg and Danny N. Bellenger (Chicago: American Marketing Association, 1977), p. 314.
3 Leonard L. Berry. 'Retail Positioning Strategies for the 1980s,' *Business Horizons,* November-December 1982: 45–50.
4 A comprehensive list of service quality dimensions is presented in Leonard L. Berry, Valarie A. Zeithaml, and A. Parasuraman, 'Quality Counts in Services. Too,' *Business Horizons,* May-June 1985: 44–52.
5 George Rieder, 'Effective Sales Remuneration: Tailoring Rewards to Desired Behaviors.' *Journal of Retail Banking,* Fall 1985: 1–10.

RELATIONSHIP APPROACH TO MARKETING IN SERVICE CONTEXTS: THE MARKETING AND ORGANIZATIONAL BEHAVIOR INTERFACE
Christian Grönroos

Christian Grönroos currently holds a position as Professor of Marketing at the Swedish School of Economics and Business Administration in Finland. He is also Head of the Marketing Department and Chairman of the Management Education Center of the Business School.

In this paper Grönroos explores the nature of relationship marketing strategy in a service context and explores a relationship definition of marketing. The paper provides a very useful insight into the critical interfaces between marketing and organisational behaviour and analyses the organisation's need for a service culture and internal marketing.

Introduction

The purpose of this article is to describe the nature and contents of the marketing function in a service organization and how this function is related to other business functions and academic disciplines, especially to personnel and organizational behavior. The approach is that of what internationally has been called the *Nordic School of Services,* originating in

Scandinavia/Northern Europe (see, e.g., Grönroos, 1983; and Grönroos and Gummesson, 1985). The expression *service contexts* implies all types of service activities, irrespective of whether they occur in so-called service firms or in public institutions, not-for-profit organizations, or manufacturers of goods.

The traditional role of marketing

Traditionally, marketing is viewed as an intermediate function, where the specialists of the marketing department are the only persons who have an impact on the customers' views of the firm and on their buying behavior. Employees in other departments are neither recruited nor trained to think marketing, nor are they supervised so that they would feel any marketing responsibilities. In this approach, the core of marketing is the marketing mix. In many consumer packaged goods situations, this conceptualization of marketing functions sufficiently well. If the product is a preproduced item with no need for service or other contacts between the firm and its customers, marketing specialists are clearly capable of taking care of the customer relationships. Good market research, packaging, promotion, pricing, and distribution decisions by the marketing specialists lead to good results.

As a general framework, the 4 Ps of the marketing mix (introduced by McCarthy [1960] based on Borden's [e.g., 1965] and Culliton's [1948] notions of the marketer as a 'mixer of ingredients'), in spite of its pedagogical virtues, is far too simplistic and may easily misguide both academics and practitioners; and it has never been empirically tested (compare Cowell, 1984; Grönroos 1989; Kent, 1986). Particularly in services marketing, and also in industrial marketing, the marketing mix approach frequently does not cover all resources and activities that appear in the customer relationships at various stages of the customer relationship life cycle (see Grönroos, in press, 1983, 1989; Grönroos and Gummesson, 1986; Gummesson, 1987a, b; as well as Håkansson, 1982; Håkansson and Snehota, 1976; Kent, 1986; Webster, 1982). Especially during the consumption process, there is a range of contacts between the service firm and its customer, which are outside the traditional marketing function as defined by the Ps of the marketing mix (compare Rathmell, 1974). Managing and operating these contacts (e.g., with bank and hotel facilities, automatic teller machines, waiters, air stewardesses, telephone receptionists and bus drivers, R&D people, design engineers, maintenance people, etc.) are the responsibilities of operations and other nonmarketing departments only. However, these buyer–seller interactions or interfaces, or the service encounter, have an immense impact on the future buying behavior of the customers as well as on word of mouth, and, therefore, they should be considered marketing resources and activities. The marketing function is spread throughout the entire organization (Gummesson, 1987a), and the customers take an active part in the production process.

A relationship approach to the buyer–seller interface

Far too often, customers are seen in terms of numbers. When someone stops being a customer, there are new potential customers to take the empty place. Customers, individuals, and organizations alike are numbers only. In reality, this is, of course, not true. Every single customer forms a customer relationship with the seller that is broad or narrow in scope, continuous or discrete, short or lasting in nature, which the firm has to develop and maintain. Customer relationships are not just there; they have to be earned. According to an alternative approach to defining marketing, this function is considered to revolve around customer relationships, where the objectives of the parties involved are met through various kinds of exchanges, which take place in order to establish and maintain such relationships.

Especially long-term relationships with customers are important (Gummesson, 1987b). In services, as in general, short-term relationships, where the customers come and go, are normally more expensive to develop. The marketing budget needed to create an interest in the firm's offerings and make potential customers accept the firm's promises are often very high. As Berry (1983) observes, 'clearly, marketing to protect the customer base is becoming exceedingly important to a variety of service industries' (p. 25). This holds true for industrial marketing as well (see Hakansson, 1982; Jackson, 1985). This is not to say that new customers who perhaps make one purchase only would not be desirable, but it means, however, that the emphasis should be on developing and maintaining enduring, long-term customer relationships. Berry (1983) introduced the concept of relationship marketing, as opposed to transaction marketing, to describe such a long-term approach to marketing strategy (see also Crosby et al., 1988; Gummesson, 1987b; Rosenberg and Czepiel, 1984). If close and long-term relationships can be achieved, the possibility is high that this will lead to continuing exchanges, requiring lower marketing costs per customer.

A relationship definition of marketing

The marketing concept as the basic philosophy guiding marketing in practice still holds. The marketing mix approach to transferring this concept to marketing in practice is, however, considered too simplistic and too narrow in scope to be more than partly useful in most service situations. In conclusion to this discussion we formulate a relationship definition of marketing (Grönroos, in press, 1989; also compare Gummesson 1987a, b; Berry, 1983). This definition states that

> Marketing is to establish, maintain, enhance and commercialize customer relationships (often but not necessarily always long term relationships) so that the objectives of the parties involved are met. This is done by a mutual exchange and fulfillment of promises.

Furthermore, this definition can be accompanied by the following supplement: The resources of the seller – personnel, technology and systems – have to be used in such a manner that the customer's trust in the resources involved and, thus, in the firm itself is maintained and strengthened. The various resources the customer encounters in the relation may be of any kind and part of any business function. However, these resources and activities cannot be totally predetermined and explicitly categorized in a general definition.

The concept of promises as an integral part of marketing vocabulary has been stressed by the Finnish researcher Calonious (1986, 1988). In establishing and maintaining customer relationships, the seller gives a set of promises concerning, e.g., goods, services or systems of goods and services, financial solutions, materials administration, transfer of information, social contacts, and a range of future commitments. On the other hand, the buyer gives another set of promises concerning his commitments in the relationship. Then, the promises have to be kept on both sides, if the relationship is expected to be maintained and enhanced for the mutual benefits of the parties involved.

Long-term customer relationships mean that the objective of marketing is mainly to go for enduring relationships with the customers. Of course, in some situations, short-term sales – what sometimes is called transaction marketing – may be profitable (see e.g., Jackson, 1985). However, generally speaking, the long-term scope is vital to profitable marketing. Thus, commercializing the customer relationships means that the cost–benefit ratio of transactions of goods, services, or systems of goods and services is positive at least in the long run.

Establishing, maintaining and enhancing customer relationships, respectively, implies that the marketing situation is different depending on how far the customer relationships have developed. From the service provider's point of view, (1) establishing a relationship involves giving promises; (2) maintaining a relationship is based on fulfillment of promises; and finally, (3) enhancing a relationship means that a new set of promises are given with the fulfillment of earlier promises as a prerequisite.

This relationship definition of marketing does not say that the traditional elements of the marketing mix, such as advertising, personal selling, pricing, and conceptualizing of the product, are less important than earlier. However, it demonstrates that so much else may be of importance to marketing than the means of competition of the marketing mix. It is based on how to develop and execute good marketing performance, rather than just on what decisions to make to do marketing.

Implications of the relationship approach to marketing

A distinct difference exists between handling the moments of truth (to use an expression introduced in the service management literature by Normann, 1984) of the buyer–seller interactions as a marketing task and executing traditional marketing activities, such as advertising, personal selling, and sales promotion. Normally, the latter are planned and implemented by marketing and sales specialists. On the other hand, the former tasks are implemented by persons who are specialists in other fields. Moreover, how the moments of truth are carried out is frequently planned and managed by nonmarketing managers and supervisors. To put it bluntly, the moments of truth with their tremendous marketing impacts are frequently both managed and executed by people who neither are aware of their marketing responsibilities nor are interested in customers and marketing.

The employees involved in marketing as nonspecialists have been called 'part-time marketers' by Gummesson (1981, 1987a; compare also Grönroos, 1988). They are, of course, specialists in their areas, and they are supposed to remain so. At the same time, however, they will have to learn to perform their tasks in a marketinglike manner so that the customers will want to return, and the customer relationships are strengthened. Hence, they, and their bosses as well, will have to learn to think in terms of marketing and customer impact.

The marketing aspect of the moments of truth is related to interactive processes, and, therefore, this part of marketing is called the Interactive Marketing Function (see, e.g., Grönroos, 1980, 1983). The impact of the 'part-time marketers' as well as the customer orientation of systems, technology, and physical resources is paramount to the success of interactive marketing. Hence, the interactive marketing function recognizes that every component – human as well as other – in producing a service, every production resource used and every stage in the service production and delivery process, should be the concern of marketing as well, and not considered operations or personnel problems only. The marketing consequences of every resource and activity involved in interactive marketing situations have to be acknowledged in the planning process, so that the production resources and operations support and enhance the organization's attempts to develop and maintain relationships with its customers.

As Gummesson (in press) observes, 'there is extreme interdependence between the traditional departments of a service firm – production, delivery, personnel, administration, finance, etc. – and marketing.' For example, marketing, personnel, operations, and technological development have to go hand in hand. These functions are linked together by the common objective of providing customers with good service. As Schneider and Rentsch (1987) formulate it, service has to become an 'organizational imperative.' Here, we shall only focus upon one interrelationship between business functions, the one between marketing and personnel/organizational behavior. Because the marketing impact of the 'part-time marketers' is curcial, efforts have to be made to secure service orientation and marketing-oriented attitudes and corresponding skills among the personnel. Next, we are going to discuss, very briefly, two important and interrelated aspects of human resources development that emerge from a service-oriented and relationship-oriented approach to marketing.

The need for a service culture

In a service context a strong and well-established corporate culture, which enhances an appreciation for good service and customer orientation, is extremely important (e.g., Bowen and Schneider, 1988, George and Grönroos, in press; Grönroos, in press; Schneider, 1986). This follows from the nature of services. Normally, service production cannot be standardized as completely as an assembly line, because of the human impact on the buyer–seller interface. Customers and their behavior cannot be standardized and totally predetermined. The situations vary, and, therefore, a distinct service-oriented culture is needed that tells employees how to respond to new, unforeseen and even awkward situations (Schneider, 1986). The culture has a vital impact on how service-oriented its employees are and, thus, how well they act as 'part-time marketers' (Bowen and Schneider, 1988).

Internal projects or activities, such as service or marketing training programs, probably have no significant impact on the thinking and behavior of e.g., employees of firms where goods-oriented standards are regarded highly. Moreover, Schneider and Bowen (1985) have found that when employees identify with the norms and values of an organization, they are less inclined to quit, and, furthermore, customers seem to be more satisfied with the service. In addition to this, '... when employee turnover is minimized, service values and norms are more transmitted to newcomers and successive generations of service employees' (Bowen and Schneider, 1988, p. 63).

Developing a service culture is clearly a means of creating and enhancing good interactive marketing performance needed for implementing a relationship marketing strategy. The corporate culture issue is closely linked to another personnel-related issue that has emerged from the research into services marketing. This is internal marketing.

The need for internal marketing

During the past 10 years or so, the concept of internal marketing has emerged first in the literature on services marketing (see, e.g., Berry, 1981; Compton *et al.*, 1987; George *et al.*, 1987; George and Grönroos, in press; Grönroos, 1978, 1981, 1985; see also Eiglier and Langeard, 1976), and then was adopted by the service management literature (see, e.g., Carlzon, 1987; Normann, 1984), and also found to be valuable in industrial marketing (Grönroos and Gummesson, 1985). Heskett (1987) recently touches upon this phenomenon as well observing that '... high-performing service companies have gained their status in large measure by turning the strategic service vision inward ...' (pp. 120–121). An increasing number of firms have recognized the need for internal marketing programs. Maybe the most spectacular internal marketing process is the one implemented by Scandinavian Airline System (SAS) (Carlzon, 1987). Today, internal marketing is considered a prerequisite for successful external marketing (see, e.g., Compton *et al.*, 1987; Grönroos, 1985).

First of all, internal marketing is a management philosophy. Management should create, continuously encourage, and enhance an understanding of and an appreciation for the roles of the employees in the organization. Employees should have holistic views of their jobs. This is illustrated by an anecdote told by Jan Carlzon, president and CEO of SAS, about two stonecutters who were chipping square blocks out of granite: 'A visitor to the quarry asked what they were doing. The first stone cutter, looking rather sour, grumbled, "I'm cutting this damned stone into a block." The second, who looked pleased with his work, replied proudly, "I'm on this team that's building a cathedral."' (Carlzon, 1987, p. 135). (It is interesting to notice that in slightly different words, this anecdote is also told by Michail Gorbatjov in his book on the perestroika in the Soviet Union [Gorbatjov, 1987].)

The focus of internal marketing is on how to get and retain customer-conscious employees. It is also a means of developing and maintaining a service culture, although internal marketing alone is not sufficient (see George and Grönroos, in press; Grönroos, 1989). Goods and services as well as specific external marketing campaigns, new technology, and new systems of functioning have to be marketed to employees before these goods and services are marketed externally. Every organization has an internal market of employees, which first has to be successfully taken care of. Unless this is done properly, the success of the organization's operations on its ultimate, external markets will be jeopardized. To put it in the words of Heskett (1987), 'Effective service requires people who understand the idea' (p. 124).

Conclusions

Joint challenges for marketing and organizational behavior

Clearly, the tasks of developing and maintaining a service culture and of internal marketing offer an important interface between marketing and organizational behavior. Hence, they also offer an arena where marketing practitioners and academics on one hand, and personnel and human resources development people and academics from the field of organizational behavior on the other hand, are challenged to work together.

This, of course, requires that among other things, the traditional borderlines that far too often have become insurmountable walls between marketing and personnel as business functions and as academic disciplines are challenged and, if necessary, torn down.

References

Berry, Leonard L., Relationship Marketing, in *Emerging Perspectives on Services Marketing*. L.L. Berry *et al.*, eds., American Marketing Association, Chicago, 1983, pp. 25–28.

Berry, Leonard L., The Employee as Customer, *Journal of Retail Banking* 3 (March 1981): 33–40.

Borden, Neil H., The Concept of the Marketing Mix, in *Science in Marketing*. G. Schwartz, ed., Wiley, New York, 1965.

Bowen, David E., and Schneider, Benjamin, Services Marketing and Management: Implications for Organizational Behavior, in *Research in Organizational Behavior*. B. Stow and L. L. Cummings, eds., JAI Press, Greenwich, CT, Vol. 10, 1988.

Calonius, Henrik, A Buying Process Model, in *Innovative Marketing – A European Perspective*. K. Blois and S. Parkinson, eds., Proceedings from the XVII Annual Conference of the European Marketing Academy, University of Bradford, England, 1988.

Calonius, Henrik, A Market Behaviour Framework, in *Contemporary Research in Marketing*. K. Moller and M. Paltschik, eds., Proceedings from the XV Annual Conference of the European Marketing Academy, Helsinki, Finland, 1986.

Carlzon, Jan, *Moments of Truth*, Ballinger, New York, 1987.

Compton, Fran, George, William R., Grönroos, Christian, and Karvinen, Matti, Internal Marketing, in *The Service Challenge: Integrating for Competitive Advantage*. J.A. Czepiel *et al.*, eds., American Marketing Association, Chicago, 1987, pp. 7–12.

Cowell, Donald, *The Marketing of Services*, Heinemann, London, 1984.

Crosby, Lawrence A., Evans, Ken R., and Cowles, Deborah, *Relationship Quality in Service Selling: An Interpersonal Influence Perspective*, Working Paper No. 5, First Interstate Center for Services Marketing, Arizona State University, 1988.

Culliton, John W., *The Management of Marketing Costs*, The Andover Press, Andover, MA, 1948.

Deshpande, R., and Webster, Jr., Frederick E., *Organizational Culture and Marketing: Defining the Research Agenda*. Report No. 87–106. Marketing Science Institute, Cambridge, MA, 1987.

Eiglier, Pierre, and Langeard, Eric, *Principes Politiques Marketing pour les Entreprises de Service*, Working Paper, Institut d'Administration des Entreprises, Aix-en-Provence, France, 1976.

George, William, R., Internal Communications Programs as a Mechanism for Doing Internal Marketing, in *Creativity in Services Marketing*. V. Venkatesan *et al.*, eds., American Marketing Association, Chicago, 1986, pp. 83–84.

George, William R., Internal Marketing for Retailers. The Junior Executive Employee, in *Developments in Marketing Science*. J. D. Lindqvist, ed., Academy of Marketing Science, 1984, Vol. VII, pp. 322–325.

George, William R., and Grönroos, Christian, Developing Customer-Conscious Employees at Every Level: Internal Marketing, in *Handbook of Services Marketing*. C.A. Congram and M.L. Friedman, eds., AMA-CON, in press.

Gorbatjov, Mikhail, *Perestroika – New Thinking for our Country and the World*, Harper & Row, New York, 1987.

Grönroos, Christian, Defining Marketing: A Market-Oriented Approach, *European Journal of Marketing* 23 (1989): 52–60.

Grönroos, Christian, New Competition of the Service Economy: The Five Rules of Service, *International Journal of Operations & Production Management* 8 (1988): 9–19.

Grönroos, Christian, Internal Marketing – Theory and Practice, in *Services Marketing in a Changing Environment*. T.M. Bloch *et al.*, eds., American Marketing Association, Chicago, 1985, pp. 41–47.

Grönroos, Christian, *Strategic Management and Marketing in the Service Sector*, Marketing Science Institute, Cambridge, MA, 1983.

Grönroos, Christian, Internal Marketing – An Integral Part of Marketing Theory, in *Marketing of Services*. J.H. Donnelly and W. R. George, eds., American Marketing Association, Chicago, 1981, pp. 236–238.

Grönroos, Christian, Designing a Long Range Marketing Strategy for Services. *Long Range Planning* 13 (April 1980): 36–42.

Grönroos, Christian, A Service-Oriented Approach to Marketing of Services, *European Journal of Marketing* 12 (1978): 588–601.

Grönroos, Christian, *Service Management and Marketing. Managing the Moments of Truth in Service Competition*. Lexington, MA: D.C. Heath Lexington Books, in press.

Grönroos, Christian, and Gummesson, Evert, Service Orientation in Industrial Marketing, in *Creativity in Services Marketing. What's New, What Works, What's Developing*, American Marketing Association, Chicago, 1986, pp. 23–26.

Grönroos, Christian, and Gummesson, Evert, eds. *Service Marketing – Nordic School Perspectives*, Stockholm University, Sweden, 1985.

Gummesson, Evert, The New Marketing – Developing Long-Term Interactive Relationships, *Long Range Planning* 20 (1987a): 10–20.

Gummesson, Evert, *Marketing – A Long Term Interactive Relationship. Contribution to a New Marketing Theory*, Marketing Technique Center, Stockholm, Sweden, 1987b.

Gummesson, Evert, Marketing Cost Concept in Service Firms, *Industrial Marketing Management* 10 (1981): 175–182.

Gummesson, Evert, Organizing for Marketing and Marketing Organizations, in *Handbook on Services Marketing*. C.A. Congram and M. L. Friedman, eds., Amacon, New York, in press.

Håkansson, Haken, ed. *International Marketing and Purchasing of Industrial Goods*, Wiley, New York, 1982.

Håkansson, Hakan, and Snehota, Ivan, *Marknadsplanering. Ett satt att skapa nya problem?* (Marketing Planning. A Way of Creating New Problems)?, Studentlitteratur, Malmo, Sweden, 1976.

Heskett, James L., Lessons in the Service Sector, *Harvard Business Review* 65 (March-April 1987): 118–126.

Jackson, Barbara B., Build Customer Relationships That Last, *Harvard Business Review* 63 (November-December 1985): 120–128.

Kent, Ray A., Faith in Four Ps: An Alternative, *Journal of Marketing Management* 2 (1986): 145–154.

Kotler, Philip, *Marketing Management, Analysis, Planning, and Control*. Prentice-Hall, Englewood Cliffs, NJ, 1984.

Levitt, Theodore, After the Sale is Over, *Harvard Business Review* 61 (September-October 1983): 87–93.

McCarthy, E. Jerome, *Basic Marketing*, Irwin, Homewood, IL, 1960.

Normann, Richard, *Service Management*, Wiley, New York, 1984.

Rathmell, John R, *Marketing in the Service Sector*, Winthrop, Cambridge, MA, 1974.

Rosenberg, Larry J., and Czepiel, John A., A Marketing Approach for Customer Retention, *The Journal of Consumer Marketing* 1 (1984): 45–51.

Schneider, Benjamin, Notes on Climate and Culture, in *Creativity in Services Marketing, What's New, What Works, What's Developing*. F. Venkatesan *et al.*, eds., American Marketing Association, Chicago, IL, 1986, pp. 63–67.

Schneider, Benjamin, and Bowen, David E., Employee and Customer Perceptions of Service in Banks: Replication and Extension, *Journal of Applied Psychology* 70 (1985): 423–433.

Schneider, Benjamin, and Rentsch, J., The Management of Climate and Culture: A Futures Perspective, in *Futures of Organizations*. J. Hage, ed., D.C. Heath Lexington Books, Lexington, MA, 1987.

Webster, Jr., Fredrick E., Management Science in Industrial Marketing, *Journal of Marketing* 1 (January 1978): 21–27.

PART TWO

Establishing a Customer-oriented Culture for Relationship Marketing

4 CLIMATE AND CULTURE

Organizational climate and culture have latterly been recognized as the foundations of long-term marketing effectiveness. By the term 'culture' we refer to the deep-seated, unwritten system of shared values and norms within an organization, which in turn dictate its climate – the policies and practices that characterize the organization and reflect its cultural beliefs.[1] The development and regulation of an appropriate organizational culture are therefore central concerns of internal marketing. Drawing on examples from service and manufacturing businesses in the USA, the UK, and Scandinavia, this chapter focuses on organizational culture and climate as critical determinants of an organization's ability to deliver superior service and quality to its customers.

The first of the readings, by Benjamin Schneider, published back in the autumn of 1980, is a penetrating investigation into the significance of organizational climate in a service business. The paper reports on the first of a series of empirical studies of service climate conducted by Schneider and his colleagues.[2-4] In his article Schneider explores the factors which have traditionally shaped the (sometimes inappropriate) policies and procedural priorities of service organizations. Short-term financial performance criteria and an overemphasis on quantitative measures have tended to create climates where bureaucracy flourishes at the expense of customer service and satisfaction. Using the findings from his research in the US retail banking sector, Schneider argues that a climate that reflects an enthusiastic service orientation is crucial to the long-term success of a service organization; and that the attitudes and actions of management are pivotal to establishing such a climate. Perhaps most significantly from a relationship marketing perspective, Schneider puts forward research findings that establish a close relationship between front-line employees' perceptions of climate and customers' opinions of service quality. Furthermore, he states that perceptions of an organization's climate are linked to both employee satisfaction and customer satisfaction, and consequently to customer retention. Climate, Schneider concludes, is transparent and cannot be hidden from the customer. Nevertheless, recognition that a link exists between employee and customer satisfaction manifested itself in an outbreak of 'smile campaigns' throughout the non-professional services sector in the 1980s. These quick-fix solutions were often no more than cosmetic attempts to improve the appearance of the customer interface, with little effort made to integrate front and back office activities or adjust organizational procedures to support the front-line workers. Such behavioural management initiatives may produce a degree of improvement in customer behaviour and perceptions of service, but they are unlikely to improve employee satisfaction or retention in the long term, making sustained improvements in customer service all the more difficult to effect. These themes, and the problems of creating a customer-orientated corporate culture in a high throughput service environment, are explored by Emmanuel Ogbonna and Barry Wilkinson in the second of the readings in this chapter.

In 'Corporate strategy and corporate culture: the view from the checkout', Ogbonna and Wilkinson describe the attempts of three British supermarket chains to change their cultures in line with changing corporate strategies. The businesses in question wished to create a strong customer orientation among their employees – particularly those in customer-facing jobs – to facilitate a move from price-based competition towards competition through customer service. A fourth business, one that chose to retain its original price-based formula, provides some interesting comparisons. In the organizations wishing to effect culture change, the writers describe how new recruitment policies – sometimes using sophisticated selection techniques – and customer services training were introduced to inculcate a customer orientation on the shop floor. Yet some seemingly counterproductive operational procedures, and the generally unattractive conditions of employment were left unchanged. In the instances described, the desired behavioural changes – most notably, smiling at the customers – did occur among front-line employees. But 'the view from the checkout' reveals that these behavioural changes were often achieved through coercion, rather than through the internalization of the new cultural values or any genuine enthusiasm for the work. The stress experienced by front-line employees as they strive to maintain an illusion of enjoyment, while undertaking work which is 'unglamorous, monotonous, and frequently intense', has been well documented in other high-throughput service situations.[5] The resistance to the new regimes encountered among some long-serving middle managers illustrates another perennial problem associated with the implementation of culture change programmes.

The third and final reading in this chapter, 'Using internal marketing to develop a new culture – the Case of Ericsson Quality' by Evert Gummesson, also takes up the theme of culture change. In this case the organization – a manufacturer of telecommunications equipment – adopts a more systemic approach to effecting culture change to create a customer orientation. The goal is customer satisfaction through total quality, instigated by the chief executive's recognition that the issue of quality would become a marketing imperative. Gummesson observes that internal marketing tools, borrowed and adapted from 'best practice' service organizations, are used to create a new quality culture. Regrettably, Gummesson expands on only one of these tools in this paper, that being the concept of the internal customer which is introduced and the multiple benefits of its application explained.

The pieces by Ogbonna and Wilkinson, and by Gummesson, share a common central theme: culture change to improve market performance and organizational effectiveness. One spotlights customer service in a service context, the other spotlights quality in a manufacturing situation. Bringing the spotlights of customer service and total quality into closer alignment with marketing is an underlying principle of relationship marketing.[6] As the distinction between the service and manufacturing sectors continues to break down, and service becomes a priority in almost every organization, there are valuable lessons to be learned from the experiences of organizations operating at both ends of the spectrum.

References

1 Webster, C. (1990). Toward the measurement of the marketing culture of a service firm. *Journal of Business Research,* **21**, 345–362.
2 Schneider, B., Parkington, J. and Buxton, V. (1980). Employee and customer perceptions of service in banks, *Administrative Science Quarterly,* **25**, 252–267.
3 Schneider, B. and Bowen, D. (1985). Employee and customer perceptions of service in banks: replication and extension, *Journal of Applied Psychology,* **70**, 423–433.
4 Schneider, B., Wheeler, J. and Cox, J. (1992). A passion for service: using content analysis to explicate service climate themes, *Journal of Applied Psychology,* **77**, 705–716.
5 Hochschild, A.R. (1983). *The Managed Heart: commercialization of human feelings,* University of California Press, California.
6 Christopher, M., Payne, A. and Ballantyne, D. (1991). *Relationship Marketing,* Butterworth-Heinemann, Oxford.

THE SERVICE ORGANIZATION: CLIMATE IS CRUCIAL
Benjamin Schneider

Benjamin Schneider is Professor of Psychology and of Business Management at the University of Maryland, College Park. He has published extensively on the subjects of service climate and culture, organizational diagnosis and change; personal selection; and work facilitation. His consultancy work includes long-term projects with Chase Manhattan Bank, AT&T, and GEICO.

In 'The service organization: climate is crucial', Schneider reports on a study of the service climate in branches of a US bank. He describes how management's attitude towards service is reflected in employees' and customers' perceptions of the organization's climate. These impressions of climate ultimately influence perceptions of service quality and employee satisfaction. From a practical perspective, the paper provides a technique for identifying the relationships between employees' descriptions of branch practices and procedures and customer opinions of the service they receive.

Behavioral science studies of work have generally concentrated on those outcomes of worker participation in the organization that can be easily counted – for example, days absent – particularly in manufacturing when production levels, absenteeism, and turnover are the 'bottom line' in evaluating the usefulness of the behavioral sciences.

I think this emphasis on the 'bottom line' is based on the fact that our theories and models about organizational dynamics come from the manufacturing sector. Thus, because the score is kept by accountants, organizations tend to monitor the easily identifiable cost. It has not been noticed that this focus on 'easily countables' gives a short-run perspective and cuts down, or even eliminates, attention paid to organizational constituencies that aren't directly involved with financial matters. Accountants, economists, and financial analysts provide the data on which decision makers base their decisions so the only constituencies that influence decisions are stockholders and banks; customers, suppliers, employees, or the families of employees are given scant attention.

The emphasis on easily countable, relatively short-run indices of human effectiveness may be shortsighted in the manufacturing sector; in the service sector, it is myopic. Yet service organizations tend to adopt a straight short-run, accounting-oriented, productivity frame of reference when they evaluate employee performance and determine organizational effectiveness. In banks, for example, tellers are evaluated on how they 'prove out' at the end of each day, rather than on how courteous they are to the bank's customers; the competence of airline reservation clerks is judged on the number of paperwork errors they make when they book passengers, rather than on the goodwill they generate when they handle a transaction to the satisfaction of the customer; and life insurance managers monitor salespersons' dollar volume rather than their 'bedside manner' as a basis for rewards. The primary measure turns out to be a short-run concern for easily countable performance standards that are relevant to short-run financial concerns.

It would be useful if the definition of 'productivity' – especially in service industries – was broadened to include at least courtesy and style of performance – particularly because the long-term effectiveness of the organization depends on service. Because the performance of employees in service organizations is directed at animate (human) objects rather than the nonfeeling, nonresponsive raw materials handled in the manufacturing world, the appropriate judges of performance should be those who are served.

The underlying thesis of this article is that in service organizations, organizational dynamics have a direct impact on the people the organization serves, as well as on employee performance and attitudes. This article focuses on the nature of employees who work in service organizations, how management's orientation to service affects employees, how management's orientation to service affects customers, and the relationship between employee and customer views of the service orientation of the organization. The project that illustrates these concerns was conducted in 23 branches of an East Coast commercial bank.

Working framework

The working framework is based on research from two viewpoints – the employee's and the customer's. Let's look at the research background from each of these vantages.

Research background: the employee side

As I've already noted, our models of organizational dynamics have been developed in, and concentrate on, manufacturing organizations – that is, organizations that transform raw materials into consumable products. Employees' efforts in such organizations are aimed at essentially nonreactive targets. In contrast, service organization employees have face-to-face contact with customers; their work involves much greater interpersonal interaction than manufacturing work. This type of work seems to result in increased stress and strain because employees try to meet conflicting demands from management and customers. Management ought to try and reduce this stress. But how? To answer this question, we must identify the types of people likely to be employed in customer contact jobs in service organizations.

We assumed that an individual's choice of occupation or organization wasn't a random process and that people *choose* the kinds of jobs they have and the kinds of organizations in which they work. Research literature on occupational and organizational choice suggests that people who choose service jobs in for-profit organizations probably have strong desires to give good service, to work with people in face-to-face relationships and, interestingly, they are probably concerned with organizational success. Therefore, management can potentially manage employee stress by establishing a climate in which employees' desires to give good service are made easier and encouraged; a climate in which service, as proved by management word and deed, is an organizational imperative.

When managers in service organizations establish policies and pro-cedures, and otherwise engage in behaviors that show concern for the organization's clients, they are service *enthusiasts*. Service *enthusiasts* engage in activities designed to satisfy the organization's customers. Service *bureaucrats*, on the other hand, are interested in system main-tenance, routine, and adherence to uniform operating guidelines and procedures. The most important difference between these orientations is the service enthusiast's emphasis on the importance of interpersonal relationships at work, concern for the customer, and flexible applica-tion of rules as opposed to the bureaucrat's avoidance of interpersonal issues and stress on rules, procedures, and system maintenance. When employee opinions about how their organization should function are not congruent with what they perceive the organization is actually emphasizing, role stress and strain – that is, role ambiguity and role conflict – usually result. Employees' role stress and strain would also

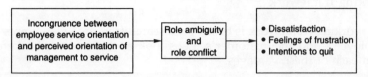

Figure 1 *How employee–management incongruence leads to employees' negative feelings*

manifest itself in other negative outcomes such as dissatisfaction, frustration, and plans to leave the organization. This framework is shown in Figure 1.

Research background: customer side

Consumers who make decisions about the goods or services offered by an organization are the ultimate judges of the quality of those goods and services in the American free-market system. What is surprising is that (1) researchers and businessmen have concentrated far more on how to attract consumers to products and services than on how to retain those customers, (2) there is almost no published research on the retention of service consumers, and (3) consumer evaluation of products or services has rarely been used as a criterion or index of organizational effectiveness. The study of organizational behavior has left relatively unexplored the questions of why consumers continue to utilize the services of a bank, an airline, a hospital, a university, an insurance agency, and so on, and of how the dynamics or processes of these organizations are related to consumer evaluation of the services they receive.

In an earlier study, I hypothesized that service consumers are responsive to the same kinds of organizational practices and procedures that affect employees. I suggested that consumers would be better served if service organizations were structured to meet and satisfy the needs of their employees. The logic for the hypothesis is quite simple: Employees in service organizations desire to give good service and when those desires are made easier by management's support, both employees and consumers are likely to react positively – that is, employees should have feelings of satisfaction, not frustration, and so on; customers should feel good about the quality of the service they receive.

It is important to note that positive outcomes for both customer and employee are a direct function of the same set of organizational dynamics – namely, the extent to which the organization, through its practices and procedures, demonstrates a 'climate for service.' Of course, positive employee outcomes are in a totally different realm from customer outcomes; the former involve the largest chunk of daytime hours (employees' total work experiences); the latter involve only a fleeting or transient relationship (a three- or four-minute visit every now and then to a bank, for example). However, these two groups share an experience with the same organizational behavior; this suggests that the way *customers* perceive their treatment when they use the organization's services should be positively related to what *employees* say about the organization's service practices and procedures. These ideas are portrayed schematically in Figure 2.

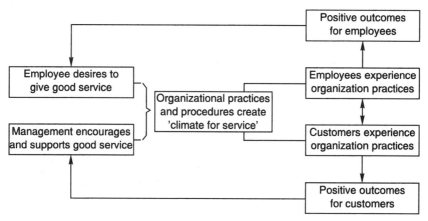

Figure 2 *Antecedents and consequences of 'climate for service' in banks*

Note also that these thoughts about the impact on *customers* of managerial orientation to *employees* represent, in fact, a 'boundary-spanning' or 'spillover' concept. This suggests that human resources processes and procedures established for customer-contact employees in service organizations have unintentional consequences because they cannot be hidden from the consumer; there is no room for 'quality control' between the employees' behavior and the customer's 'purchase.' The climate for service 'shows' to those who are served.

It could be no different. Service organizations are established to attract and retain customers through service; their reason for being is (or should be) the customer. In fact, this logic indicates that when employees feel their service organization is *not* customer-oriented, both employees and customers should report the customer has less positive experiences. Conversely, in organizations where employees report that management displays characteristics of the service enthusiast and establishes customer-oriented policies and procedures, *customers* should report higher levels or quality of service and they should be more likely to keep their service accounts with the organization.

The research process

Data for this project were collected in three distinct phases: preparation of the organization for the data collection process, interviews with bank branch employees and customers, and survey development and administration to employees and customers.

Preparation of the organization

It took the researcher five years to find a bank in which to test these hypotheses because banks, like most service organizations, separate their employee 'attitude' research from their customer 'opinion' research; this thwarted any opportunity to examine relationships between employees and customers. Fortunately, the management of the bank that eventually cooperated (financially as well as psychologically) realized that while customer opinions about quality were an index of branch effectiveness, actual attempts to change branch practices and procedures would be nonproductive unless techniques were available for measuring how higher-quality differed from lower-quality branches. My research framework provided a technique for identifying the relationships, if any, between customer opinions about service and employee descriptions of branch practices and procedures. Because these descriptions referred specifically to actual branch routine and the research provided diagnostic data that were useful for organizational change, the bank finally agreed to participate.

Both parties to the project took on specific responsibilities. The bank was expected to:

- *Arrange a meeting with branch managers to solicit their cooperation.* This gave those branch managers who would participate in the study an opportunity to meet and observe the research team and to ask questions about their roles.
- *Arrange corporate newspaper announcements describing the research and research team.* This alerted the whole organization to the research effort and helped allay false rumors.
- *Arrange for all customer and employee interviews and conduct the customer interviews after the research team trained the interviewers.* The idea of using bank employees to conduct the customer interviews was to get nonbranch people (especially marketing types) to speak to actual customers.
- *Appoint a liaison team to work with the research team.* The liaison team acquainted researchers with some of the language of the organization (every organization has its own language) and specified 'obvious' ways to conduct the research. This team was used as a sounding board and critic and was particularly valuable in critiquing the proposed surveys.
- *Print and mail surveys to all sampled customers and employees, and select the customer samples (all employees in the relevant branches were asked to respond).*

The research team had the duty to:

- *Explain the research effort to participating bank employees* – on a face-to-face basis with bank branch managers and in writing to other branch employees.
- *Interview branch employees.*
- *Develop the survey drafts for both customers and employees, and check them with the liaison team.*
- *Analyze data and write reports.*
- *Feed data back to branch managers and employees.*

Manager and employee interviews

As preparation for the employee survey, the branch manager, one nonteller, and one teller were interviewed from each branch. Some interviews were 'one-on-one,' while others were conducted in groups. Groups were always composed of employees holding jobs at the same level – all managers or all tellers, for example. These interviews were tape-recorded and concentrated on the following issues:

- What happened to and around them on a typical day that made them feel particularly good or particularly bad about their work.
- What came to mind when they thought about customer service and the bank.
- What they thought giving good service involved; what are the components of good service.
- How they felt when they weren't giving good service; what prevented them from providing good customer service.

Customer interviews

Customers were interviewed from each of the branches by randomly selecting three account holders from mailing lists, telephoning them, and asking them to participate in an interview for which they would be paid $15. Interviews were conducted at a branch convenient to the customer and were conducted 'one-on-one.' Customers were asked the following questions:

- In a few words, how would you describe the service you generally receive at the branch where you do most of your banking?
- Can you tell me about a time you went to your branch and received service you thought was particularly good? Please tell me what happened, who was involved, how you felt, and why you think you were treated well.
- Now tell me about a time when service was particularly bad.

Survey development and administration

Based on an informal analysis of the interviews, one survey was designed for employees and one for customers. The surveys differed from the interviews in the level of the detail of the questions and, very importantly, in the number of people from whom we were able to collect data. The latter difference permitted more systematic, quantitatively based exploration of the hypotheses.

In all, survey responses came from 263 employees and 1,657 customers from 23 branches of the bank; about 70 customers and about 11 employees per branch.

Results of employee interviews

The employee interviews suggested a complex set of issues in the service orientation of branches. At a more general level, as expected, employees responded to our questions with the themes of both enthusiasts and bureaucrats. The issues that reflected an enthusiastic orientation referred to the branch's philosophy of a flexible and interpersonally open form of involvement with the branch's customers and the community in the delivery of service. In the survey, the enthusiastic orientation was measured by these items, for example: keeping a sense of 'family' among branch employees, having the branch involved in community affairs, and giving customer service in new and creative ways. In contrast, the bureaucratic orientation was measured by constraints on giving good service – for example, stress on rules, procedures, and system maintenance that, we were told, often diverted energy away from providing good customer service. Other measures of the bureaucratic theme included strict adherence to rules and procedures, routine performance of one's job, and the use of only established methods for solving customers' problems.

On an everyday activity level, employees said that the activities that represented good service included the degree to which the branch manager assumed the traditional managerial functions of giving good service (planning, coordinating, goal setting, establishing routine), the extent to which extra effort in serving customers was rewarded and appreciated, and the degree to which there was an active attempt to retain customers in the branch.

Employees also told us about some primarily central bank-controlled (as compared with predominantly branch-controlled) support systems that would help them give better or poorer customer service. Four apparently independent and identifiable support systems were noted:

- *Personnel support* ('The employees sent by Personnel are not able to do their jobs well.')
- *Central processing support* ('Having all customer records in a central location makes it easier on the branch.')
- *Marketing support* ('We are well-prepared by Marketing for the introduction of new products and services.')

● *Equipment/supply support* ('Equipment and machinery in the branch are well-serviced and rarely break down.')

The managerial functions scale is presented in Table 1 as an illustration of the kinds of items in a complete scale from the employee survey.

Table 1 *Items composing the managerial function scale from the employee survey*

Item number	Item
4	My branch manager supports employees when they come up with new ideas on customer service.
7	My branch manager sets definite quality standards of good customer service.
9	My branch manager meets regularly with employees to discuss work performance goals.
13	My branch manager accepts the responsibilities of his/her job.
20	My branch manager gets the people in different jobs to work together in serving branch customers.
21	My branch manager works at keeping an orderly routine going in the branch.
29	My branch manager takes time to help new employees learn about the branch and its customers.

Parenthetically, it is worth noting that the three interviewers were remarkably unanimous in their agreement about the very strong desire of the employees in this system to give customers good service. Indeed, a central theme coming out of the interviews was a sense of *frustration*, – that is, the feeling that 'the system' set up obstacles that frustrated their desire to provide the best possible customer service.

Results of customer interviews

In response to the open-ended questions about service, customers identified ten issues associated with the climate for service at their branch. These ten, with an example of the kind of statements used in the customer survey, are:

1 *Teller courtesy* ('Tellers care about customers as people in my branch.')
2 *Officer courtesy* ('Some officers in the branch know me by name.')
3 *Teller competence* ('Tellers in the branch seem to be well-trained and knowledgeable.')

4 *Adequate staff* ('My branch seems to have enough employees to handle its customers.')

5 *Branch administration* ('It sometimes seems to me that tellers have to walk all over the place to get things done.')

6 *Handling services* ('Deposits are promptly credited to my account(s).')

7 *Convenience* ('I like the fact that the bank has a large number of branches.')

8 *Employee turnover* ('There seems to be a high turnover of employees in my branch.')

9 *Selling* ('Officers of the bank have tried to get me to open new accounts.')

10 *Employee attitudes* ('My impression is that the branch employees really try to give the customers good service.')

Statements from the branch administration scale from the customer survey are presented in Table 2.

Table 2 *Items involved in the branch administration scale from the customer survey*

Item number	Item
3	An officer (or someone else) takes charge of things when the bank becomes overcrowded.
−4	It sometimes seems to me that tellers have to walk all over the place to get things done.
−12	When I've opened new accounts or had to change old ones, something usually got messed up.
34	My branch has an adequate supply of deposit and withdrawal tickets.
−36	I sometimes feel lost in the branch, not knowing where to go for a certain transaction.
−39	It is difficult to know who to call or where to write when I need specific kinds of bank-related information.

Note: A minus sign before the item number indicates that the item was reverse-scored.

Survey findings

Results of the survey will be presented in two parts: (1) data on employee desires to give good service, and what happens when the stress of customer vs. management demands is encountered, and (2) data on the relationships between the way employees and customers experience service.

Employee desires to give good service

To explore employee desires to give good service, we took a two-pronged approach: First we asked employees to tell us how essential both the enthusiastic approach and the bureaucratic approach were to good service. Then we asked the same employees to tell us how essential they felt *management* thinks both the enthusiastic and the bureaucratic approaches are to giving good service.

Ascertaining employees' perceptions of management's perspective, as well as their own, permitted the examination of two interesting questions: First, do service employees generally see themselves emphasizing different approaches to service than they believe management wants? As shown in Table 3, the answer is 'Yes'; employees see themselves more as enthusiasts and less as bureaucrats than they believe management is. The second question is considerably more subtle: it asked for the consequences of a discrepancy between the way employees believe service should be given and the way they think management wants service provided.

Table 3 *Employee views on own and management's service orientation*

Approach to service	Average employees' own views	Average employees' views of management
Bureaucrat	1.92	2.33
Enthusiast	2.48	2.35

Note: All responses were made on a three-point scale. The differences between employees' own views and employees' views of management are both statistically significant.

Answers to the second question provided information that enabled us to calculate, for each employee, the *discrepancy* between employee emphases and perceived management emphases and then to relate that discrepancy to employee reports of role stress – that is, of role conflict and ambiguity, job dissatisfaction, frustration over being unable to give good service, and intentions to change jobs. Following the logic presented earlier, it was assumed that the larger the discrepancy, the more negative feelings employees would experience. In fact, as shown in Table 4, this was the case. This means that a host of negative consequences follow when employees think customer service should be handled in ways that differ from the way they believe management wants service given.

Additional analyses, not shown here, revealed that the service orientation discrepancy *first* creates role conflict and ambiguity, and then

Table 4 *Correlations between service orientation discrepancy and employee outcomes*

Employees' negative feelings	Correlation
Role conflict	0.45
Role ambiguity	0.20
Dissatisfaction	0.42
Frustration	0.33
Turnover intentions	0.32

Note: A large discrepancy means less agreement; all correlations are significantly different from zero.

the other negative outcomes. Thus incongruence between employee desires and the perceived orientation of management *first* seems to lead to role stress; it is this stress that *then* seems to result in frustration, dissatisfaction, and intentions to quit.

Relationship between customer and employee views of service

It is one thing to be aware that employees may suffer feelings of conflict or frustration when they disagree with management's orientation to service, but it is another thing to find out that management's orientation to service is related to other indices of organizational success. The present study defines organizational success in terms of customer evaluations of the level or quality of service rendered by their bank branch.

At this point our frame of reference switched from how individual employees experience their work world to the ways in which employees and customers, as groups, experience their bank branches. Thus, the reference is not to individuals but to organizations – that is, bank branches. Therefore, the focus shifts from the 263 branch employees, to the 23 branches. This change was necessary because organizations are really aggregates of people and, in evaluating organizational effectiveness, meaningful aggregates constitute the appropriate frames of reference.

Customer data combined with employee data provided the answer to the question: Are employees' descriptions of customer service in their branch related to what *customers* have to say about the service they receive? Once again, the answer was yes.

For example, Figure 3 shows how customer views of service are related to employee views of service in the 23 branches. The dots in the figure each represent a branch.

The data for employees were based on their responses to the question: 'How do you think the customers of your branch view the general quality

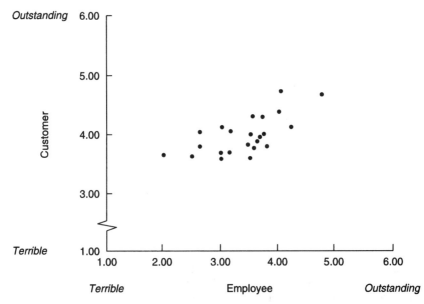

Figure 3 *Relationship between customer and employee perceptions of customer service*

of the service they receive in your branch?' Customers were asked to: 'Describe the general quality of the service you receive in your branch.' Both groups graded service on the following six-point scale: outstanding, excellent, good, not so good, bad, terrible. The analysis showed that customers report better service in branches when employees report that:

- There's a more enthusiastic service emphasis.
- The branch manager emphasizes service as he or she carries out the role of the branch manager.
- There's an active attempt to retain all customer account holders, not only large accounts.
- The personnel department provides a sufficient number of well-trained tellers.
- Equipment is well-maintained and supplies are plentiful.

In fact, the correlation of the data from the analyses of employee and customer responses was so consistently strong that it was possible to isolate a few customer perceptions that warrant particular note – that is, it was possible to identify which facets of service from the *customer's* view were most strongly related to selected facets of service as described by *employees*.

For example, when employees describe their branch as one in which the manager emphasizes customer service as he or she carries out the traditional managerial role, customers report not only generally superior service but, more specifically, that:

- The tellers are courteous.
- The tellers are competent.
- The staffing level is adequate.
- The branch is administered well.
- Teller turnover is low.
- The staff has positive work attitudes.

Similar findings were observed when branches were described by employees as having more of an enthusiast approach and also when employees reported they worked in a branch that actively tries to retain all categories of account holders.

Summary

These results may be summarized as follows: When branch employees perceive a strong service orientation in their branch, the customers of those branches report not only that they receive generally superior service, but that specific facets of service are handled in a superior manner. In addition, employees *themselves* experience less negative consequences at work when their branch has more of an enthusiastic orientation to service. Thus, employees are *less* dissatisfied and frustrated, *more* likely to plan to remain in their branch, and they experience *less* role conflict and role ambiguity when the branch is more like employees feel it should be – that is, more enthusiastic in its approach to service.

A major conclusion from this study: Employees and customers of service organizations will each experience positive outcomes when the organization operates with a customer service orientation. This orientation seems to result in superior service practices and procedures that are observable by customers and that seem to fit employee views of the appropriate style for dealing with customers.

More specifically, this research supports the following assumptions:

- Employees perceive themselves to be more enthusiastic and management to be more bureaucratic in service orientation. This suggests gaps between the goals of employees *vis-à-vis* service and the management goals that employees perceive. It is important for organizations to be aware of *where* these differences exist so they can take steps to remedy them. Figure 4 pinpoints these differences for the branch employees in this study and, thus, where the bank needed to change to be more congruent with the employees' more enthusiastic, less bureaucratic orientation to service.
- Employees who work in settings that are more congruent with their own service orientation experience less role ambiguity and role conflict and, as a result, are generally more satisfied, experience less frustration in their efforts to give good service, and are more likely to report they

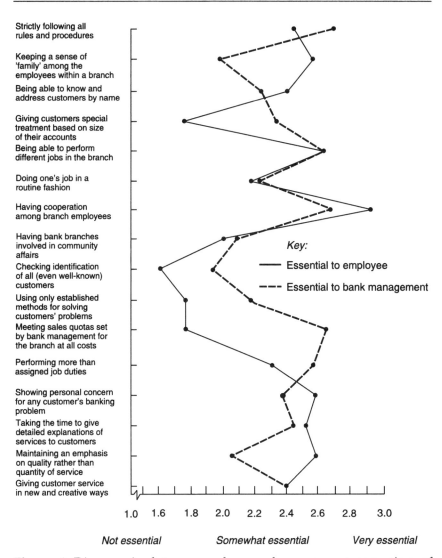

Figure 4 *Discrepancies between employee and management perceptions of service facets*

intend to keep working for the organization. This assumption was clearly supported; it also suggests that what management frequently perceives as employee disinterest or lack of motivation is really employees' lack of enthusiasm for carrying out management policies that are incongruent with their own desires. In fact, employees in this study seemed very interested in meeting *customer* service needs, but less interested in satisfying management's bureaucratic needs.

- Even though they view service from a different perspective, employee and customer perceptions of organizational effectiveness are positively related. Support for this assumption was quite strong; that is, when employees report that their branch emphasized service by word and deed, customers report superior banking experiences. These data, and my earlier work with bank customers also show that customers who report a more positive service climate are less likely to switch their accounts to other banks. These findings clearly indicate that management emphasis in a service organization cannot be hidden from those who are served: climate shows in service organizations.

This idea of an organization's climate being apparent to customers goes to the heart of issues presented in the introduction about the determination of organizational effectiveness. A finance-oriented conspiracy seems to promote a short-run productivity orientation rather than a more long-term, holistic perspective to determine organizational effectiveness. A more succinct way of summarizing this issue is through the concept of 'goodwill.'

An organization accrues good will over long periods of time by varied behaviors. Goodwill is reflected in the way people who have direct (that is, employees), indirect (that is, employees' families), and in-between (that is, customers, suppliers) contact with an organization think and speak about it; goodwill is the organization's reputation – that is, the way it is viewed by the multiple constituencies it affects and by which it is affected.

While the present study concentrated on the goodwill perceptions of customers, there probably would have been similar results from research concentrated on other branch constituencies. Thus suppliers to the branches could have been asked for their opinions about the branch, and branch employees could have been asked about how suppliers are treated. Or employees' families could have reported their opinions about the way the bank affects their spouse/parent and so on, and employees might have reported on the general quality of consideration given them as employees. Perhaps more interestingly, *potential* branch employees could have been surveyed about what they think it would be like to work in a particular branch, and those perceptions could have been related to what *incumbents* report it is like to work there.

In each of these hypothetical research efforts, the interesting issue would be the way in which climates created in the branch are 'picked up' by the various groups important to the long-term survival of the organization. I suspect these questions are infrequently asked, and rarely if ever pursued systematically. Yet, organizations need the goodwill of families when an employee is making turnover decisions; they need to have a positive reputation as a place to work in order to attract good employees; and, especially in a time of strife (for example, in a situation like that of the Chrysler Corporation), they need the goodwill of suppliers.

A very general conclusion, then, culled from this research effort: It is just as important for an organization to be interested in its relationships with the many groups that affect its long-term viability as it is for it to be concerned with the short-run-financial considerations affecting stock-holders and creditors, and so on.

Selected bibliography

For a more technical treatment of the research reported here, see 'Employee and Customer Perceptions of Service in Banks,' by Benjamin Schneider, John J. Parkington, and Virginia M. Buxton, in *Administrative Science Quarterly*, June 1980; 'Some Correlates of Experienced Job Stress: A Boundary Role Study' by John J. Parkington and Benjamin Schneider, in *Academy of Management Journal*, June 1979; and 'The Perception of Organizational Climate: The Customer's View,' by Benjamin Schneider, in *Journal of Applied Psychology*, June 1973.

For conflicting views on the role of service organizations in a consumer society, the industrialization of service is promoted by Theodore Levitt in *The Harvard Business Review*, September October 1972 and 1976; the consumer's view is promoted by Alan Gartner and Frank Riessman in *The Service Society and the New Consumer Vanguard* (Harper & Row, 1974).

For further discussion of the multiple constituency view of organizational effectiveness, see 'Toward a Workable Framework,' by Johannes M. Pennings and Paul S. Goodman in their book *New Perspectives on Organizational Effectiveness* (Jossey-Bass, 1977).

For a general treatment of the organizational climate construct, see 'Organizational Climates: An Essay,' by Benjamin Schneider, in *Personnel Psychology*, Winter 1975, and (the less biased treatment) 'Climates in Organizations' by William F. Joyce and John W. Slocum in Steven Kerr's (ed.) *Organizational Behaviors* (Grid, 1979).

The nature of boundary roles in organizations and the stress experienced by employees who occupy those roles is well described in 'Inter-organizational Processes and Organization. Boundary Activities' by J. Stacy Adams in the book *Research in Organizational Behavior, Volume 2,* edited by Barry M. Staw and Larry L. Cummings (JAI Press, 1980).

CORPORATE STRATEGY AND CORPORATE CULTURE: THE VIEW FROM THE CHECKOUT
Emmanuel Ogbonna and Barry Wilkinson

Emmanuel Ogbonna is a Lecturer in Organizational Behaviour and Director of the Postgraduate Diploma in Business Administration programme at the Cardiff Business School. He has published a variety of articles on the subjects of corporate strategy, corporate culture and human resource management. Barry Wilkinson is Professor of Human Resource Management and Coordinator of the Japanese Management Research Unit at the Cardiff Business School. His research is in the area of industrial and organizational sociology, focusing on the human and organizational implications of new manufacturing systems and technologies. He is author of three books and many articles reflecting his research interests.

'Corporate strategy and corporate culture: the view from the checkout' describes the human resource management techniques adopted by three British supermarket chains in bids to change their corporate cultures, to support the move from price to service-based competition. The behavioural management techniques employed by the supermarkets were successful in that employees were more likely to behave politely and hide their feelings when dealing with difficult customers. However, the measures did not succeed in changing the underlying values of the customer-facing staff, where high staff turnover, a reliance on part-time workers and the unattractive nature of the work limited the programmes' effectiveness.

In our previous article on strategy and culture in British supermarkets[1] we described the attempts of the managements of three major British supermarkets to transform their cultures in line with the shifting strategic emphasis away from price competition towards competition based on customer service. The new culture is intended to be one in which the customer is *king*, not a *punter*. We described the means by which the customer-comes-first philosophy was to be achieved, particularly the human resource strategies aimed at gaining employee commitment and instilling a customer ethos among staff at all levels, especially 'front-line' staffs. The implied changes to individuals' working lives are of considerable significance. The four companies described in this article alone employ between them around 200,000 people; and attempts to transform organisational cultures have taken hold not just in supermarkets but in banks, building societies, clothing and other retail sectors.

Of course, there are limits to what may be learned from describing top management ambitions, especially on the subject of 'culture', and since writing that article interviews have been conducted at store level with store managements, supervisors and checkout operators in the same three supermarket chains plus one other (company D, which provides interesting contrasts) in order to ascertain the impact of customer care campaigns and the extent of internalisation of values espoused by the top managements of the major supermarket corporations. If the super-markets were achieving the transformation in values they desire after several years of instilling a corporate philosophy, then one might expect checkout operators not only to smile but to mean it, and their work to be as much for love as it is for money.

In this article then, the view from the checkout is presented. First, we briefly re-cap the human resource strategies adopted in the 1980s intended to create a match between corporate strategy and corporate culture. Second, we focus on the measures explicitly intended to inculcate a customer orientation. Third, we describe in some detail the impact on the supermarket staff, particularly checkout operators, and document employee responses. Finally, we discuss the implications of our findings, and examine the prospects for the customer ethos in the British supermarket industry.

Matching strategy and culture

During the 1980s there has been a clear shift in the basis of competition among Britain's major supermarket chains. The shift has been away from price (although price undoubtedly remains important) towards 'meeting customer needs'.[1,2] With only one or two exceptions, this has involved the major supermarkets in:

● Shifting location to convenient out-of-town sites with car parking facilities;
● Designing supermarkets with modern and 'pleasing' architecture, décor and layout on 'green' sites;
● Extending the range of goods on offer, including high quality wines and exotic or organically grown fruits and vegetables;
● Attempting to transform the culture of the organisation and the values of employees such that a high quality of personal service is enjoyed by the customer.

The first of the three changes have been well documented[2,3] and it is the fourth initiative on the list which is of concern in this article. We use the term 'culture' to refer to the habitual and traditional ways of thinking, feeling and reacting that are characteristic of a particular organisation.[4] This means that we are concerned not just with peoples' behaviour, but the meanings, values and assumptions which underlie that behaviour.[5] According to Robbins[6] a *strong* culture is one in which there is a set of guiding values which are widely shared, clearly ordered and intensely held. The 'excellent companies' described by Peters and Waterman[7] have been held up as examples of such strong cultures. Many of Britain's major supermarkets are pursuing exactly such a culture based on a customer ethos. The desired culture has been pursued through various human resource management practices, from an emphasis on 'attitude' in selection to extensive customer care campaigns. Before documenting employee responses to the new expectations, we will describe the human resource measures being undertaken in the four companies which were subject to study.

Pursuit of the customer ethos

Three of the four chains under study are actively pursuing a customer ethos, this being symbolised in one company where the use of the term *punter* has been abolished from the store manager's vocabulary. In the fourth chain, which is exceptional among Britain's major supermarkets, the 'pile it high, sell 'em cheap' philosophy is deliberately maintained. One long-serving manager in a supermarket pursuing the customer ethos captured the 'old ways' as follows:

> ... ten years ago when I first joined the company if you had queues all the way back in the checkout you were doing well ... now if you've got more than two people you want to get another checkout operator to serve the customers.

A store manager at another branch of the same chain reinforced the point:

> Thirteen years ago customer service was way down the list of our priorities. All the company was really interested in was getting the shelves filled. ... We didn't deal with customer complaints as we do now and we used to say no to customers most of the time. The managers were just there to run the business in the best way and in those days, the best way was to stock at the cheapest price and sell at the cheapest price ... that's how we were taught.

No longer is this how they are taught – a manager in the same store commented:

> The company decided about two years ago to change from the price wars to the customer services factors. We now see the customer as the most important animal who has to be pleased.

Store managers in each of the three supermarkets pursuing a customer ethos (hereafter referred to as companies A, B and C) provided similar sentiments regarding the present emphasis on the customer and the transformation from 'cheapest is best' to 'quality and service is best' philosophies in the 1980s. The exceptional supermarket chain, company D, has deliberately continued to pursue cost-minimisation and cheapest price policies, and has been successful in extending its market share in the 1980s (in fact doubling it over the last few years), largely through filling the 'vacuum' created as the majority of large supermarket chains move 'up-market' and 'out-of-town'.

So how do companies A, B and C go about creating the sort of organisational culture in which staff – particularly front-line staff on the shopfloor – put the customer first?

At companies A, B and C the attempt to establish a strong culture begins with selection, where there is an attempt to recruit people with the ability to develop a customer orientation. Occupational and psychological tests have been introduced in company C, the other two relying on the ability of managers to spot capable candidates during interviews. Most managers claimed they knew what they were looking for in potential staff, though some in company B were unsure how to take the message from head office that 'like-minded' people should be recruited: 'What is a like-minded person, that's what I would like to know? . . . I employ people that want the job and are presentable'.

Selection is followed by induction and training when management expectations of staff are established. At company A a staff training officer has been established at every single store, part of her (typically the officer is female) responsibility being to ensure customer service briefings and training are provided to every employee. In each of the three companies videos are used to get the 'customer is king' message across. One store manager at company A commented:

> They are told to smile all the time and if the customer has a particular problem then they should try and get them through the checkout and contact a supervisor or manager to deal with it.

An operator at the same store indicated that she had got the message:

> We are given customer care training when we join the company and as an ongoing thing. We are told to smile all the time and that the customer is always right.

A store manager at company C appreciated the difficulty which checkout operators might face on some occasions and how training might help:

> . . . it's quite a difficult job . . . they are the ones that come into contact with the customers most . . . they have to deal with the niggles directed at the company. Because they wear (company C) badges, the customers see them as the company's representatives . . . We tell them not to let out their emotion and to be as polite as possible and to tell themselves that the customers are not having a go at them but at the company and the system.

At company B training in customer care is effectively on-the-job and continuous:

> We tell them to try and deal with minor complaints as pleasantly as possible but we emphasise that if they sense they will have a problem they should refer the customer to the deputy manager or

myself (store manager) . . . We encourage them to stay when we are dealing with such customers so that they can learn.

At the same company shelf fillers are trained to spot and help the 'lost customer', who is a customer 'unsure of what they want or where to find what they want'. At company C all staff are expected to carry a plastic card (credit card-size) which reminds them how to deal with customers – in ten points it states that one should smile, make eye contact, greet the customer, apologise for any delay, etc.

Company D provides a contrast with regard to customer care training. Here, customer service is the tenth item on the employee induction checklist, being preceded by a range of rules regarding attendance, etc. The timeclock card is third on the list. Training is minimal. Nonetheless, employees are told in an induction video that 'the customer makes pay day possible'.

In companies A, B and C the customer care message is put across frequently through a variety of media. For instance, at company A there are posters at all entrances onto the shopfloor which read 'smile, you're on (company C) stage'. The same company runs an employee-of-the-month competition where staff nominate persons who have contributed most to helping customers or fellow employees. The winning member of staff has his or her name posted on the staff notice-board and may feature in the company magazine. At the end of the year marks are totted up for an employee-of-the-year award. There are customer care committees in every store, whose job it is to generate ideas on how to improve customer service. Ideas go up through regional and national level managements and may eventually be implemented (and celebrated in the company newspaper) nationally. The child changing facilities now available in some stores is one example of an idea orginating from such committees. Companies B and C have similar initiatives and schemes.

Company D is preoccupied with keeping the shelves filled and speed of through-put at the checkout and so far has not introduced any smile or customer care campaigns. In 1988 it introduced an in-house magazine, but unlike companies A, B and C, it is not given out to all employees. Rather, two copies are firmly secured to a table in the canteen. This is symptomatic of the stringent cost controls operating at company D where, in contrast to A, B and C, there are no staff discount, profit-sharing or welfare schemes, and no formal employee involvement schemes. As one store manager commented: 'management's only interest is to stack the goods on the shelves and sell them'.

Customer care at companies A, B and C is taken seriously by top managements, and their influence can be direct, as one checkout supervisor made clear:

> We have people from head office coming along all the time to see how we are getting along . . . this means that we have to be on our toes and provide the best possible service.

In turn, the checkout supervisors constantly monitor the behaviour of checkout operators. A supervisor at company A commented:

> We are able to detect when a checkout operator is not smiling or even when she is putting on a false smile . . . we call her into a room and have a chat with her.

The checkout operator's work is also, of course, subject to constant scrutiny by customers. The effect is obvious: '. . . you have to be very careful and polite because they can report you to the manager'.

Some supermarkets in recent years have gone so far as to employ consultancies which send bogus shoppers into stores and report on the level of service they get.[8] With such visibility of behaviour, supermarket managements with customer ethos ambitions clearly have an inherent advantage from the start.

The view from the checkout

Most checkout and other shopfloor personnel in companies A, B and C certainly appear to have 'got the message' regarding customer care. The following quotation was typical: 'The customer is always right . . . the customer comes first . . . we have to smile all the time and make them feel welcome.'

Many also pointed out the benefits of customer care not only to the company but also personally in that checkout operator–customer relations could be smoothed, or (more rarely) that there was a moral obligation to provide good service:

> You can't let the customer know what your worries are. You have to put on a smile and this disarms the customer and helps us to do our job so we even try to build up personal relationships with some of the customers.
>
> You have to differentiate between your home life and work . . . you forget your problems when you come to work . . . I am a mother and I go to many shops and I know that there's nothing worse than asking somebody a question and she says I don't know, with a long face . . . that's awful.
>
> Sometimes you feel like being rude because some of them can be really nasty but you can't. Some customers come in thinking that they can have a go at us because they believe that we are just shop workers, but being nice and polite to them means that they are usually taken aback and some of them then change their attitude.
>
> When they get angry you try to calm them down. Some customers are really very funny . . . We are told to smile all the time . . . sometimes it's very hard . . . I succeed because I try to put up an act . . . my mother thinks I'm very good at it and that I should have been an actress.

'Disarming' the customer with an actress's smile was frequently recognised as beneficial, but company loyalty, a characteristic expressly sought by companies A, B and C, was exceptional. The following comment is such an exception: 'I think you always have to be loyal to them because they pay you . . . it's good to be loyal because if you are happy with the company it reflects on your attitude to the customers.'

Even this quotation suggests a degree of instrumentality, as does 'I would like to stay in (company A) for a long time. It suits me. I would not go to any other company because I don't think the pay will be good enough . . . I enjoy my work sometimes but I come out for the money.'

Very often, operators are subject to a high degree of emotional stress, and virtually all those interviewed could relate instances where they had to bottle up their feelings in order to keep the customer happy:

> . . . a customer came in and was very rude to me; I tried to keep calm and was smiling but he went on and on . . . he was standing very close to me and was very rude . . . he upset me so bad that I ended up bursting into tears.
>   . . . the worst thing is that you are on the till trying to go as fast as you can and you can hear them moaning that you are slow . . . there are times that I just want to look up and say shut up but you have to be busy and keep smiling.
>   . . . I get a difficult customer at least once a week . . . older customers tend to be more difficult . . . they seem to want more for their money . . . there's one lady that usually comes in here and moans all the time . . . when we see her come in we boil but we don't let her see it . . . we just keep a smile on our faces.
>   . . . we do get a lot of customers moaning and groaning and that's where we can get nervous. We are supposed to look after the customer but some can be rude but you have to keep all that inside you; you are not allowed to let it out and this adds to the stress of the job. You can easily let your emotion out on the next customer who still expects you to smile.
>   . . . carrier bags are the most sensitive issue that I have come across. Some customers get very angry when you tell them to pay for carrier bags . . . some even throw their shopping at you and walk out of the store.
>   I try just to be polite and try to keep them happy. If they are not happy I try to call the supervisor . . . Sometimes I get nervous and want to let out the emotion but I can't because the job doesn't allow it.
>   We do get some very difficult customers . . . but customer service is something we pride ourselves in so we have to learn to manage our feelings. When you get too angry you just go into the office and have a good swear at them and you come out smiling.

Checkout operators have to be very careful in the signs they give off to customers. An USDAW officer recounted an extreme example of what can happen if the message given by the operator is misread:

A woman customer walked into the store with her husband and saw a checkout girl smiling at him. The husband returned the smile and eye contact and his wife went beserk accusing the checkout operator of flirting with her husband . . . It was a serious case and the manager had to be called in to resolve it.

Most often, and the following quotes are both verbatim and typical of checkout operators, there is a degree of resigned acceptance of the customer ethos, and sometimes even a hostility towards it:

I try and find out what the problem is and try and be polite but if I can't handle it I call the manager . . . I smile because I'm told to . . . sometimes you don't want to smile but you have to . . .

. . . sometimes I feel like I could kick them . . . why should I smile at them . . . they don't know the problems I have at home . . . but at the end of the day it's the customer that pays the wage . . . when this (smile campaign) first came about I had a few arguments about it because you can't always be happy all the time . . . I might not be smiling but it doesn't mean that I'm unhappy . . . at the beginning I never thought I could walk around with my face full of smile but now I can go on smiling at customers.

. . . the company has to be realistic . . . it's all right for somebody to tell you to smile but you can't smile at someone who's calling you a stupid bitch.

Relations with supervisors, of course, varied from store to store, but complaints were commonplace in most. The following are examples:

When the system (EPOS) is at fault, the checkout operator could easily correct it . . . but we are not allowed to. Sometimes the supervisor can take up to 10 minutes to come and this makes the customers very angry.

On the whole we work well with supervisors. Occasionally we get hard done by and we blow up. We feel guilty saying no to work overtime though most of us have young kids at home. Once you want a day off, the supervisor says sorry you can't have it. We feel that we give a lot and get very little in return.

The management could do a lot more. We get a feeling that once they get what they want, they don't care about anybody else.

The supervisors themselves tended to be more optimistic about customer care and the wisdom in offering loyalty to their company. Many enjoyed the status and promotion prospects they were given, and most agreed with the philosophy of customer care. One expressed the following additional benefit: 'I also have to be a Claire Rayner. Everybody comes to me with their problems. It's keeping me sane; I worry about everybody else's problems and tend to forget mine.'

There were also complaints though, particularly about the long hours (45 to 50 hours was not untypical in stores of companies A, B and C). One complained that 'The twilight shift is fine in theory but you only need a few staff to be ill and the supervisor will do the shelf filling. I'm really a "glorified shelf filler"'.

If the above comments are characteristic of companies A, B and C, how would staff respond to the cost-conscious management of company D? There were some complaints, for example about the fact that overtime was generally expected but unpaid: '. . . they tend to take advantage of the staff loyalty. They don't pay us for overtime but we are expected to do it. If you have to work overtime I think you should be paid for it. I work one hour extra every day and I don't get paid for it.'

One operator at company A who had worked previously for company D contrasted the demands of the two managements:

> It's quite difficult (at company D) . . . you have to learn all the prices . . . you are constantly thinking about the prices even when you go home . . . it takes over your mind and once you stop thinking about it you tend to make mistakes . . . you are tested every so often and if your till is wrong either way by a certain amount every week you get three warnings and you're out . . . At (company D) you can't chat to the customers but here (company A) you can . . . at (company D) you sign a contract to work extra hours if any employee is sick but at (company A) they ask you politely and you don't have to work if you have other engagements.

Similar sentiments were expressed by another checkout operator (at company B) who had previously worked for company D: 'At (company B) there's emphasis on making the customer happy. You are encouraged to chat to the customers. At (company D) you are not allowed to talk to the customer; they just want the customer to spend and get out.'

However, although company D staff were less likely to smile and express deference towards customers, awareness of customer needs, loyalty to the company, and enthusiasm about the job were equally evident as in companies A, B and C. Witness the following comments:

> . . . the customer is the most important person because he makes pay day possible.
> . . . all right we are not as glossy as (company B) but that's what keeps the prices down and the customers simply come here for the prices . . . that's their main concern.
> (Company D) is a way of life for me . . . I left after six years to do something else and I missed it so much that I had to come back . . . I enjoy the challenge of having to learn the prices, that's what I like most about the job.

Analysis and conclusions

The comments above almost unanimously suggest that supermarket shopfloor staffs have not taken on board the values and assumptions espoused by their senior managements via training films and campaigns. Nonetheless there is evidence that staff have been responsive in terms of the behaviours they display at work. Employees of companies A, B and C are more likely to smile and behave politely towards customers, and to hide their feelings in the case of difficult customers. However, the interviews revealed little evidence of any internalisation of espoused values to the extent that we could refer to these supermarkets as 'strong culture' organisations. Rather, the motives behind the behaviour patterns displayed on the shopfloor were almost invariably either instrumental ('this disarms the customer') or under threat of sanction ('I smile because I'm told to'; 'you have to be very careful and polite because they can report you to the manager'). The checkout operator's job is, of course, highly visible, and not smiling or even 'putting on a false smile' can result in being 'called into a room for a chat' with the supervisor. Random visits by bogus shoppers and head office managements reinforce the threat of sanctions for undesirable behaviour or expressing one's true feelings to difficult customers. Some stores also have TV monitors in the manager's office so that the store manager can see what is happening at checkouts without even having to visit the shopfloor.

The polite and sometimes deferent behaviour of shopfloor staffs in supermarkets tends, then, to be an act (in the theatrical sense) which demands acting skills ('when we see her come in we boil but we don't let her see it ... we just keep a smile on our faces'; 'I succeed because I try to put up an act ... my mother thinks I'm very good at it and that I should have been an actress'). Hochschild[9] in a penetrating description and analysis of the work of airline stewardesses at an American airline, uses the term 'emotion management', a psychologically demanding process, to explain how employees control their feelings and give a convincing performance. The same skills are now being asked of checkout operators and other shopfloor staffs in British supermarkets and other service sector organisations. However, the training is not so long or intense (typically a few days for supermarket staffs compared with six weeks in-camp training at Delta airlines) and professional stress counselling and advice on how to cope emotionally (apart from occasional 'Claire Rayner' sessions) is less likely to be given. Some individual managers gave advice to staff on emotion management ('we tell them ... to tell themselves that the customers are not having a go at them but at the company and the system'). And some operators have devised their own methods ('when you get too angry you just go into the office and have a good swear at them and you come out smiling'). But occasionally there is a casualty ('he upset me so bad that I ended up bursting into tears').

Limits to success in establishing a customer ethos also come from the very nature of the work, which is unglamorous, monotonous, and frequently intense. 'Sitting down on the till all day makes you bored' was a frequent comment. Three and three-quarter hour stints at the till are typical. A USDAW officer explained anger and frustration at the smile campaign among staffs as follows:

> They underestimate their staff ... training people to smile implies that they really don't have such skill in everyday life ... we know how to smile ... we don't smile because we are understaffed, overworked, not respected and underpaid ... one is hardly motivated to smile in such situations.

A recent USDAW conference, she continued, 'was devastated about the assumptions management has of the workers ... they should be treated like adults and not children in a playschool.'

The Grocer magazine recently gave further reason why customer care campaigns might meet with anger or frustration. In a chain where workers are compelled to wear name badges, 'over-familiarity' had become a common complaint, and some checkout girls had become the victims of harrassment by customers who wrote them obscene letters.[10]

In sum, analysis of the view from the checkout reveals that it is the acting skills of employees, developed in the context of instructions from management and carried out under threat of sanction in an inherently 'visible' environment, which account in large part for their polite or deferent behaviour. A senior director in company C expressed the view that he wanted his employees not only to smile but to mean it. What appears to be in the process of development is somewhere between the two. The checkout operator with good acting skills may be seen to mean to smile but still does not necessarily mean it. Whether this matters to management is an open question; for the checkout operator subject to three and three-quarter hour stints of putting on an act and managing emotions, twice a day and week in week out, it does.

Finally, there are two further reasons why cultural and behavioural change in supermarkets may be limited. These relate first to internal resistance to change, and secondly to broader market factors beyond the control of individual companies.

Regarding internal resistance to change, despite the above comments of the USDAW officer and the frustrations we documented ourselves, there was no evidence of overt resistance to change from shopfloor staffs; rather, a resigned behavioural compliance was evident. Given the constant visibility of behaviour this is perhaps not surprising. There was, however, a degree of resistance to change among older managers in some stores. This is because, first, they have previously been instilled with the 'cheap is best' philosophy, and, second, because of the perceived loss of autonomy, close scrutiny and routinisation of work they perceive as operational controls have been centralised. A manager at one store commented:

It's going to be a very long process . . . we've got people who've been working with the store for 15 years or more and they have seen the full changes in (company A) especially in the last few years with customer service.

A manager at a different company A store reinforced the point:

It's difficult for an old store such as this to achieve the type of change required because people are used to the old standards and the physical environment . . . it would be easier to achieve change in a new store with new people.

A long-serving manager at company B complained of the effects of rapid expansion in the 1980s:

. . . there was a time that I could pick up a phone and speak to somebody in head office and know exactly who I was speaking to and what they did . . . now we are in a position where we don't know who's up there and what they do.

Two younger managers explained the older managers' attitudes in terms of loss of autonomy and the centralisation of decision making as the supermarket chains have attempted to standardise service across the country and take advantage of economies of scale, especially in purchasing:

In the past the managers had autonomy to do what they wanted to do but now they are subjected to checks and they find it difficult to accept . . . The older managers are against the fact that their task is now more routinised and they are reacting against the discipline of routine.

A lot of managers are used to buying stock directly from suppliers . . . but they can't adjust themselves to a different way of working . . . they're thinking their jobs are going down the drain but they should realise that their job is adapting . . .

Regarding customer campaigns themselves, most managers were enthusiastic, but we met occasional scepticism. For instance:

When the whole concept of customer care was started people were told to smile at the customers and there was a very strong reaction to it . . . they looked to America . . . the way it's done in America is not the way it's done over here . . . British people don't like to smile at people . . . 99 per cent of people are courteous and all they need do is act in the same way as they do in everyday life.

There are several factors beyond the control of individual supermarket chains which are additional constraints on the establishment of a customer ethos. The most obvious may be the relatively low wages and high turnover of staff in the supermarket industry. This is a bigger problem in some areas – particularly the South East – than others. We have not measured the extent of differences, and our own interviews in stores were limited to Wales and the West Country, but managers were aware of the importance of regional differences and the following comment was typical: '(staff loyalty) would depend on which area of the country which you are working in . . . turnover in Wales and the North of England is quite low if compared with figures in the South of England.'

Another problem is that of rapid expansion which means promotion from within, arguably central in developing a strong culture, is less likely.[1] And a third point is that the employment of large numbers of part-time, mainly female, workers is likely to continue to be crucial to competitive strategy for the foreseeable future. This is because of long opening hours, and the need to staff to meet peak daily, weekly and seasonal demand. As one manager put it: '. . . the 16 to 18-year-old temporary workers (at company B) are largely college students who need extra cash. The percentage of such staff who identify strongly with the company is quite low. The part-time staff are also not as committed as full-time staff as they don't feel that they have a career with the company.'

The fourth important constraint is that workforce composition is predicted to change in the 1990s with a shortage of young women, and older women coming back into the labour force.[11] One manager's comment may overstate the case, but indicates the perceived potential problem: 'I would like to take younger staff because I could develop them . . . I could brainwash a 16-year-old and make him understand our ways more than I could do with somebody of 21.'

Many shopfloor employees, who are mostly women, came to work in supermarkets with instrumental attitudes ('for the money') which was used to maintain or improve a certain quality of family life. Indeed some shopfloor staffs interviewed claimed they had rejected the offer of a supervisory position on the grounds that the long hours would conflict with family demands. The changing composition of the workforce is clearly likely, then, to exacerbate the difficulties supermarkets face in generating a 'strong' organisational culture: older women are more likely to have family demands and may be less likely to be susceptible to 'brainwashing'.

Our main conclusions for the prospects for cultural change in the British supermarket industry are, then, twofold. First, changes in 'culture' are likely to be behavioural rather than value changes. The culture being created is one in which, in Schein's[5] terms, particular behavioural patterns are established, but the underlying values and assumptions of the actors remain unchanged. Second, there are clear limits, sometimes beyond company control, to the development of a customer ethos. Both value and behavioural change are limited by staff turnover, rapid expansion, the use of part-time workers, changes in workforce composition, and by the values carried by the actors derived from non-work life.

References

1 Ogbonna, E. and Wilkinson, B., 'Corporate Strategy and Corporate Culture: The Management of Change in the UK Supermarket Industry', *Personnel Review*, Vol. 17 No. 6, 1988, pp. 10–14.
2 Ogbonna, E., 'Strategic Changes in UK Grocery Retailing: Present Trends and Future Prospects', *Management Decision*, Vol. 27 No. 6, 1989.
3 'Recent Changes in Grocery Retailing', *Retail Business*, No. 340, 1986, pp. 21–5.
4 Schwartz, H. and Davis, S.M., 'Matching Corporate Culture and Business Strategy', *Organizational Dynamics*, Summer 1981.
5 Schein, E.H., *Organization Culture and Leadership*, Jossey-Bass, San Francisco, 1985.
6 Robbins, S.P., *Organization Theory*, Prentice-Hall, London, 1989.
7 Peters, T. and Waterman, R.H., *In Search of Excellence*, Harper & Row, New York, 1982.
8 *The Independent*, 3 May 1989.
9 Hochschild, A.R., *The Managed Heart: Commercialization of Human Feelings*, University of California Press, California, 1983.
10 *The Grocer*, 10 December 1988, p. 5.
11 USDAW, *Retailing in the 1990s*, Report submitted by the Executive Council to the 1988 Annual Delegate Meeting.

USING INTERNAL MARKETING TO DEVELOP A NEW CULTURE – THE CASE OF ERICSSON QUALITY
Evert Gummesson

Evert Gummesson is a Professor of Services Management and Marketing at Stockholm University. His research and teaching interest are marketing management, services management, quality management, and research methods. He is the author of several books and numerous journal articles, and co-founder of the Stockholm Consulting Group.

In 'Using internal marketing to develop a new culture – the case of Ericsson Quality' Gummesson looks at the step-by-step implementation of an internal marketing programme in a large company operating in a business-to-business setting. The example illustrates how closely the concepts of internal marketing, service quality, total quality and corporate culture are intertwined.

On internal marketing and corporate culture

The concept of internal marketing, along with its concomitant techniques, has received particular attention in Northern Europe and in the research carried out by the 'Nordic School of Services.'[2,3] It has emerged out of services marketing. In service firms, where the interface with the customers is broad and intense, all contact personnel must be well attuned to the mission, goals, strategies, and systems of the company. Otherwise they cannot represent their firm well and successfully handle all those crucial contacts, known as 'the moments of truth,' that occur in the interaction with customers. Human resources are thus a key factor in developing and maintaining a successful service business.

The idea behind internal marketing is to apply the marketing concept, originally developed for the company's external marketing, to the 'internal market' as well. The knowhow developed over the years for successfully approaching the market can be made applicable, with some modification, to the internal market as well.

The interface between a firm's employees and its customers can be extensive even if the firm is not traditionally thought of as a service firm. This is particularly true of firms that market complex equipment or systems, be it to consumers or to businesses. Even where the interface is limited, however, companies look for better ways of preparing their employees for organizational changes, the introduction of new products and services, new technologies, new routines, and the like. Traditional ways of reaching out – using internal memos and magazines, meetings, training courses, and more recently video and computer techniques – leave a lot to be desired. Changing a culture is more than 'shooting off' a communications program.

In recent years the interest in corporate culture has increased. *In Search of Excellence*, Peters and Waterman's unprecedented success, and the spate of management literature that followed in its wake, are basically about the culture of companies and how a culture of excellence is created and maintained. Despite the flood of such recipes for success, many of them both intellectually and emotionally exciting, the more mundane reality of having to implement these grand ideas on a daily basis soon becomes a more difficult proposition than at first meets the eye. In other words, conceiving new ideas may be a great feat, but their actual implementation is an even greater one.

The Ericsson Group

Ericsson, which has developed a new 'quality culture,' gives us an example of internal marketing on a large scale in a business-to-business setting. With its headquarters in Stockholm, Sweden, Ericsson is a truly international corporation. Its home market can absorb only 20% of its output; the rest is being sold and partly manufactured globally. In 1985 its sales were $4.5 billion. The company is organized into seven business areas and the total number of subsidiaries and partly owned operations number almost 200.

Since Ericsson was founded 110 years ago it has had a stable record of growth and a healthy financial status, and above all it has been at the forefront of applied telecommunications technology. During the past few years, however, it has suffered some financial setbacks.

With the exception of one business area, the customers are few and large, consisting primarily of telecommunications administrations which are state monopolies. The obvious exception to a monopoly situation is the United States, where, since the recent deregulation, the market consists of seven large, privately owned Bell companies, plus a host of large and small independent operating companies. With a limited number of key customers on one hand and 75,000 employees in 70 countries on the other, one can ask where the biggest marketing problem rests: in the external market or in the internal market?

Why quality?

It is difficult to separate the content of a program from its form (cf. McLuhan's statement that 'the medium is the message'). Although we are discussing internal marketing rather than quality, some aspects of quality have particular relevance for the proper understanding and broadening of the concept of internal marketing.

In 1983 a quality program was triggered by the CEO of Ericsson. The rationale behind the program was a strong conviction that quality was to become the most important weapon in the marketing warfare. Quality has always been a major ingredient in Ericsson's strategy but this approach was a new one.

Quality has a long-standing tradition in manufacturing, but contributions to quality were needed from all functions of the firm. From a management perspective the focus of quality on manufacturing issues was suboptimal. The traditional manufacturing-oriented approach to quality has been challenged by U.S. thinkers, notably J. Edwards Deming, J.M. Juran, and Philip B. Crosby. The quality concept has been further developed by the Japanese, who could certainly be candidates for the Guinness Book of Records as world champions in combining the roles of quality thinkers and quality doers. The PIMS results[10] show a correlation between high profits and high quality although the cause-and-effect relationship is not fully evident. A recent issue of *Fortune*[8] points in the same direction: 'As in the past, respondents to *Fortune's* survey point to quality of management and quality of products and services as by far the most important attributes in judging corporate reputations.'

Basic differences between the old and the new approaches to quality at Ericsson are rejected in the following statements:

from a product and manufacturing quality concept *to* a total quality concept where every function contributes to quality;

from quality being a production management issue *to* quality being a top management issue; from quality being assessed by technicians to the customer being the judge of quality;

from focus on errors and their appraisal and remedy *to* focus on prevention: doing right from the start;

from accepting a certain error ratio as being 'normal' *to* aiming at zero defects;

from the notion that high quality leads to high costs *to* the notion that high quality leads to increased productivity, increased customer satisfaction, and increased profits.

In conclusion, a change of mindsets coupled with a change in behavior with regard to quality would be likely to have positive effects on Ericsson's future.

The EQ Program

Thus, as can be seen, many new ideas were waiting to be brought into the Ericsson culture. How was it, then, brought about?

The decision was taken to launch the extensive EQ Program. A three-year budget of $4 million and a full-time staff of seven were allocated. The task of the staff was to stimulate line managers to initiate quality activities. Advice was asked from many consultants – from the United States, Japan, and Sweden – on quality thinking as well as on the planning and execution of activities.

To initiate EQ, 'The EQ 16-Step Program' was presented. At its core was a list of measures that would be necessary in order to change the quality culture. Here is a sample of these:

- Analyze customer perceptions of Ericsson and its products and services.
- Assess the quality systems at Ericsson and improve them.
- Develop more precise quality goals, goal-setting procedures, and reporting procedures.
- Develop better quality cost definitions and procedures for measuring and reporting quality costs.
- Create an annual Quality Report (an equivalent to the annual financial report).

These and other activities were aimed primarily at creating an environment receptive to quality improvements. This 'setting of the stage' is a must if new ideas are to thrive. If programs for change are limited to communication activities, then even if the communication is professional, it does not lead to any substantial changes in behavior.

The achievements expected from EQ are summed up in Figure 1. EQ (1) could influence attitudes, perceptions, and know-how. (2) But even if that step is successful, what guarantees are there that behaviour will change (3), that quality will improve (4), and finally that profits will increase (5)? None, of course, but one has to be persistent, show stamina, and aim at success in the long term. Changing a culture is never a one-shot activity. Also, one must not forget other influences (6) that may speed up or delay this process, such as the business cycle, activities of the competition, and technological advances, as well as the operational units' own initiatives, taken independently of EQ.

The first goal of EQ at Ericsson was to move to square 2 and change the mindsets of people. This was a move in which communication skills were important, and a program based on established marketing and educational techniques was set up.

But even in such communication there are pitfalls and traps. The sequential description in Figure 1 is deceptive. Although it is logically neat to postulate that attitudes and knowhow come first and action and results later, it could just as well be the other way around: square 3, and even 4 and 5, may have to be entered before 2 is reached. Mao once said that 'if you want to know what a pear tastes like, you have to change the pear by eating it.' Until you yourself have been directly involved in a change, you may not be able to understand what it is all about. It is 'learning by doing.'

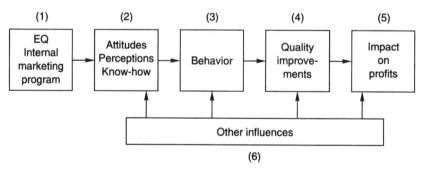

Figure 1

On implementation and the internal customer

We will concentrate here on a few issues that are of particular significance for the implementation of changes and the achievement of concrete results.*

---

* A more complete overview of EQ may be found in Larsson and Nylander.

We have discussed the necessity of getting past the mere communication activities and getting down to direct action. Arriving at squares 3 to 5 of Figure 1 can be a long and arduous process, a fact that academic researchers largely ignore.[4,5] Recent work by Bonoma eloquently spells this problem out: (1) 'The preoccupation of managers with implementation problems came as a great surprise to me, because I was eminently well prepared to help management find its way out of strategic darkness but blind as a bat about the factors important in actually getting a strategy executed.'[1]

The concept most often referred to as a powerful tool for implementation is the Japanese QC Circle (or 'quality circle'). It is well known everywhere today. It is also used by Ericsson but in a slightly amended form, called EQ Teams. This is a way of engaging everyone in quality improvement work and letting them 'taste the pear.'

A less well-known concept that fits in well here is the *internal customer*. According to this concept, everyone at Ericsson is said to have customers inside the firm and everyone should act as a supplier to these customers. It then becomes just as important to deliver high-quality products and services to the internal customer as it is to deliver high quality to the external customer. Eventually, quality is a satisfied external customer, the road to which is paved by satisfied internal customers.

This concept was not fully clear when EQ started, but its significance has grown during the project. It is likely not a new concept and its origin is not known, but it is used in Japan, for example, by Nissan Motor Company.

The larger problem of corporations, especially big ones, is often integration, not specialization. For example, a design problem is just as often an interface problem with marketing, manufacturing, finance, and other areas as it is a problem that can be solved inside the design department. The internal customer concept then becomes an 'integrator' helping to make every function, individual, and activity a stronger link in the chain of events which leads to greater customer satisfaction.

The practical use of the internal customer concept requires everyone to interview his internal customers and find out what he does well and what could be done better – from the internal customer's point of view. Interviews can be person-to-person or group-to-group.

Where does this concept take us? It fulfills three essential criteria: it is simple, it involves everyone, and it is implementable. It is certainly not a high-tech concept of the space age, and it involves no fancy statistical formulas and computer programming; it is back to basics. It is back to the need for understanding one's contribution to the success of the firm. In a complex industrial environment few people, even in high tiers of the hierarchy, fully see their role in the firm's total operations. The concept creates natural feedback; people learn whether their performance is appreciated or not.

The effect of internal marketing is strongly reinforced by the concept of the internal customer. The concept brings communication down to face-to-face interaction where the actual implementation takes place: on the shopfloor, in the office of designers, planners, clerks, and others.

EQ Results

EQ is followed up carefully at Ericsson. On two occasions an external consultant has been brought in to evaluate certain aspects of the acceptance of EQ. Quality activities and results are reported regularly by operational units. It is too early to assess the overall effect of EQ, but two examples will illustrate the types of concrete results that are within the spirit of EQ.

The first example is from an Ericsson factory which produces printed circuit boards for telephone switching systems. Letting everybody take part in the EQ training sessions and introducing the concept of the internal customer have had a dramatic effect on operations. In the first six months of 1985, compared with the previous six months, there was a 40% increase in productivity (thus lowering costs), an increase from a 50 to 90% rate of on-schedule deliveries (thus increasing customer satisfaction), and reductions of 'error points' (an internal measure of defects) from 100 to 30 (thus reducing future service costs).

The second example concerns the product and service quality of computers. A change of focus from appraisal and remedy to prevention initiated field quality task forces to investigate defects in the assembly and delivery to local markets. As a result, a receiving inspection is no longer necessary at the local subsidiary (lowering costs) and there has been a dramatic reduction in defects; for example, keyboard quality has improved in six months from 70% to 98% perfect, including such things as being completely clean (increasing customer satisfaction and lowering service costs).

These are just two of the results from individual Ericsson units. The role of EQ in this improvement is not clear-cut. In all honesty, we do not know what would have happened had EQ not existed. We can say, however, that EQ has spotlighted the issue of quality, helped to support quality thinking, and introduced new techniques for practical application, thereby increasing the likelihood that line managers give priority to quality improvements.

After three years EQ is now entering its 'second wave' and will concentrate on specific quality issues. Planning is currently in full progress.

Conclusions

Experience with this and other projects indicates that internal marketing is a potent concept not only for service firms but for industrial firms as well. It must not be limited to a superficial communications program but should stress action and profits. The notion of the internal customer is a useful contribution for making internal marketing more efficient.

References

1 Bonoma, Thomas V., *The Marketing Edge*. New York: The Free Press, 1985.
2 Grönroos, Christian, *Strategic Marketing and Management in the Service Sector*. Cambridge MA: Marketing Science Institute, 1983.
3 Grönroos, Christian, and Evert Gummesson, eds., *Service Marketing – Nordic School Perspectives*. Stockholm, Sweden: University of Stockholm. Department of Business Administration, Research Report R 1985:2 (1985).
4 Gummesson, Evert, 'Organizing for Strategic Management – A Conceptual Model,' *Long Range Planning*, 7, No. 2 (April 1974), pp. 13–18.
5 Gummesson, Evert, *Resultatinriktad marknads föring* (Result-Oriented Marketing). Stockholm, Sweden: Norstedts, 1984.
6 Gummesson, Evert, *Quality – The Ericsson Approach*. Stockholm, Sweden: Ericsson, 1987.
7 Gummesson, Evert, *Academic Researcher andor Management Consultant*. London: Chartwell-Bratt, in press.
8 Hutton, Cynthia, 'America's Most Admired Corporations,' *Fortune*, 6 January 1986, pp. 32–43.
9 Larsson, Carl-Göran, and Per Nylander, 'Ericsson Quality,' *Ericsson Review*, No. 1, (1986), pp. 2–10.
10 Luchs, Robert, 'Successful Businesses Compete on Quality – Not Costs,' *Long Range Planning*, 19, No. 1, (1986), pp. 12–17.

5 ACHIEVING EMPLOYEE COMMITMENT

A competent employee who is committed to delivering customer satisfaction is a valuable asset in any organization. Retaining such individuals, and attracting and developing others like them, became a burning issue in the late 1980s, when organizations' aspirations of growth were curtailed by skills shortages and readily defecting key personnel.[1] In many instances these concerns were short-lived. Measures adopted to stem the defections were quickly abandoned with the advent of recession. Such short-term thinking ignored the fact that employee retention is an important part of the relationship marketing equation. The impact of high staff turnover on customers' perceptions of service quality, and on customer satisfaction and retention, has frequently gone unrecognized in the past. Fortunately, some organizations are beginning to understand the costs involved, and realize that reducing voluntary staff turnover should be a perennial concern. They are also learning to appreciate that – given greater latitude and encouragement – their employees can become a significant source of competitive advantage.

The readings in this chapter deal with some of the concepts associated with improving employee commitment, and look at how these concepts have been applied by organizations keen to realise the fuller potential of their workforces. 'Empowerment' is often vaunted as the way to release this hidden potential and engender commitment among the workforce. But what does empowerment really mean? A review of the literature on the subject to date reveals a great deal of evangelism, but very little substance. The readings in this chapter include some notable exceptions.

In 'The empowerment of service workers: what, why, how and when', David E. Bowen and Edward E. Lawler make an important contribution to the field with a careful examination of the concept of empowerment. They show that empowerment is in many ways the antithesis of the production-line approach to service management. According to Bowen and Lawler, both have their merits. In this paper they identify a range of forms or levels of empowerment, from involvement in suggestion schemes to fully self-managing teams. They show that the concept has great potential as a means of improving employee commitment, but caution that it should not be regarded as a universal panacea. There are costs as well as benefits associated with the empowerment.

Following on from Bowen and Lawler's theoretical examination of empowerment, Jane Pickard's case-based article looks at empowerment in action. It describes how and why three organizations in the UK have chosen to empower their employees. The three cases described by Pickard illustrate well the amorphous nature of the concept, showing how empowerment varies between organizations. In two of the examples empowerment is an evolving phenomenon resulting, in one instance, in different forms of empowerment emerging within units of the same business. Certain commonalities do exist between the cases, for example managers' roles either disappear or are transformed from one of controller to coach. All three programmes described by Pickard experienced difficulties in the early stages of implementation, but survived to show increases in levels of employee involvement and commitment; resulting in improvements in company performance.

To further the empowerment theme, we go on to look at 'Enfranchisement'. The term is used by Leonard A. Schlesinger and James L. Heskett to describe the effects of combining the concept of empowerment with performance-related reward systems.[2,3] 'Enfranchisement of service workers' describes how enfranchisement programmes have achieved remarkable results in a number of service businesses. Using examples drawn mainly from the US retail sector, Schlesinger and Heskett show that while methods of implementation vary considerably between cases, all the examples provide evidence of considerable improvements in employees' commitment, reductions in voluntary staff turnover, and dramatic improvements in performance. Crucial to the success of these programmes is that the administration of the performance-related reward systems must be seen to be fair. The issue of evenhandedness is highlighted in the examples of Fairfield Inns and Nordstrom, and the latter illustrates the possible consequences of failure on this point.

Certain important questions remain unanswered at the end of Schlesinger and Heskett's paper, such as whether rewards should be based on group or individual performance. The impact of enfranchisement is relatively easy to assess in a retail sales context, but more difficult in a back-room situation where employees, individual contributions are less readily quantifiable. Schlesinger and Heskett acknowledge that the long-term sustainability of enfranchisement programmes has yet to be established. Maintaining their momentum when disappointing results are due to factors beyond the control of employees, or the organization as a whole, is likely to present the greatest challenge to the programmes' long-term survival.

Empowerment and enfranchisement are still emerging – and rapidly evolving – management concepts: concepts that are nevertheless becoming central to many customer service improvement initiatives. These articles illustrate the degree to which tools such as empowerment or enfranchisement are also crucial facilitators of organizational delayering and business process redesign. Their application, whether motivated by marketing or other concerns, is likely to have profound implications for all aspects of the organization's activities.

References

1 Atkinson, J. (1989). Four stages of adjustment to the demographic downturn. *Personnel Management*, August, 20–24.
2 Schlesinger, L. and Heskett, J. (1991a). Breaking the cycle of failure in services. *Sloan Management Review*, **32**, No. 3, Spring, 17–28.
3 Schlesinger, L. and Heskett, J. (1991b). The service-driven service company. *Harvard Business Review*, **69**, No. 5, September/October, 71–81.

THE EMPOWERMENT OF SERVICE WORKERS: WHAT, WHY, HOW AND WHEN
David E. Bowen and Edward E. Lawler

David E. Bowen is Associate Professor of Management at Arizona State University West. His research and consulting interests include managing organizational culture and human resources, with special emphasis on the empowerment of service employees; managing customer involvement in co-producing services; and creating customer-focused corporate staffs. Edward E. Lawler is director of the Centre for Effective Organizations, Graduate School of Business Administration, University of Southern California. He is recognized as an important contributor to the fields of organizational development, organizational behaviour and compensation.

'The empowerment of service workers: what, why, how and when' provides a thoughtful and critical dissection of the concept of empowerment, clearly identifying what the writers believe are its essential components. Bowen and Lawler put forward a table of five contingencies which, with careful consideration, should help managers to identify an appropriate level of empowerment for their own organizations – or indeed whether to empower at all.

Empowering service workers has acquired almost a 'born again' religious fervor. Tom Peters calls it 'purposeful chaos'. Robert Waterman dubs it 'directed autonomy'. It has also been called the 'art of improvisation'.

Yet in the mid-1970s, the production-line approach to service was the darling child of service gurus. They advocated facing the customer with standardized, procedurally driven operations. Should we now abandon this approach in favor of empowerment?

Unfortunately, there is no simple, clear-cut answer. In this article we try to help managers think about the question of whether to empower by clarifying its advantages and disadvantages, describing three forms that empower employees to different degrees, and presenting five con-tingencies that managers can use to determine which approach best fits their situation. We do not intend to debunk empowerment, rather we hope to clarify why to empower (there are costs, as well as benefits), how to empower (there are alternatives), and when to empower (it really does depend on the situation).

The production-line approach

In two classic articles, the 'Production-Line Approach to Service' and the 'Industrialization of Service', Theodore Levitt described how service operations can be made more efficient by applying manufacturing logic and tactics.[1] He argued:

> Manufacturing thinks technocratically, and that explains its success ... By contrast, service looks for solutions in the performer of the task. This is the paralyzing legacy of our inherited attitudes: the solution to improved service is viewed as being dependent on improvements in the skills and attitudes of the performers of that service.
>
> While it may pain and offend us to say so, thinking in humanistic rather than technocratic terms ensures that the service sector will be forever inefficient and that our satisfactions will be forever marginal.[2]

He recommended (1) simplification of tasks, (2) clear division of labor, (3) substitution of equipment and systems for employees, and (4) little decision-making discretion afforded to employees. In short, management designs the system, and employees execute it.

McDonald's is a good example. Workers are taught how to greet customers and ask for their order, including a script for suggesting additional items. They learn a set procedure for assembling the order (for example, cold drinks first, then hot ones), placing items on the tray, and placing the tray where customers need not reach for it. There is a script and a procedure for collecting money and giving change. Finally, there is a script for saying thank you and asking the customer to come again.[3] This production-line approach makes customer–service interactions uniform and gives the organization control over them. It is easily learned; workers can be quickly trained and put to work.

What are the gains from a production-line approach? Efficient, low-cost, high-volume service operations, with satisfied customers.

The empowerment approach

Ron Zemke and Dick Schaaf, in *The Service Edge: 101 Companies That Profit from Customer Care*, note that empowerment is a common theme running through many, even most, of their excellent service businesses, such as American Airlines, Marriott, American Express, and Federal Express. To

Zemke and Schaaf, empowerment means 'turning the front line loose', encouraging and rewarding employees to exercise initiative and imagination: 'Empowerment in many ways is the reverse of doing things by the book.'[4]

The humanistic flavor of empowerment pervades the words of advocates such as Tom Peters:

> It is necessary to 'dehumiliate' work by eliminating the policies and procedures (almost always tiny) of the organization that demean and belittle human dignity. It is impossible to get people's best efforts, involvement, and caring concern for things you believe important to your customers and the long-term interests of your organization when we write policies and procedures that treat them like thieves and bandits.[5]

And from Jan Carlzon, CEO of Scandinavian Airlines Systems (SAS):

> To free someone from rigorous control by instructions, policies, and orders, and to give that person freedom to take responsibility for his ideas, decisions, and actions is to release hidden resources that would otherwise remain inaccessible to both the individual and the organization.[6]

In contrast to the industrialization of service, empowerment very much looks to the 'performer of the tasks' for solutions to service problems. Workers are asked to suggest new services and products and to solve problems creatively and effectively.

What, then, does it really mean – beyond the catchy slogans – to empower employees? We define empowerment as sharing with frontline employees four organizational ingredients: (1) information about the organization's performance, (2) rewards based on the organization's performance, (3) knowledge that enables employees to understand and contribute to organizational performance, and (4) power to make decisions that influence organizational direction and performance. We will say more about these features later. For now, we can say that with a production-line approach, these features tend to be concentrated in the hands of senior management; with an empowerment approach, they tend to be moved downward to frontline employees.

Which approach is better?

In 1990, Federal Express became the first service organization to win the Malcolm Baldrige National Quality Award. The company's motto is 'people, service, and profits'. Behind its blue, white, and red planes and uniforms are self-managing work teams, gainsharing plans, and empowered employees seemingly consumed with providing flexible and creative service to customers with varying needs.

At UPS, referred to as 'Big Brown' by its employees, the philosophy was stated by founder Jim Casey: 'Best service at low rates.' Here, too, we find turned-on people and profits. But we do not find empowerment. Instead we find controls, rules, a detailed union contract, and carefully studied work methods. Nor do we find a promise to do all things for customers, such as handling off-schedule pickups and packages that don't fit size and weight limitations. In fact, rigid operational guidelines help guarantee the customer reliable, low-cost service.

Federal Express and UPS present two different faces to the customer, and behind these faces are different management philosophies and organizational cultures. Federal Express is a high-involvement, horizontally coordinated organization that encourages employees to use their judgment above and beyond the rulebook. UPS is a top-down, traditionally controlled organization, in which employees are directed by policies and procedures based on industrial engineering studies of how all service delivery aspects should be carried out and how long they should take.

Similarly, at Disney theme parks, ride operators are thoroughly scripted on what to say to 'guests', including a list of preapproved 'ad libs'! At Club Med, however, CEO Jacques Giraud fervently believes that guests must experience *real* magic, and the resorts' GOs (*gentils organisateurs*, 'congenial hosts') are set free to spontaneously create this feeling for their guests. Which is the better approach? Federal Express or UPS? Club Med or Disney?

At a recent executive education seminar on customer service, one of us asked, 'Who thinks that it is important for their business to empower their service personnel as a tool for improving customer service?' All twenty-seven participants enthusiastically raised their hands. Although they represented diverse services – banking, travel, utilities, airlines, and shipping – and they disagreed on most points, they all agreed that empowerment is key to customer satisfaction. But is it?

Empowering service employees: why, how, and when

Why to empower: the benefits

What gains are possible from empowering service employees?

● *Quicker on-line responses to customer needs during service delivery.* Check-in time at the hotel begins at 2 p.m., but a guest asks the desk clerk if she can check in at 1:30 p.m. An airline passenger arrives at the gate at 7:30 a.m., Friday, for a 7:45 a.m. departure and wants to board the plane with a travel coupon good Monday through Thursday, and there are empty seats on the plane. The waitress is taking an order in a modestly priced family restaurant; the menu says no substitutions, but the customer requests one anyway.

The customer wants a quick response. And the employee would often like to be able to respond with something other than 'No, it is against our rules', or 'I will have to check with my supervisor'.

Empowering employees in these situations can lead to the sort of spontaneous, creative rule-breaking that can turn a potentially frustrated or angry customer into a satisfied one. This is particularly valuable when there is little time to refer to a higher authority, as when the plane is leaving in fifteen minutes. Even before greeting customers, empowered employees are confident that they have all the necessary resources at their command to provide customers with what they need.

● *Quicker on-line responses to dissatisfied customers during service recovery.* Customer service involves both delivering the service, such as checking a guest into a hotel room, and recovering from poor service, such as relocating him from a smoking floor to the nonsmoking room he originally requested. Although delivering good service may mean different things to different customers, all customers feel that service businesses ought to fix things when service is delivered improperly. Figure 1 depicts the relationships among service delivery, recovery, and customer satisfaction.

Fixing something after doing it wrong the first time can turn a dissatisfied customer into a satisfied, even loyal, customer. But service businesses frequently fail in the act of recovery because service employees are not empowered to make the necessary amends with customers. Instead, customers hear employees saying, 'Gee, I wish there was something I could do, but I can't', 'It's not my fault', or 'I could check with my boss, but she's not here today'. These employees lack the power and knowledge to recover, and customers remain dissatisfied.

● *Employees feel better about their jobs and themselves.* Earlier we mentioned Tom Peters' thinking on how strict rules can belittle human dignity. Letting employees call the shots allows them to feel 'ownership' of the job; they feel responsible for it and find the work meaningful. Think of how you treat your car as opposed to a rented one. Have you ever

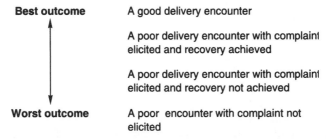

Figure 1 *Possible outcomes during service delivery and recovery (From* Service Breakthroughs: Changing the Rules of the Game *by James L. Heskett, W. Earl Sasser Jr and Christopher W. L. Hart. Copyright © 1990 by James L. Heskett, W. Earl Sasser Jr and Christopher W. L. Hart. Adapted with permission of The Free Press, a Division of Macmillan, Inc.*

washed a rental car? Decades of job design research show that when employees have a sense of control and of doing meaningful work they are more satisfied. This leads to lower turnover, less absenteeism, and fewer union organizing drives.

● *Employees will interact with customers with more warmth and enthusiasm.* Research now supports our long-standing intuition that customers' perceptions of service quality are shaped by the courtesy, empathy, and responsiveness of service employees.[7] Customers want employees to appear concerned about their needs. Can empowerment help create this? One of us has done customer service research in branch banks that showed that when the tellers reported feeling good about how they were supervised, trained, and rewarded, customers thought more highly of the service they received.[8] In short, when employees felt that management was looking after their needs, they took better care of the customer.

In service encounters, employees' feelings about their jobs will spill over to affect how customers feel about the service they get. This is particularly important when employee attitudes are a key part of the service package. In banking, where the customer receives no tangible benefits in the exchange other than a savings deposit slip, a sour teller can really blemish a customer's feelings about the encounter.

● *Empowered employees can be a great source of service ideas.* Giving frontline employees a voice in 'how we do things around here' can lead to improved service delivery and ideas for new services. The bank study showed that the tellers could accurately report how customers viewed overall service quality and how they saw the branches' service climate (e.g., adequacy of staff and appearance of facilities).[9]

Frontline employees are often ready and willing to offer their opinion. When it comes to market research, imagine the difference in response rates from surveying your employees and surveying your customers.

● *Great word-of-mouth advertising and customer retention.* Nordstrom's advertising budget is 1.5 percent of sales, whereas the industry average is 5 percent. Why? Their satisfied-no-matter-what customers spread the word about their service and become repeat customers.

The costs

What are the costs of empowerment?

● *A greater dollar investment in selection and training.* You cannot hire effective, creative problem solvers on the basis of chance or mere intuition. Too bad, because the systematic methods necessary to screen out those who are not good candidates for empowerment are expensive. For example, Federal Express selects customer agents and couriers on the basis of well-researched profiles of successful performers in those jobs.

Training is an even greater cost. The production-line approach trains workers easily and puts them right to work. In contrast, new hires at SAS are formally assigned a mentor to help them learn the ropes; Nordstrom department managers take responsibility for orienting and training new members of the sales team; customer service representatives at Lands' End and L.L. Bean spend a week in training before handling their first call. They receive far more information and knowledge about their company and its products than is the norm.

The more labor intensive the service, the higher these costs. Retail banking, department stores, and convenience stores are labor intensive, and their training and selection costs can run high. Utilities and airlines are far less labor intensive.

- *Higher labor costs.* Many consumer service organizations, such as department stores, convenience stores, restaurants, and banks, rely on large numbers of part-time and seasonal workers to meet their highly variable staffing needs. These employees typically work for short periods of time at low wages. To empower these workers, a company would have to invest heavily in training to try to quickly inculcate the organization's culture and values. This training would probably be unsuccessful, and the employees wouldn't be around long enough to provide a return on the investment. Alternatively, the organization could pay higher wages to full-time, permanent employees, but they would be idle when business was slow.

- *Slower or inconsistent service delivery.* Remember the hotel guest wanting to check in early and the airline passenger requesting special treatment at the gate? True, there is a benefit to empowering the employee to bend the rules, but only for the person at the front of the line! Customers at the back of the line are grumbling and checking their watches. They may have the satisfaction of knowing that they too may receive creative problem solving when and if they reach the counter, but it is small consolation if the plane has already left.

Based on our experiences as both researchers and customers, we believe that customers will increasingly value speed in service delivery. Purposeful chaos may work against this. We also believe that many customers value 'no surprises' in service delivery. They like to know what to expect when they revisit a service business or patronize different outlets of a franchise. When service delivery is left to employee discretion, it may be inconsistent.

The research data show that customers perceive reliability – 'doing it right the first time' – as the most important dimension of service quality. It matters more than employees' responsiveness, courtesy, or competency, or the attractiveness of the service setting.[10] Unfortunately, in the same research, a sample of large, well-known firms was more deficient on reliability than on these other dimensions. Much of the touted appeal of the production-line approach was that procedurally and technocratically driven operations could deliver service more reliably and consistently than service operations heavily dependent upon the skills and attitudes of employees. The production-line approach was intended to routinize service so that customers would receive the 'best outcome' possible from their service encounters – service delivery with no glitches in the first place.

We feel that service managers need to guard against being seduced into too great a focus on recovery, at the expense of service delivery reliability. We say 'seduced' because it is possible to confuse good service with inspiring stories about empowered employees excelling at the art of recovery. Recovery has more sex appeal than the nitty-gritty detail of building quality into every seemingly mundane aspect of the service delivery system, but an organization that relies on recovery may end up losing out to firms that do it right the first time.

- *Violations of 'fair play.'* A recent study of how service businesses handle customer complaints revealed that customers associate sticking to procedures with being treated fairly.[11] Customers may be more likely to return to a business if they believe that their complaint was handled effectively because of company policies rather than because they were lucky enough to get a particular employee. In other words, customers may prefer procedurally driven acts of recovery. We suspect that customers' notions of fairness may be violated when they see employees cutting special deals with other customers.
- *Giveaways and bad decisions.* Managers are often reluctant to empower their employees for fear they will give too much away to the customer. Perhaps they have heard the story of Willie, the doorman at a Four Seasons Hotel, who left work and took a flight to return a briefcase left behind by a guest. Or they have heard of too many giveaways by empowered Nordstrom employees. For some services, the costs of giveaways are far outweighed by enhanced customer loyalty, but not for others.

  Sometimes creative rule breaking can cause a major problem for an organization. There may be a good reason why no substitutions are allowed or why a coupon cannot be used on a certain day (e.g., an international airfare agreement). If so, having an empowered employee break a rule may cause the organization serious problems, of which the employee may not even be aware.

These are some of the costs and benefits of empowerment. We hope this discussion will help service businesses use empowerment knowledge-ably, not just because it is a fad. But we must add one more caveat: There is still precious little research on the consequences of empowerment. We have used anecdotal evidence, related research (e.g., in job design), and our work on service. More systematic research must assess whether this array of costs and benefits fully captures the 'whys' (and 'why nots') of empowerment.

How to empower: three options

Empowering service employees is less understood than industrializing service delivery. This is largely because the production-line approach is an example of the well-developed control model of organization design and management, whereas empowerment is part of the still evolving 'commitment' or 'involvement' model. The latter assumes that most employees can make good decisions if they are properly socialized, trained, and informed. They can be internally motivated to perform effectively, and they are capable of self-control and self-direction. This approach also assumes that most employees can produce good ideas for operating the business.[12]

The control and involvement models differ in that four key features are concentrated at the top of the organization in the former and pushed down in the organization in the latter. As we have discussed above, these features are the following: (1) information about organizational performance (e.g., operating results and competitor performance); (2) rewards based on organizational performance (e.g., profit sharing and stock ownership); (3) knowledge that enables employees to understand and contribute to organizational performance (e.g., problem-solving skills); and (4) power to make decisions that influence work procedures and organizational direction (e.g., through quality circles and self-managing teams).

Three approaches to empowering employees can be identified (see Figure 2).[13] They represent increasing degrees of empowerment as additional knowledge, information, power, and rewards are pushed down to the front line. Empowerment, then, is not an either/or alternative, but rather a choice of three options:

1 *Suggestion involvement* represents a small shift away from the control model. Employees are encouraged to contribute ideas through formal suggestion programs or quality circles, but their day-to-day work activities do not really change. Also, they are only empowered to recommend; management typically retains the power to decide whether or not to implement.

   Suggestion involvement can produce some empowerment without altering the basic production-line approach. McDonald's, for example, listens closely to the front line. The Big Mac, Egg McMuffin, and McDLT all were invented by employees, as was the system of wrapping burgers that avoids leaving a thumbprint in the bun. As

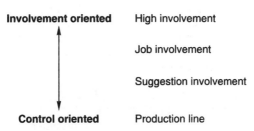

Figure 2 *Levels of empowerment*

another example, Florida Power and Light, which won the Deming quality award, defines empowerment in suggestion involvement terms.

2 *Job involvement* represents a significant departure from the control model because of its dramatic 'opening up' of job content. Jobs are redesigned so that employees use a variety of skills. Employees believe their tasks are significant, they have considerable freedom in deciding how to do the work, they get more feedback, and they handle a whole, identifiable piece of work. Research shows that many employees find enriched work more motivating and satisfying, and they do higher-quality work.[14]

Often job involvement is accomplished through extensive use of teams. Teams are often appropriate in complex service organizations such as hospitals and airlines because individuals cannot offer a whole service or handle a customer from beginning to end of service delivery. Teams can empower back-office workers in banks and insurance companies as well.

Employees in this environment require training to deal with the added complexity. Supervisors, who now have fewer shots to call, need to be reoriented toward supporting the front line, rather than directing it. Despite the heightened level of empowerment it brings, the job involvement approach does not change higher-level strategic decisions concerning organization structure, power, and the allocation of rewards. These remain the responsibility of senior management.

3 *High-involvement* organizations give their lowest-level employees a sense of involvement not just in how they do their jobs or how effectively their group performs, but in the total organization's performance. Virtually every aspect of the organization is different from that of a control-oriented organization. Business performance information is shared. Employees develop skills in teamwork, problem solving, and business operations. They participate in work-unit management decisions. There is profit sharing and employee ownership.

High-involvement designs may be expensive to implement. Perhaps most troublesome is that these management techniques are relatively undeveloped and untested. People Express tried to operate as a high-involvement airline, and the ongoing struggle to learn and develop this new organizational design contributed to its operating problems.

Today, America West is trying to make the high-involvement design work. New hires spend 25 percent of their first year's salary on company stock. All employees receive annual stock options. Flight attendants and pilots develop their own work procedures and schedules. Employees are extensively cross-trained to work where they are needed. Only time will tell if America West can make high-involvement work as it struggles with its financial crisis stemming from high fuel costs and rapid growth.

Federal Express displays many high-involvement features. A couple of years ago, it began a companywide push to convert to teams, including the back office. It organized its 1,000 clerical workers in Memphis into superteams of five to ten people and gave them the authority and training to manage themselves. These teams helped the company cut customer service problems, such as incorrect bills and lost packages, by 13 percent in 1989.

When to empower: a contingency approach

Management thought and practice frequently have been seduced by the search for the 'one best way to manage'. Unfortunately, business does not lend itself to universal truths, only to 'contingency theories' of management. For example, early job enrichment efforts in the 1960s assumed that all employees would prefer more challenging work and more autonomy. By the 1970s it was clear that only those employees who felt the need to grow at work responded positively to job enrichment.[15] As the research on it is still thin, it is at least possible that empowerment is a universal truth, but historical evidence weighs against its being the best way to manage in all situations.

We believe that both the empowerment and production-line approaches have their advantages, and that each fits certain situations. The key is to choose the management approach that best meets the needs of both employees and customers.

Table 1 presents five contingencies that determine which approach to adopt. Each contingency can be rated on a scale of 1 to 5 to diagnose the quality of fit between the overall situation and the alternative approaches. The following propositions suggest how to match situations and approaches. Matching is not an exact science, but the propositions suggest reasonable rules of thumb.

Proposition 1: The higher the rating of each contingency (5 being the highest), the better the fit with an empowerment approach; the lower the rating (1 being the lowest), the better the fit with a production-line approach.

Proposition 2: The higher the total score from all five contingencies, the better the fit with an empowerment approach; the lower the total score, the better the fit with a production-line approach. A production-line approach is a good fit with situations that score in the range of 5 to 10. For empowerment approaches, suggestion involvement is a good fit with situations that score in the range of 11 to 15, job involvement with scores that range from 16 to 20, and high involvement with scores that range from 21 to 25.

Proposition 3: The higher the total score, the more the benefits of increasing empowerment will outweigh the costs.

In what follows, we describe each contingency's implications for a production-line or empowerment approach.

Table 1 *The contingencies of empowerment*

Contingency	Production-line approach						Empowerment
Basic business strategy	Low cost, high volume	1	2	3	4	5	Differentiation, customized, personalized
Tie to customer	Transaction, short time period	1	2	3	4	5	Relationship, long time period
Technology	Routine, simple	1	2	3	4	5	Nonroutine, complex
Business environment	Predictable, few surprises	1	2	3	4	5	Unpredictable, many surprises
Types of people	Theory X managers, employees with low growth needs, low social needs, and weak interpersonal skills	1	2	3	4	5	Theory Y managers, employees with high growth needs, high social needs, and strong interpersonal skills

Basic business strategy

A production-line approach makes the most sense if your core mission is to offer high-volume service at the lowest cost. 'Industrializing' service certainly leverages volume. The question is: what is the value-added from spending the additional dollars on employee selection, training, and retention necessary for empowerment? This question is especially compelling in labor-intensive services (e.g., fast food, grocery stores, and convenience stores) and those that require part-time or temporary employees.

The answer depends on what customers want from the service firm, and what they are willing to pay for. Certain customer segments are just looking for cheap, quick, reliable service. They do want quality – a warm hamburger rather than a cold one. But they are not necessarily expecting tender loving care. Even if they wanted it, they wouldn't pay for it.

These customers prefer a production-line approach. A recent study of convenience stores actually found a negative relationship between store sales and clerks being friendly with customers.[16] Customers wanted speed, and friendly clerks slowed things down. The point is that customers themselves may prefer to be served by a nonempowered employee.

At Taco Bell, counter attendants are expected to be civil, but they are not expected or encouraged to be creative problem solvers. Taco Bell wants to serve customers who want low-cost, good quality, fast food. Interestingly, the company believes that as more chains move to customized, service-oriented operations, it has more opportunities in the fast, low-price market niche.

The production-line approach does not rule out suggestion involvement. As mentioned earlier, employees often have ideas even when much of their work is routinized. Quality circles and other approaches can capture and develop them.

An empowerment approach works best with a market segment that wants the tender loving care dimension more than speed and cost. For example, SAS targets frequent business travellers (who do not pay their own way). The SAS strategy was to differentiate itself from other airlines on the basis of personalized service. Consequently, the company looked at every ingredient of its service package to see if it fit this segment's definition of service quality, and, if so, whether or not customers would pay for it.

Tie to the customer

Empowerment is the best approach when service delivery involves managing a relationship, as opposed to simply performing a transaction. The service firm may want to establish relationships with customers to build loyalty or to get ideas for improving the service delivery system or offering new services. A flexible, customized approach can help establish the relationship and get the ideas flowing.

The returns on empowerment and relationship-building are higher with more sophisticated services and delivery systems. An employee in the international air freight industry is more likely to learn from a customer relationship than is a gasoline station attendant.

The relationship itself can be the principal valued commodity that is delivered in many services. When no tangibles are delivered, as in estate planning or management consulting, the service provider often is the service to the customer, and empowerment allows the employee to customize the service to fit the customer's needs.

The more enduring the relationship, and the more important it is in the service package, the stronger the case for empowerment. Remember the earlier comparison between Disney, which tightly scripts its ride operators, and Club Med, which encourages its GOs to be spontaneous? Giraud, Club Med's CEO, explains that Disney employees relate to their guests in thousands of brief encounters; GOs have week-long close relationships with a limited number of guests. The valuable service they sell is 'time'.

Technology

It is very difficult to build challenge, feedback, and autonomy into a telephone operator's job, given the way the delivery technology has been designed. The same is true of many fast-food operations. In these situations, the technology limits empowerment to only suggestion involvement and ultimately may almost completely remove individuals from the service delivery process, as has happened with ATMs.

When technology constrains empowerment, service managers can still support frontline employees in ways that enhance their satisfaction and the service quality they provide. For example, managers can show employees how much their jobs matter to the organization's success and express more appreciation for the work they do. In other words, managers can do a better job of making the old management model work!

Routine work can be engaging if employees are convinced that it matters. Volunteers will spend hours licking envelopes in a fundraising campaign for their favorite charity. Disney theme park employees do an admirable job of performing repetitive work, partly because they believe in the values, mission, and show business magic of Disney.

Business environment

Businesses that operate in unpredictable environments benefit from empowerment. Airlines face many challenges to their operations: bad weather, mechanical breakdowns, and competitors' actions. They serve passengers who make a wide variety of special requests. It is simply impossible to anticipate many of the situations that will arise and to 'program' employees to respond to them. Employees trained in purposeful chaos are appropriate for unpredictable environments.

Fast-food restaurants, however, operate in stable environments. Operations are fairly fail-safe; customer expectations are simple and predictable. In this environment, the service business can use a production-line approach. The stability allows, even encourages, management with policies and procedures, because managers can predict most events and identify the best responses.

Types of people

Empowerment and production-line approaches demand different types of managers and employees. For empowerment to work, particularly in the high-involvement form, the company needs to have Theory Y managers who believe that their employees can act independently to benefit both the organization and its customers. If the management ranks are filled with Theory X types who believe that employees only do their best work when closely supervised, then the production-line approach may be the only feasible option unless the organization changes its managers. Good service can still be the outcome. For example, most industry observers would agree that Delta and American Airlines are managed with a control orientation rather than a strong empowerment approach.

Employees will respond positively to empowerment only if they have strong needs to grow and to deepen and test their abilities – at work. Again, a checkered history of job enrichment efforts has taught us not to assume that everyone wants more autonomy, challenge, and responsibility at work. Some employees simply prefer a production-line approach.

Lastly, empowerment that involves teamwork requires employees who are interested in meeting their social and affiliative needs at work. It also requires that employees have good interpersonal and group process skills.

The future of service work

How likely is it that more and more service businesses will choose to face the customer with empowered employees? We would guess that far more service organizations operate at the production-line end of our continuum than their business situations call for. A recent survey of companies in the 'Fortune 1000' offers some support for this view.[17] This survey revealed that manufacturing firms tend to use significantly more employee-involvement practices than do service firms. Manufacturing firms use quality circles, participation groups, and self-managing work teams far more than service firms.

Why is this so? We think that the intense pressure on the manufacturing sector from global competition has created more dissatisfaction with the old control-oriented way of doing things. Also, it can be easier to see the payoffs from different management practices in manufacturing than in service. Objective measures of productivity can more clearly show profitability than can measures of customer perceptions of service quality. However, these differences are now blurring as service competition increases and service companies become more sophisticated in tracking the benefits of customer service quality.

As service businesses consider empowerment, they can look at high-involvement manufacturing organizations as labs in which the various empowerment approaches have been tested and developed. Many lessons have been learned in manufacturing about how to best use quality circles, enriched jobs, and so on. And the added good news is that many service businesses are ideally suited to applying and refining these lessons. Multisite, relatively autonomous service operations afford their managers an opportunity to customize empowerment programs and then evaluate them.

In summary, the newest approaches to managing the production line can serve as role models for many service businesses, but perhaps not all. Before service organizations rush into empowerment programs, they need to determine whether and how empowerment fits their situation.

References

1 T. Levitt, 'Production-Line Approach to Service.' *Harvard Business Review*, September-October 1972, pp. 41–52; and T. Levitt, 'Industrialization of Service,' *Harvard Business Review'*, September-October 1976, pp. 63–74.
2 Levitt (1972).
3 D. Tansik, 'Managing Human Resource Issues for High-Contact Service Personnel,' in *Service Management Effectiveness*, eds. D. Bowen, R. Chase, and T. Cummings (San Francisco: Jossey-Bass, 1990).
4 R. Zemke and D. Schaaf, *The Service Edge: 101 Companies That Profit from Customer Care* (New York: New American Library, 1989), p. 68.
5 As quoted in Zemke and Schaaf (1989), p. 68.
6 J. Carlzon, *Moments of Truth* (New York: Ballinger, 1987).
7 V. Zeithaml, A. Parasuraman, and L.L. Berry, *Delivering Quality Service: Balancing Customer Perceptions and Expectations* (New York: The Free Press, 1990). See also: B. Schneider and D. Bowen, 'Employee and Customer Perceptions of Service in Banks: Replication and Extension,' *Journal of Applied Psychology* 70 (1985): 423–433.
8 Schneider and Bowen (1985).
9 *Ibid.*
10 Zeithaml, Parasuraman, and Berry (1990).
11 C. Goodwin and I. Ross, 'Consumer Evaluations of Responses to Complaints: What's Fair and Why,' *Journal of Services Marketing* 4 (1990): 53–61.
12 See E.E. Lawler III, *High-Involvement Management* (San Francisco: Jossey-Bass, 1986).
13 See E.E. Lawler III, 'Choosing an Involvement Strategy,' *Academy of Management Executive* 2 (1988): 197–204.

14 See for example J.R. Hackman and G.R. Oldham, *Work Redesign* (Reading, Massachusetts: Addison-Wesley, 1980).
15 Ibid.
16 R.J. Sutton and A. Rafaeli, 'Untangling the Relationship between Displayed Emotions and Organizational Sales: The Case of Convenience Stores,' *Academy of Management Journal* 31 (1988): 461–487.
17 E.E. Lawler III, G.E. Ledford, Jr., and S.A. Mohrman, *Employee Involvement in America: A Study of Contemporary Practice* (Houston: American Productivity & Quality Center, 1989).

THE REAL MEANING OF EMPOWERMENT
Jane Pickard

Jane Pickard is Features Editor for *Personnel Management* magazine. She is a regular contributor to the magazine, reporting on a range of contemporary issues in human resource management.

Pickard's article uses three case studies to show how empowerment can increase employee involvement and improve motivation, performance and job satisfaction. The article looks at the aims and objectives of the empowerment programmes, outlining some of the techniques used in their implementation. Pickard describes lucidly the meaning of empowerment from the perspective of the newly empowered, explaining how their jobs were redefined and their responsibilities reapportioned.

Cleaning out the area where puddings are served used to be one of the most hated jobs in a Harvester restaurant. Sweet sauces, mixed with chocolate shavings, nuts and ice cream formed a revolting cocktail on the serving table.

A year ago, when waitress Vanessa Quigley started work at the Harvester in Dulwich, south London, staff would make any excuse not to do it. The waitress who drew the short straw was left to get on with the job. Now everyone volunteers and two or three waitresses will muck in and help each other. As a result, the serving area is kept cleaner throughout the evening.

They don't get anything extra out of it. It does not affect their bonus or entitle them to a set of cut-glass goblets. 'They do it for the job satisfaction they get at the end of the day. There is a real pride in the job,' says Quigley.

Her story is a typical tale of empowerment. The change in attitude arose, according to staff, because they were 'empowered'. *PM* spoke to telesales staff in a financial services company, operators in a chemical plant and waitresses in a restaurant and, despite differences in their employers' approaches to empowerment, they all agreed on one thing: it made the job more interesting and hugely increased their motivation and sense of involvement.

The same story is reported by academics and consultants who have studied the subject, such as Bill Byham or Tom Peters in the United States and Tom Lambert or Richard Whipp in this country.

TOM PETERS, *author and consultant*: 'Oddly enough, it's managers who are having the toughest time making the shift. Well, it's not so odd, on second thoughts. Many of their jobs are disappearing'

But what exactly is empowerment? Is it any more than old-fashioned employee involvement? If not, how does it differ? Are there any benefits other than improved motivation? What are the problems?

Vanessa Quigley must be one of empowerment's biggest fans. It is not often one sits chatting to a waitress about American management theory. But Harvester, part of the Forte group, has been talking to Tom Peters' organisation in California, and Quigley knows all about 'Liberation management – necessary disorganisation in the nano-second nineties', has seen the video, read the hand-outs and is converted.

She could easily have felt the opposite. For Harvester, empowerment has been highly structured, is inextricably linked to delayering and was regarded as highly threatening by many staff. A year ago, when empowerment was brought in, following a pilot, a layer of management was taken out in the restaurants. They now have a branch manager who works with a 'coach', who handles all training and some other personnel issues. Everyone else is a team member of some description.

W EDWARDS DEMING, *a founder of TQM*: 'Oh those words! Empowerment? Nonsense! They need to know what their jobs are'

Staff turnover rose in the first six months after empowerment was brought in last year. Quigley herself lost status: she had been taken on as an assistant manager for the whole restaurant, Harvester's biggest, with 67 staff. Two weeks later, she was told the job was disappearing.

She was now to be a mere waitress again, albeit in a role which Harvester describes as 'team expert'. This is not a team leader, but someone who has mastered all the special responsibilities, which Harvester calls 'accountabilities', delegated to the team. The whole team can be made up of experts. Although experts like Quigley were often appointed in the early stages, they are now elected by the team.

Everyone has one or more 'accountabilities', which include recruitment, drawing up rotas and keeping track of sales targets in the restaurant (as opposed to the kitchen or the bar). These are not allocated by Quigley but shared out among staff at their weekly team meetings.

Sue Newton, operations director for Harvester and its former personnel and training director, who has been responsible for bringing in empowerment, says that the flatter structure meant promotion had to be horizontal.

Harvester restaurant staff gather badges for achieving certain standards: a silver badge, which puts you on the bonus scheme, for demonstrating you can deliver accountabilities, a technical skills badge for delivering most of the team accountabilities and a team expert badge for people in Quigley's position.

The very, very few – so far six in all out of the 2,000 workforce – become 'associates' for a successful, original contribution.

So if teams are responsible for recruitment and promotion and the coach looks after training, what is left for the branch manager, Bernard O'Neill? 'My role is mainly one of marketing. I am spending much more time now going out into the community getting business.

PETER SENGE, MIT *Sloan School of Management*: 'This fad of empowerment . . . What they mean by empowerment varies dramatically . . . many of them are really talking about firing middle management. But companies which are really serious are talking about the orderly distribution of power and authority'

'For instance, we linked up with a festival in the park opposite on the August Bank Holiday, and I talk to local groups such as the police to attract specialist custom.' He has also had to act as a facilitator, encouraging people to believe they could organise themselves in such a new way. It was not easy for waitresses or chefs to grasp that they were suddenly accountable for ordering their own stock, carrying out their own hygiene checks, sorting out their own problems, dealing with customer complaints, or cashing up.

There are even four people, as well as O'Neill and his coach, who are empowered – as 'appointed people' – to open up in the morning and lock up at night.

Atmosphere

Each team on each shift also has a co-ordinator. Apart from new recruits, all the team members will at different times take on this role. It is a recognition that, in the highly charged, fast-moving atmosphere of a packed restaurant someone needs to make snap decisions.

Whoever is accountable for the rotas in that team decides who is to be the co-ordinator on a particular shift, and that decision can also come up for discussion at a team meeting.

To have driven out hierarchy to this extent in the space of a year could not have been achieved, in Sue Newton's view, without an immensely tight structure.

The staff are empowered to do virtually anything except decide whether they will be empowered. The system of team experts, co-ordinators, coaches, team meetings and so on is all handed down and is the same for each restaurant. Only within that framework can they make their decisions.

They also have tight targets to meet: for instance every waitress at the Dulwich restaurant is expected to sell a side order to every table. If they don't do this, the team want to know what went wrong.

There is an American flavour to the system, with lots of competition encouraged between restaurants through an incentive scheme and some slightly cringe-making expressions, such as 'Doinks' to describe a good idea and 'wowed' to describe the feeling of empowerment. Sue Newton is compiling a book of the best stories about Doinks to motivate others.

The American style is not because of the Peters influence: the basic work was done before Harvester came into contact with Peters' organisation, and the communication between them has been two-way.

After the initial contact, when Harvester was effectively discovered by an associate of Peters' working in Britain, Sue Newton and a colleague went to California and addressed a conference, and since then they have swopped information for advice. They are now featured in a book by Jim Kouzes, president of the Tom Peters Group.[1]

The approach to empowerment at Ciba UK, the British arm of the Swiss-based chemicals multinational, Ciba Geigy, forms a striking contrast to Harvester. In place of a highly structured system imposed from headquarters, a general philosophy has been cascaded out from the centre, with the details of policy being left to each business.

This is partly because, like most modern multinationals, Ciba-Geigy allows business units great independence. It may also be due to the group's source of inspiration.

The company was influenced by Peter Koestenbaum, emeritus professor of philosophy at San Jose State University in California, who has written extensively on leadership theory and empowerment. In his view, people who are 'empowered' need a combination of 'autonomy, direction and support'.

He advised Ciba-Geigy's Basle headquarters and helped to devise its 'Vision 2000', illustrated by a three-piece jigsaw representing the firm's

How Ciba measured results

Ken Gilliver and his training department colleagues at Ciba UK have been conducting their own surveys of small samples among managers in the 5,000-strong workforce to find out if they are developing the right behaviour to support empowerment. Over 1991 and 1992 they surveyed 298 people. Further surveys this year brought the total to 358.

Those surveyed, and some of their subordinates, were asked to rate the individual, from one to five, on nine dimensions:

- ensures openness
- promotes co-operation
- delegates authority
- manages performance
- develops people
- provides rewards and recognition
- communicates effectively
- resolves issues
- encourages innovation.

The subordinates' views were slightly less flattering than the subject's own. But the two were averaged out against each dimension. The average of this figure was then taken for the 298 and, in July this year, for the 358.

The latest figures show a slight improvement. For instance, against the 'ensures openness' dimension, the 298 in 1992 scored an average of 3.0. This year, the 358 scored 3.08.

The same scores appear against 'communicates effectively', while on 'delegates authority', scores moved from 3.1 to 3.14.

With many caveats, such as pointing out that the samples in each survey are of different people and that the improvement was marginal in the extreme, Gilliver is encouraged.

He believes the survey is a useful way of measuring the general climate of opinion over the long term.

---

industrial, social and environmental responsibilities. This was launched in 1990 along with a restructuring into 14 virtually autonomous and product-related business units. Empowerment was central to the vision, but the group felt that, by definition, business units could not be forced to become empowered.

Ken Gilliver, Ciba UK's head of management development and training, says: 'Empowerment is not a verb. "You" cannot empower "me". It is more a state of mind and way of working.'

Cascaded down

So the vision was transmitted through a series of senior management seminars, known as SMS 90, and cascaded down the chain, so that now a training officer in a chemicals factory in Manchester has the jigsaw pinned onto her door and Koestenbaum's theory lodged in her brain.

But the process of dissemination has had the effect that, two years on, empowerment can differ between business units and even between different production or marketing centres.

In the additives business, for instance, which in the UK consists of a 24-person marketing operation, it has meant that the managing director's secretary, Pat Hunstone, has taken in the role of personnel administrator as well and now sits on the unit's operations management committee, not to take notes, but to take part in decision-making.

Success stories

A group of three warehousemen at Ciba's Clayton Aniline factory were faced with a greatly increased workload as a result of a new automated warehouse. One hundred metres long, it could only accommodate pallets of a certain size and weight. Instead of merely unloading and loading pallets from trucks, they now had to 'repalletise' much of the material.

They complained about this. In the ensuing discussion, one suggestion was to abandon the new warehouse. Requested to think again, they came up with the idea of persuading all suppliers to send in materials on pallets made to Clayton Aniline's requirements.

This was 18 months ago. Most suppliers have now complied. The team has a log on their wall showing the number of successes and how many are still holding out. They are not giving up until everyone has come round.

At Harvester, one restaurant in a tourist area was so seasonal that staff decided to give up summer holidays altogether and take them instead in the winter. Another held a barbeque in the snow to offset the effect of bad weather on trade.

Frizzell's two pilot teams, set up in September last year, suggested cutting out several stages in the system of recording a new vehicle on an existing motor insurance policy. Instead of forms going to and fro between the department, the customer and the underwriters, the staff now complete the customer's form and send it straight off.

Sue Bristow, one of the team members involved, says the process used to take 35 minutes over 22 days and now takes 13 minutes over two days. Departmental manager Ian Woolley says the saving over a year is equivalent to six members of staff. And, of course, it makes life easier for the customer.

'I don't think of Mike Kerr as my boss, more as a working partner. I draft the revenue budget and estimate for the year for him, which I didn't do before. This budget comes from the divisional accountant and at stages through the year, estimates can be changed. I look at the spend for each quarter and decide if estimates should be adjusted and put forward my view to help Mike make a decision.'

In additives, teamworking is not central to empowerment. But in the chemicals and dyestuffs factory at Clayton Aniline, in Manchester, it is, simply because teams already exist. Now, instead of taking orders which filter down the hierarchy from manager to superintendent to supervisor to worker, they receive questions and challenges to which they supply the answers. They also frequently supply the questions as well.

However, that is where any likeness to Harvester ends. Teams do not have to comply with a centrally dictated structure or way of working. Each part of the factory has a different approach.

David Crabtree, the warehousing and distribution manager, says: 'If you tell people they have the authority and responsibility to act on their initiative and pursue improvements as far as they can and you establish that within a rigid framework, then you don't really have empowerment, do you?'

Everyday language

Crabtree rejects jargon, preferring to use what he calls 'everyday, normal language'.

In his area, which covers warehouses and their support staff for the 57-acre site, empowerment was never labelled as such. One of the warehousemen, Dave Clarke, asked by *PM* what he felt about being 'empowered', was struck dumb. He had never heard of the word.

It was gradually introduced from the summer of 1991 onwards, with Crabtree slowly pushing the responsibility for problem-solving onto the front-line workforce.

Questioning the corporate culture

Frizzell Financial Services was one of the first companies to use Saville and Holdsworth's corporate culture questionnaire, after taking part in the trials.

The questionnaire, which was publicly launched in March, asks employees to grade 126 statements about their organisation from 'strongly agree' to 'strongly disagree'. They include topics such as the amount of workload, the degree of bureaucracy, or whether customers are treated seriously.

The results are then collated and grouped into 21 subjects which can be marked on a scale of one to 10, with 5.5 being the average for all organisations culled from Saville and Holdsworth's three-year trials.

Various aspects of culture can be measured this way. For instance, if people feel empowered, they are likely to show a high score against job involvement, the seventh subject on the list of 21.

The third Frizzell survey, which was conducted last year, shortly after the pilot teams were empowered, showed a score of seven out of 10 for job involvement among pilot team members, but only four out of 10 for employees working traditionally.

Similarly, the pilot teams scored 10 against 'employee influence on decisions' and 'concern for the longer term' compared with three and eight respectively for the others.

While acknowledging the pilot teams were on a high, because they felt privileged, training manager Tony Miller believes that structural changes must have made some impact.

There are no targets, only a policy of continuous improvement. People are expected to keep a written record of their own or their team's productivity and the line, while it rises and dips, is supposed to maintain a general upward curve.

Neither are there any new titles or accountabilities: everyone is responsible. There are still 'workers' and 'supervisors', but their relationship has changed. As in other empowered work-places, the supervisor no longer commands and checks: he or she coaches, discusses and assesses training needs.

In addition to natural work teams, the site also established cross-functional teams as part of its empowerment programme, although many of these had a fairly short life and ceased to meet after a particular project was completed.

Doing it by the book

Bill Byham, author of *Zapp!*, the best-selling book on empowerment, is concerned that many copies have gone to managers who try to 'do empowerment' by handing out books to read. 'They think orientation is training. A whole lot of *Zapp!* books went to companies who thought that all they had to do was give people the book. I'm not complaining about the number of copies we've sold, but I feel bad about it,' he confessed.

In an interview with *PM*, Byham, like the other consultants and academics we talked to, underlined the fact that there was no one model of empowerment. 'It's not an on-off switch. It's a matter of degree. We have a seven-point scale to indicate how empowered an organisation is. There is no Japanese company in the world which gets past five, but they are doing pretty good, so you can't assume more is better.'

Asked if it had just become a buzzword, Byham agreed: 'It's getting that way. One of the big problems is that companies are committing themselves to empowerment without knowing what it means, and therefore they are not getting anything out of it.'

The results of Ciba's policy, like many others, are hard to assess, even though it has been in operation three years. Gilliver admits that progress is patchy.

But warehouseman Dave Clarke says it has made his job more interesting. 'We are able to speak directly to the suppliers now, to sort out any problems or tell them when we need our next delivery. It means we can work faster and more efficiently'.

To try to measure success, Gilliver has established an empowerment practice record which demonstrates a slow improvement in the degree of empowerment since 1991.

Another company which is busy trying to measure its success with empowerment is Frizzell Financial Services. Nine months after introducing empowered teamworking into its telesales and service area, senior managers are convinced it is bringing benefits.

Measure of culture

The company is using a new measure of culture change devised by Saville and Holdsworth which shows a positive shift in employees' own perceptions of whether they are empowered or not, when the scores of the pilot empowered teams are compared to non-empowered teams. This could be partly because the empowered teams feel 'special'. But the results have pleased managers.

Telesales and service – the people who record policies, sell them, and answer customer queries – are in a huge open-plan office and have always worked in informal teams, with a supervisor. Unlike Harvester, Frizzell has not done away with the supervisors' jobs altogether, although they are now called 'team managers' and they no longer have deputies. But the role has completely changed: in place of allocating and checking on targets and rotas, the supervisor is a facilitator and coach, encouraging the team to set up and measure their own systems.

Teams, each with around 10 people, are empowered to draw up rotas, organise their workload and provide ideas for improvements.

There appears to be more of an air of experimentation than at Harvester.

But, like Harvester, there are some tight guidelines. At first these were oral and informal. Experience showed they needed to be formalised and written down.

Ian Woolley, divisional director, consumer relations, worked out parameters with the teams to clarify what was expected in terms of output and internal relations. Written guidelines summarise company objectives and team targets. Terms of reference give more detail.

Consumer advisers

For instance, 'consumer advisers', the new name for the workers on the end of the telephone, are expected to be logged into the computer for 90 per cent of the time they are in the office and on the phone for at least 55 per cent of the day. They can exceed the targets. But if they fail to meet them, the team managers will discuss how they can improve.

The guidelines also lay down what Harvester would call 'account-abilities': each team must have its co-ordinator, taking up to two hours a day to represent and lead the team, a quality controller and someone to mastermind holidays, overtime and flexi-shifts.

Many teams also have a sub-co-ordinator and a social events organiser. All five are elected, and most teams rotate them about every three months between the most suitable and experienced people. Weekly rotation was tried but failed, since the person had no time to get established. Unlike Harvester, Frizzell has no system for conferring eligibility for these roles.

Teams have weekly meetings with the team manager. There are two agendas (one from the manager, one from the team) from which key items are agreed for discussion.

Woolley says: 'In the early months it tends to focus on things like: "Why can't we park our cars under the building?" But it very quickly moves to: "How can we improve the service to our customers?" or "How do we cut costs?"'

Guidelines are reviewed every quarter or half year and can be modified after discussion.

Each individual also has a statement of expectations, defining what the team manager will expect of the team member and vice versa. These constitute 13 to 20 bullet points varying from expectations of politeness and cheerfulness to 'never turn a blind eye to anything you think is wrong or silly'.

TOM LAMBERT, *consultant and author of 'Key management tools',* which includes a chapter on Frizzell, says: 'One of the problems with empowerment is that everyone lays claim to it, but when you go and look at it, many of them aren't doing very much. It's a bit like TQM. To me it means people using their own judgement in the interests of the organisation and the customer within a disciplined context. The problem is that some of the yankeedoodle gurus have created a band-wagon which I think could bring chaos'[2]

The influences are varied. Training manager Tony Miller claims several authorities, including Bill Byham, Tom Peters, and, unusually, Rensis Likert, the American writer, who demonstrated in the 1960s that the most participative organisations were the most successful.

The trickiest position is that of the ex-supervisor. Team manager Anne-Marie Griffiths admits: 'The hardest thing was to hand over to someone else and trust them to do it as well as I would.' Many other companies, including Rover and Vauxhall have found the supervisor is the stumbling block to empowerment.

Bonus scheme

Pay has been affected: in place of the old bonus scheme linked to individual achievement of targets, the bonus now goes to the best teams. Fast workers find they are carrying the slow coaches and some don't like it.

But most revel in the ability to influence their own jobs. There are 'silly boards' dotted around the office on which anyone can list silly tasks which in their view could be changed or eradicated. Teams have come up with some highly effective ideas over the year which they have researched and implemented.

However, empowerment at Frizzell has not been without hiccups. When it was first introduced, there was a sense that, as Woolley puts it, 'The revolution had begun'.

Supervisor Ann-Marie Griffiths says: 'Everyone came back from their training and thought: "Right, that's it; we're running the company." In the first few weeks, everyone thought of themselves. They were going home early, having long lunch breaks and having a smoke when they wanted.' Darrin Vingoe, a co-ordinator for the team Griffiths supervises, adds: 'People would go for a fag and hope someone else would answer the phone. We weren't being totally irresponsible, but we were less productive.'

In fact, the teams were so unproductive that certain senior managers started to get cold feet and very nearly withdrew backing. But they were persuaded by the enthusiasts in the company to stay their ground and are now convinced this was the right decision.

Personnel manager David Tomlinson still doesn't like the term 'empowerment', describing it as 'just a buzzword'. He views it as a 1990s form of job enrichment or employee involvement. 'We are going back to basic principles trying to gain commitment from people by giving them a sense of ownership,' he says.

But he likes what is happening. A recent calculation of the productivity increase since February among the 170 people, including managers, who are involved in servicing existing clients shows a 62 per cent gain. Among those in the sales operation, who were empowered 10 weeks later and were less enthusiastic, the comparable increase was 18 per cent.

RICHARD WHIPP, *Professor of human resources management and deputy director of Cardiff Business School*, who advised Ciba UK, likes the definition of empowerment coined by Jan Carlson, chief executive of Scandinavian Airline Systems. 'He says the purpose of empowerment is to free someone from rigorous control by instructions and orders and give them freedom to take responsibility for their ideas and actions, to release hidden resources which would otherwise remain inaccessible'

Training manager Tony Miller claims well over £250,000 savings resulting from empowerment. Although some of these are arguably associated with the general re-engineering of the company, with multi-skilling and new computer systems, others can be directly attributed to people's increased responsibility.

Problem-solving

Woolley says: 'Empowerment has definitely saved 18 jobs among managers and support staff.' Localised problem-solving has saved £198,000. There has also been a drop in sickness absence, an increase in calls handled and a rise in total sales, some of which is put down to empowerment. However, it should be pointed out that Frizzell is currently undergoing a rapid expansion anyway. It might be harder for the senior managers to create the same wave of enthusiasm in hard times.

Staff might also be wary of saving six jobs if they thought that spelt six redundancies. At present, such savings can be absorbed without such traumatic results and the teams admit they never gave a thought to such a possibility.

Empowerment may have become a buzzword, as Tomlinson says. Even one of its greatest disciples, Bill Byham, admits that. But that does not mean it should be denigrated. Many a cliché expresses a great truth, and the latest approach to employee involvement does appear to be having a radical effect on the way people work.

References

1 *Credibility* by James Kouzes and Barry Posner, published by Maxwell Macmillan, 1993.
2 *Key management tools* is published by Pitman, 1993.

Reproduced from Pickard, J. (1993). The real meaning of empowerment! *Personnel Management*, November. By permission of *Personnel Management*.

ENFRANCHISEMENT OF SERVICE WORKERS
Leonard A. Schlesinger and James L. Heskett

Leonard A. Schlesinger is Associate Professor of Business Administration and James L. Heskett is UPS Foundation Professor of Business Logistics, at the Harvard Business School. The authors have produced several important papers which explicitly link human resource management policies to successful services marketing.[1,2]

In the 'Enfranchisement of service workers' Schlesinger and Heskett look at 'enfranchisement'; a combination of empowerment and performance-related reward schemes. They identify several critical success factors which characterize successful attempts to enfranchise employees, and outline some commonly encountered barriers to its implementation.

The customer pointed out to the Nordstrom salesperson that she had bought a pair of shoes at Bloomingdales (a competitor) that were too small for her. She liked the style, but Bloomingdales didn't have her size. After being fitted with the same shoe of the proper size, the customer started to pay for the shoes. The salesperson instead suggested that she merely take the too-small shoes in exchange for the new purchase. When the customer reminded the salesperson that she hadn't bought the first pair at Nordstrom, the salesperson said to her, 'If I take these shoes for you, you won't have any reason to return to Bloomingdales.'[1]

This typifies the kinds of stories told by customers of Nordstrom, the well-known fashion department store chain. Such results are possible only when an organization gives its employees latitude to satisfy customers and rewards the employees for their efforts. It is what we refer to as 'enfranchisement'.

Enfranchisement is a way of granting freedom and responsibility to an employee within a franchise without requiring a monetary investment or ownership on the part of the employee. It is achieved through a combination of what has come to be known as 'empowerment'[2] coupled with compensation methods that pay people for their performance.[3] It has the potential for producing extraordinarily responsive service, extra employee effort, and unusually high rewards to those who are enfranchised. The efforts of service organizations to enfranchise their employees address several major concerns.

- A major source of frustration for employees is that management may publicly proclaim that it wants to serve its customers but will actually impede its employees, or fail to provide them with the necessary resources, or will even penalize them for attempting to do so.[4]
- The time 'window' for recovery from many service errors is small. If a service error is not corrected quickly, especially for high-cost services, it becomes nearly impossible to regain the level of customer satisfaction that would have been achieved had the service been performed correctly the first time.[5]
- In many services, there is greater risk in not empowering employees than in giving them too much latitude. As Jan Carlzon, CEO of Scandinavian Airlines System, noted:

  What's the danger of giving away too much? Are you worried about having an oversatisfied customer? That's not much of a worry. You can forget about an oversatisfied customer, but a dissatisfied customer is one of the most expensive problems you can have ... the danger is not that employees will give away too much. It's that they won't give away anything – because they don't dare.[6]

Employees often need to be encouraged – through performance-based programs – to use the discretionary latitude which they are given.

Achievements to date

The most significant and successful enfranchisement programs have occurred in the field of retailing. Retail organizations, both large and small, have turned to a combination of empowerment and pay-for-performance to fuel rapid internal growth and to increase sales productivity. Advocates of enfranchisement argue that it can dramatically improve sales and earnings, while at the same time require less direct supervision from corporate management and provide increased employee earnings, job satisfaction, and retention. Employee retention is of particular importance in retailing because it can have a positive impact on customer retention, which in turn has been found to be an important determinant of profit in many companies.[7]

Table 1 provides evidence from two retail chains, Ito Yokado in Japan and Nordstrom in the United States that demonstrates the positive effects of enfranchisement. Furthermore, the efforts of the two companies have become a matter of intense curiosity (if not an actual model) for their competitors and other retailers.

Ito Yokado's reform program

The Ito Yokado Group is a Japanese chain of department stores, convenience stores, and other retail shops and restaurants.[8] It is one of several large, non-traditional Japanese retailing organizations that got their start during Japan's retailing boom of the late 1950s by offering a wider range of utilitarian goods to a broader spectrum of the Japanese public than more traditional department stores. In 1988, its sales were approximately $16 billion.

Faced with the prospect of slower growth, and unable to distinguish its profit performance from that of its major competitors, the Group's founder initiated the 'Reform Program' in 1982. The program is centered on understanding customers' needs, concentrating inventory management decisions to achieve ample in-stock inventory positions, and redesigning and merchandising stores to reflect this new emphasis on providing value to customers.

The Reform Program was designed to be consistent with Ito Yokado's emphasis on seniority and job flexibility (rather than a particular job as a symbol of status), the heavy use of part-time employees, and a culture that supports the delegation of decision making to a large number of people. Given its mission to improve asset management, the Reform Program focuses on the buying function. It was implemented by selecting large numbers of full- and part-time employees to be buyers of small portions of the total product line; supplying them with the best computerized decision tools and complete current information; fully training them in the use of these resources; giving them full responsibility for decision making; and rewarding them at above-market rates and, in part, on the basis of the organization's overall performance.[9]

Six years after its initiation, the Reform Program enabled Ito Yokado to achieve a return on sales that was more than double and a return on assets that was nearly double that of its four major competitors. At the same time, it grew at a significantly faster rate than these same competitors (see Table 1).

Table 1 *Comparative data for Ito Yokado and Nordstrom*

	Ito Yokado[a]	Nordstrom[b]
Annual sales volume	14.9 billion	2.7 billion
Annual growth rate, Past five years:		
Subject company	8.0%	24.2%
Major competitors	5.1%	8.3%
Return on sales:		
Subject company	2.8%	4.5%
Major competitors	1.1%	2.1%
Return on assets:		
Subject company	3.4%	8.4%
Major competitors	1.9%	3.5%
Degree of empowerment	Extensive	Extensive
Amount of incentive, as % of total compensation	Up to 33%	Up to 100%
Nature of incentive	Group	Individual
Levels enfranchised	Managers and employees	Managers and employees
Employees included	All full-time and 1/3 of part-time	All full-time
Primary concentration	Buying, inventory control	Sales
Role of management	'Teachers & advisors'	'Satisfying customers'
Results:	Fewer stockouts, lower inventory levels, less inventory loss, higher merchandise quality, employee commitment	Sales per sales hour and sales per square foot of selling space roughly double industry averages, low recruiting and advertising costs, average costs for sales labor and real estate in relation to sales, high employee and customer loyalty

[a] Operating data are for 1983–1988, and exclude franchised operations
[b] Operating data are for 1983–1988

Nordstrom's 'obsession' with customer satisfaction

Expanding from a chain of shoe stores in 1963, Nordstrom has grown into a chain of 61 fashion department stores operating largely on the West Coast of the United States and realizing sales at an annual rate of roughly $2.7 billion.[10] Members of the family (of which most of senior management is composed) attribute their rapid growth and success in apparel to their application of the principles of the shoe business: offer an unusually wide selection of merchandise in attractive stores with a high level of service and competitive prices.

Nordstrom's store personnel have been told for years that their single responsibility is to satisfy customers. While this broad statement allows for a wide range of interpretation, it is brief, clear, and well-understood by the entire organization. Furthermore, it is indicative of the wide latitude given managers and associates at all levels in the organization.

Nordstrom is the generally recognized leader in paying its salespeople a commission not only on what they sell, but on the extent to which they exceed their superiors' projected sales forecasts. Nordstrom's practice of discarding the term 'employee' in favor of 'associate' has been emulated throughout U.S. retailing. The philosophy of enfranchisement is exemplified by its public display of the results achieved by all personnel and by the frequent celebration of associates' accomplishments. Some of the extraordinary services performed on behalf of Nordstrom's customers include such things as warming up customer's automobiles in cold weather, delivering products to their offices or homes, or taking them to the airport in emergencies.

The contractual arrangement between sales associates and Nordstrom assumes that associates will do what they deem necessary to enhance sales per hour during the time they are 'clocked in' on the job. This may include spending time 'off the clock' writing thank-you notes or reminders to customers or running errands for them. All of this is intended to enhance associates' sales per hour for officially recorded selling hours. This is the basis for the guaranteed base hourly wages established periodically between Nordstrom's management and its sales associates as well as for the commission that is paid in addition to the base wage (usually about 6.75% of sales).[11]

The combination of excellent locations, store ambience, and complete merchandise selection along with a focus on customer satisfaction, the heavy use of commissions and other incentives, and efforts to build an intense loyalty among associates to Nordstrom and its mission has produced remarkable results. They include sales per square foot that are more than twice industry averages, with an attendant high return on assets. Sales associates have been compensated at rates ranging from two to four times industry averages. Customers readily profess unusually high levels of loyalty to Nordstrom, its people, and its service. And the profits generated by the enfranchisement concept have fueled unusually high internal growth.

Productivity

Noting Nordstrom's success, managements of other retailing organizations have adopted aspects of its enfranchisement strategy to help solve other problems, including low space productivity and rising labor costs. Two of the more recent and notable companies are Younkers and Dayton-Hudson. Efforts are being made to implement such concepts in consumer services other than retailing, as illustrated by the Fairfield Inn hotel experience.

Younkers' Satisfaction Plus

Younkers, a 37-store chain of department stores in the Midwest, implemented its 'Satisfaction Plus' program on April 1, 1988.[12] It was part of an effort to inject new life into a 100-year-old, traditionally managed chain that had enjoyed unusually high market share for much of its history and whose sales and profits had stagnated.

Satisfaction Plus involves careful selection of personnel, with heavy reliance on referrals from associates and on training and recognition. It

Table 2 *Results achieved by recent enfranchisement programs at two U.S. department store chains*

	Younkers[a]	Dayton Hudson[b]
Number of stores	34[c]	34
Total sales, 1989	$0.3 billion	$1.7 billion
Average per hour sales	+20%	+25%
Average per hour compensation	+24%	+17%
Percentage of new hires from associates' recommendations	Doubled to 60%	Not measured
Quality of service	+18%[d]	+5%
Employee morale	'Dramatically improved'	Not available[e]
Turnover of sales personnel (one year after initiation of the process)	−50%	+22%
Cost of sales labor to sales	+10%	+33%
Cost of recruiting and personnel development	Lower	Lower

[a] Measurements are for all stores for a period beginning in March 1988, and ending in July 1990.
[b] Based on information from four stores implementing the concept in 1987 and 1988.
[c] Since the initiation of Satisfaction Plus, Younkers has closed three of its stores.
[d] This represents the increase in the proportion of acceptable or higher mystery shops.
[e] In the process of being measured.

has been integrated with long-standing methods of recognition such as the company's Hall of Fame, which now bases its admission decisions on the sales per hour measure used for Satisfaction Plus. Unlike Nordstrom, Younkers does not pay a commission on sales, but wage rates are adjusted every six months based on a trailing twelve-month sales-per-hour basis. A percentage of sales factor is used to determine a negotiated sales-per-hour rate on which compensation will be based. Failure to meet the agreed sales level may trigger a downward adjustment of the base wage, additional training, or eventual dismissal.

Quality of customer service is encouraged through an effort called '30/30 STAR', which refers to the desire to have sales associates acknowledge customers within 30 seconds of their arrival in a department at a distance of no more than 30 feet. In addition, through a 'mystery shopping program' (the evaluation of service quality conducted by a cadre of professionally trained shoppers), evaluations of associates' efforts are based on Smile, Time spent with the customer, Attention to the customer's needs, and Respect shown the customer. One unsatisfactory mystery shopping experience produces a warning, two eliminates a person from consideration for the Hall of Fame for a given year, and three is grounds for dismissal. However, unsatisfactory mystery shops are accompanied by increased training activities to help associates improve.[13]

The results of Younker's program (as shown in Table 2) have been quite remarkable, especially in view of the fact that for most of the period during which Satisfaction Plus has been in effect, the company has been publicly offered for sale. In spite of the uncertainty and reduced morale created by the imminent sale, Younker's sales productivity, compensation levels, and quality of service have all increased significantly. At the same time, the turnover of sales associates has been cut in half. While the cost of labor relative to sales has risen, this has been offset, in part, by the lower costs of recruitment.

Dayton Hudson's Performance Plus

Dayton Hudson, a chain of 34 upscale full-line department stores and three home stores, was created from a merger of the Dayton and the Hudson department store chains.[14] Dayton Hudson stores located in the Detroit area retain the name 'Hudson's' and stores in the Minneapolis area operate under the name 'Dayton's'. The company achieved sales of $1.7 billion in 1989.

Building on its history of excellence in customer service, the company initiated its Performance Plus program in 1987. This program focuses on selection, training, and incentives aimed at providing superior customer service performed by sales 'consultants' (comparable to Nordstrom's and Younkers' 'associates') who 'go the extra mile' for the customer.

Initially, the company implemented the program in two departments across the entire company. After further consideration, management decided to switch to a store-by-store implementation. By the end of 1988, four stores had fully implemented the program and another seven were added in 1989.

The company encourages its sales consultants to be creative in serving customers. This is emphasized in its training and reinforced by recognition and rewards on the selling floor. While on the sales floor, consultants are encouraged to take customers into different departments when needed and to develop a repeat clientele by sending thank you notes and informing customers of sales or new merchandise. Sales consultants are rewarded on a pay-for-performance basis similar to Nordstrom's.

The company believes that selection plays an important role as well. Interviewers look for candidates hoping to make retail sales a career. After being hired, new employees go through a two-day 'Celebration Training' in which the underlying theme is 'it's my company.'

Even though Performance Plus is in early stages of implementation, results to date, when comparing Performance Plus with non-Performance Plus stores, suggest that per hour sales have increased substantially along with average earnings per sales consultant (as shown in Table 2). The rate of salesperson turnover in stores one year after implementation has increased 22%; this is attributed by management to the self-selection still taking place among its sales consultants, and is typical of other firms in our study. However, reduced turnover is still a long-term objective of the program. A combination of increased compensation and greater opportunity for personal development has given stores operating under Performance Plus greater access to college graduates. As a result, the proportion of selling managers who are promoted from sales consultants in those stores has risen by roughly 150%, according to management estimates. Just as important, increases in customer service levels (based on the company's 'Extra Mile' measures that are obtained from customer interviews) are 56% greater in Performance Plus stores than in the stores that have yet to implement it. Overall service quality measures also have risen faster in Performance Plus than in other Dayton Hudson stores.

Quality

High quality and its favorable long-term impact on profit is at the heart of several other efforts being made to implement enfranchisement.

Fairfield Inn

Fairfield Inn, a division of Marriott Corporation, seeks to impress (not just satisfy) guests with rooms often priced as low as $39 per night.[15] To staff its 135-room economy priced inns, Fairfield Inn carefully selects only those people who have the appropriate attitudes and capabilities to deliver two things: the friendliest atmosphere and the cleanest rooms. Whether they are hired as managers, desk clerks, or housekeepers, they must be the kind of people who respond favorably to frequent measurement and rewards based on performance, even though the incentive offered represents only a 10% premium over prevailing wages.

Fairfield Inn has developed a method of selection, performance measurement, and incentives that incorporates a guest-driven, computer-assisted Scorecard measurement system as the focal point of its human resource and control strategies. Even though Fairfield Inn opened its first economy inn only as recently as 1987, when confronted with particularly competitive labor markets, its management has been able to alter its template to set itself apart from other employers.

Consider, for example, Fairfield Inn's approach to the employment and management practices for the job category of housekeepers, known as 'GRAs' (guest room attendants) at Fairfield Inn. Empowerment of GRAs occurs through the assignment of 14 rooms to clean as the equivalent of an 8-hour work day. If the rooms can be cleaned faster, a full day's compensation is paid. Further, on particularly busy days GRAs can 'bid' on additional rooms for which they are paid an additional half-hour in wages for each additional room cleaned. ('Overtime' is paid in cash at the end of the shift, reflecting the typical short-term needs for compensation that often motivate GRAs to clean additional rooms on a given day.) This allows Fairfield Inn to maintain a relatively small core of regular housekeepers who are given incentives to expand their work at busy times. Housekeepers earn paid leave through regular attendance on the job. But they have the option of maintaining their regular attendance by taking responsibility for finding an already-trained replacement on days when they are not able to appear for work.

Finally, each inn establishes two discretionary budgets of $150 each for each 28-day period. The first is an employee relations budget which is spent at the discretion of the inn's manager for anything ranging from 'employee of the month' awards to morale-building events. The second is a guest relations budget which frequently is managed by employees. In the words of a recent Fairfield Inn general manager, the budgets are managed with great care and spent with considerable creativity:

> One of our properties in Kansas is not unusual. Here, a guest service representative keeps a careful log of the preferences of frequent customers, those regional business travelers by auto who may log 40 to 50 nights per year at our inns and who return to the same places quite frequently. Preferences are collected by all staff members. The list of incoming guests is checked in advance. If a particularly frequent guest likes a certain kind of cookie, a GSR or GRA will go to the store for them. It is handled entirely by the hourly employees; managers don't have time to do it. This is so important to us that managers are cautioned to make sure the budgets are spent, regardless of short-term preferences.[16]

Indices of performance for Fairfield Inn in the third year of its existence are shown in Table 3. These include comparisons with other economy lodging chains obtained through an independent survey. They suggest

Table 3 *Early results of Fairfield Inn's effort to enfranchise employees*

	Fairfield Inn	Other economy lodging chains
Index of compensation Rates, hourly employees:[1]		
Wage	1.00	1.00
Incentives	1.10	1.00
Employee turnover (annual)		
1990:	100–120%	167%
1989:	120–140%	167%[2]
Occupancy rates percentage of rooms filled on average[3]		
1989–90:	70–75%	60%
Average number of trips per year among economy business travellers[4]	50–70	30–40
Management salary index[5] (unit level)	1.05	1.00
Nonmanagement labor costs as a percentage of revenue (unit level)[6]	18–20%	16–19%
Indices of customer satisfaction[4]		
Overall cleanliness of hotel	80–90	55–85
Overall value for money	70–80	55–65
Overall maintenance and upkeep of hotel	80–90	45–80
Hotel service overall	80–90	50–70
Speed and efficiency of check-in and check-out	70–80	40–70
Friendliness of hotel personnel	70–80	50–60

Notes:

1 Based on competitive wage surveys in various markets. Hourly incentives include bonus and bonus leave.
2 1989 Gallup Survey.
3 Average of competitors, based on Smith Travel Research Data. Fairfield Inn numbers exclude inns open less than one year. Competitor chains are believed to average 55–75%.
4 Based on Economy Business Transient Tracting Study, 1990, commissioned by FFI.
5 This is an average, index for a particular FFI manager can be much higher due to bonus potential.
6 Range based on various competitor operating statements.

that Fairfield Inn has in a short time achieved higher 'product' quality, higher customer loyalty, a significantly higher occupancy rate, and a comparable cost structure. Its employee turnover rate is 60–70% of that of its competitors. Further, in a recent poll, 92% of employees indicated that the scorecard measurement and reward system should be maintained. Also, as with several of the examples of enfranchisement programs cited earlier, one major benefit is the need for less traditional supervision. Housekeeping supervisors are being eliminated at some Fairfield Inns. This not only allows for a reduction in an important cost of operation, but also represents a reallocation of a unit manager's time to more positive activities of selecting and motivating employees.

Conditions for effective enfranchisement

These successful efforts to enfranchise employees reveal the conditions under which the concept works best.[17] They include:

- Each effort reflects the culture of the organization or individual department in which it is being implemented. In particular, employees have to be comfortable with a pay-for-performance-oriented atmosphere. Beyond this, an important question is whether rewards should be based on individual or group performance. Nearly every U.S. retailing executive with whom we have spoken argues that rewards based on individual performance are most appropriate, particularly for sales-related jobs. On the other hand, rewards at Ito Yokado are based on the company's performance, with loyalty to the company emphasized as a major motivating force.
- Enfranchisement is only one part, albeit sometimes the most visible, of a process that begins with recruitment and selection of people and continues through to training, development, assignment, and recognition.[18]
- Each of the programs we have described grants employees varying degrees of control over both operating decisions and compensation.
- All of the programs involve efforts to encourage communication from lower to higher ranks of the organization.
- All of the efforts are accompanied by controls covering what is thought to be the critical core of the organization's activities. At Nordstrom, for example, the critical core is defined as customer satisfaction. At Younkers, it is embodied in the quality control effort.[19]
- Employee turnover is largely management-initiated. Non-performers are dismissed so that those remaining feel they are associated with a high-performance organization. While voluntary turnover is dramatically lowered, the involuntary turnover is roughly comparable to that of competitors who have not enfranchised their employees (or those who have not taken the trouble to replace non-performing employees).
- A large proportion of new people are hired on the basis of referrals from existing employees. This is a result of the excellent compensation

and working conditions provided by companies that emphasize employee enfranchisement. It is critical to the creation of a self-selected work force whose values and expectations are consistent with those of the organization.

- An array of resources is made available to the enfranchised employees to help them succeed. At Ito Yokado, these resources include current information and computerized inventory management decision tools. At Nordstrom they include excellent store locations and ambience and great depth of merchandise selection, which is especially important for fashion retailing to an affluent market segment. At Younkers, the resources range from an exchange of information about selling skills and ideas to a greater effort to focus merchandising efforts on a particular market target. (For example, when Younkers faced a recent recession and loss of customers in the markets it serves, it encouraged sales associates to increase average sales per customer. It did this by making available carefully-selected 'Satisfaction Plus' add-on items, displaying them prominently, and training its sales associates to suggest these items to customers to achieve more add-on sales.) At Dayton Hudson, implementation of Performance Plus is accompanied by a review of merchandise 'content', intended to provide better or a greater depth of goods for sales associates to sell. At Fairfield Inn, employees are provided with good working conditions, clear-cut objectives, and a measurement and reward system that appeals to them.

Would these conditions produce superior performance without enfranchisement? We are doubtful. Enfranchisement not only makes the value of these changes visible, but provides improved performance that helps defray their cost.

A more important question is how much of what we have observed in these examples is the result of the so-called Hawthorne Effect: improved morale and performance resulting from increased attention of any kind paid to a long-neglected group of workers?[20] Undoubtedly, some portion of early results that we have reported can be attributed to this phenomenon. However, what we have observed are much more basic changes concerning selection as well as job design, compensation, and the development of supporting devices, all of which are intended to 'lock in' significant improvements in performance over time.

Longer-term tracking of results from sites such as these should provide evidence of the sustainability of these incentives and results. Similar studies in both manufacturing and service-producing settings have yielded mixed results, although each of the programs observed differed in substantial ways from those we have reported here.[21] Already, the efforts we have observed have produced changes in output and quality far in excess of those observed in other experiments.[22] We have no reason to believe that they are not sustainable, although early experience suggests that there are major challenges to be encountered in implementing such programs.

Major challenges to implementation

Enfranchisement can be highly satisfying and rewarding during times of success, at least for those who share in that success. Even then, of course, the concept may not be appropriate for all employees. However, a negative environment producing disappointing sales results can challenge the fortitude of even the most avid believer in the concept. Major challenges include:

- Unit managers with the human and technical skills to interpret policies associated with enfranchisement and to make them work may be in short supply. Because decisions are often pushed down into an organization under these kinds of programs, fewer managers with operating knowledge may be needed at the corporate level. But the wider latitude of decision making involved at the unit level will require managers with good business insight and particularly strong human resource skills to 'stroke' winners, work to help losers develop into winners, and make losers feel like winners as they leave the firm. It is this shortage of managers that proponents of the concept discuss most frequently.
- Middle management may be unwilling to support enfranchisement. Under this kind of program, the role of middle managers shifts from operating the firm to coaching and advising unit managers. Middle managers go beyond the mere identification of problems in their units, making sure that unit managers have the resources to solve them. Because many middle managers in service organizations are promoted from the unit management ranks, it is difficult for them to resist the inclination to continue to participate in the actual management of units under their supervision. Furthermore, it is difficult for them to see their unit managers making what appear to be poor decisions without stepping in to assume command.
- Senior managers may not be able to allow enfranchisement to work. In enfranchisement programs, the role of senior management shifts from an operational to a strategic orientation. Supervisory roles are replaced by planning, policy setting, and negotiating of major contractual arrangements. Experience suggests that senior management may accept of these role shifts as long as performance is good. However, when either growth in sales or profitability level off – often for reasons totally unrelated to internal efforts – there is a natural tendency for senior management to begin to 'tinker' with apparently sound enfranchisement policies. Senior managers often are encouraged in this practice by disenchanted operating managers who may see their compensation declining for reasons beyond their control and who wish to abrogate their 'contracts'.
- Managers may be perceived as being unfair by associates. Under most enfranchisement programs, assignments influence rewards. At Nordstrom, Dayton Hudson, and Younkers, the hours assigned to sales associates determine in some measure the amount of merchandise they

may be able to sell. Similarly, the number of salespeople assigned to a given department will influence the amount that any one of them may be able to sell. A Fairfield Inn with an unusually high occupancy rate may be one at which higher or even acceptable customer satisfaction ratings – on which compensation is based – may be particularly difficult to achieve. This produces an anomaly where the employees of the most profitable units are personally penalized. To the extent that participants feel that the enfranchisement program is being managed unfairly, the program will be a target for criticism within the organization.

● Participants' expectations may be inadequately conditioned. There is a natural tendency for parties to enfranchisement programs to assume that a positive result will be achieved that will benefit both parties. Too little emphasis may be placed on spelling out in advance the expected behavior by both parties if such results are not continually achieved. In effect, enfranchisement gives employees a kind of contractor status. This can be a problem, especially if employees don't see themselves as contractors, particularly when adverse conditions arise.

It is impossible to place too much emphasis on the conditioning of expectations. Enfranchisement is not a benign program. It rewards winners and punishes losers. It asks participants to accept the bad with the good. When the worst does happen, individuals are often psychologically unprepared and disappointed.

● Programs may be improperly designed and implemented. The design of an enfranchisement effort must fit the culture of the organization. A major concern is the extent to which individuals should have a choice regarding their participation. In most of the enfranchisement efforts in the U.S. to date, participants indicate the compensation level they wish to achieve, which in turn influences the sales goal set for them. While actual compensation for sales above the goal may be on a commission basis, it is a negotiated commission level. Such design features have been intended in part to reduce the appearance of arbitrariness.

When implementing enfranchisement, one of the first concerns is whether to implement it in all operating units simultaneously or to install it progressively on a unit-by-unit basis. Younkers' managers introduced its 'Satisfaction Plus' program in all 36 of its department stores simultaneously to avoid what management termed the 'grapevine effect' – communication from employees at stores with the program to those in stores yet to implement it. Their assumption was that negative responses often travel more rapidly and tend to be more exaggerated or distorted than positive ones. By contrast, Dayton Hudson opted for a store-by-store implementation, beginning with stores where reactions might be the most positive. These decisions are extremely critical, because improperly designed or implemented programs will not only disrupt the status quo, they may be seen as grounds for grievances, union organizing drives, or even government intervention.

● Organized labor may be uncomfortable with the concept of individual employees as contractors. Union organizations generally have seen one of their roles as being contractors for groups of employees. Enfranchisement, to the extent that it is seen as regarding employees as contractors, may run counter to the role model assumed by union leadership. Further, given the difficulty of separating nonperforming employees from potentially lucrative jobs (especially those employees who may have achieved substantial seniority), efforts to enfranchise employees can be targets for disgruntled employees. For example, employees at one store where Dayton-Hudson's Performance Plus program has yet to be implemented have voted to accept unionization.[23]

In perhaps the most-publicized case of this occurrence, a union representing a small proportion of Nordstrom employees in the state of Washington has had a complaint upheld by the Washington State Labor and Industries Department. It was charged that the company did not pay sales associates for time spent performing non-selling activities such as home deliveries, company meetings, and preparation of personal correspondence with customers. It ruled that Nordstrom had to compensate associates retroactively for time spent in such activities even though they were being paid on the basis of a commission. Now the union has filed a suit to require Nordstrom to make similar restitution in every state in which it operates in the United States.[24]

These events have triggered several reactions. They have somewhat divided employees in Nordstrom's stores involved in the complaint, with one group loyal to the company actively seeking to have the union decertified so that it no longer represents them. The events have also influenced Nordstrom's emulators to take a more cautious approach to the implementation of similar programs in their companies. This situation has fueled a great deal of speculation as to the possible reasons for the dispute at Nordstrom, with cited causes including: senior management's sincere belief that all activities, whether selling or not, are recognized in a commission-base compensation system; too much empowerment for managers who might have allowed practices that abused the spirit of the program; inadequate corporate control over human resource management practices in the store: disgruntled associates unable to succeed under a pay-for-performance program; and inadequate conditioning of associates' expectations regarding the workings of the concept. The common theme running through much of this speculation is whether or not adverse reactions in this and other cases could have been avoided with more effective ongoing communication between senior management, associates, and union representatives.

Conclusion

Our data reflect results obtained from what most researchers would term extreme examples or experiments. They were selected for that reason in order to illustrate what is possible.

An important unanswered question, however, is whether or not these results are sustainable. Although only time will tell, the Nordstrom experience suggests that under conditions in which both empowerment and pay-for-performance are important elements of a basic, long-term business strategy, substantial positive long-term benefits from enfranchisement are achievable.

Theoretically, enfranchisement should be a win-win concept, the cornerstone of truly outstanding service performance. Not only are there rewards for both managers and associates, but customers benefit as well from the improved service that enfranchisement provides. The customers develop such strong loyalty to companies practising it that their favorable word-of-mouth recommendations to others often replace some part of the advertising budget for a company. In most cases, companies practising enfranchisement have become preferred employers – a particularly important advantage at a time of tight labor markets.

Why then isn't enfranchisement more widely accepted and practised? One of the biggest reasons is the demands it places on people to manage two highly volatile concepts, empowerment and pay-for-performance. When combined, these concepts can become explosive, especially in the hands of one or more empowered, but misguided managers. Once it reaches that stage, it becomes an understandably appropriate matter of interest for other parties, including associates, unions, and state and federal agencies.

As attractive as it seems, enfranchisement will continue to encounter a number of challenges, including: an unsupportive culture of the organization itself; a shortage of unit managers with the requisite technical and human skills, of middle managers willing to support the program, and of senior managers who are able to let it work; the inability to condition participants' expectations; the improper design and implementation of the concept; and the perceived threat that it may represent to labor union organizations.

Such challenges can be overcome with effective communication between all levels of management and employees with the objective being to establish realistic expectations on everyone's part in advance. Labor organizations should not be excluded from the process, but it will require that their leadership reassess the kind of representation that the enfranchised require. It will involve greater emphasis on working conditions and benefits and less on compensation per se. More important, it will inevitably alter evaluations of what is 'fair treatment' and strike to the very heart of the employee grievance procedure itself. Further, it may challenge union notions of individuals' loyalty to the labor movement just as it does those of employees' loyalty to the company.

Enfranchisement can be a potent long-term competitive force, but only when it is part of an organizational culture and strategy that is built on careful selection and development of people to whom the concept appeals and for whom it functions well. By itself, it will not produce the relatively spectacular results shown here. Nor is it for everyone.

The concept, so seemingly universal in its appeal, will continue to be controversial. To the extent that it requires a sharing of both rewards and risks in good times and bad, long-term adherence to the concept will require an unusual level of management dedication. Given the special qualities of supporting behavior and restraint that it requires of managers, not all who adopt it will be able to make enfranchisement work. Nevertheless, for those who can make it work, enfranchisement is a potent competitive strategy.

References

1 James L. Heskett, W. Earl Sasser, Jr., and Christopher W.L. Hart. *Service Breakthroughs* (New York, NY: The Free Press, 1990), pp. 13–14.
2 Empowerment is perhaps an overworked and underdefined term. We use it here as the rough equivalent of what industrial psychologists and political economists alike term 'participation' in decision making. See, for example, David I. Levine and Laura D'Andrea Tyson, 'Participation, Productivity, and the Firm's Environment,' in Alan S. Blinder, ed., *Paying for Productivity* (Washington, D.C.: The Brookings Institute, 1990), pp. 183–243.
3 Edward E. Lawler III addresses pay-for-performance issues in *Strategic Pay* (San Francisco. CA: Jossey-Bass Publishers, 1990), especially pp. 55–131.
4 For evidence concerning this kind of stress, see the work of J.J. Parkington and Benjamin Schneider, 'Some Correlates of Experienced Job Stress: A Boundary Role Study,' *Academy of Management Journal*, 22 (1979): 270–281. Also see Warren Bennis, 'Beyond Bureaucracy,' in Warren Bennis, ed., *American Bureaucracy* (Chicago, IL: Aldine, 1970), pp. 3–17; and Peter M. Blau, *On the Nature of Organizations* (New York, NY: John Wiley and Sons, 1974), pp. 80–84.
5 In our service management classes we require students to write and mail letters of complaint (as well as commendation) about services they have experienced recently. In more than half the cases in which service providers respond, often with substantial offers of restitution, students tell us that they feel no more positively about poorly performed services after getting their responses than before. This suggests the difficulty of correcting a service poorly performed or delivered long after the time of the error.
6 'The Art of Loving,' *Inc.* (May 1989), p. 36.
7 Frederick F. Reichheld and W. Earl Sasser, 'Zero Defections: Quality Comes to Service,' *Harvard Business Review* (September/October 1990), pp. 105–111.
8 Information in this section is drawn from Ito Yokado, Case No. 9–589–116 (Boston, MA: Publishing Division, Harvard Business School, 1989).
9 *Ibid.*

10 Information in this section is drawn from Nordstrom. Case No. 9–579–218 (Boston, MA: Publishing Division, Harvard Business School, 1979) and Francine Schwadel, 'Nordstrom's Push East Will Test Its Renown For the Best in Service. '*The Wall Street Journal*. August 1, 1989, pp. A1 and A4.

11 The actual process involves establishing a guaranteed base wage and dividing it by the commission rate (6.75% of sales in most cases) to obtain a targeted sales per hour. Overtime (for more than 40 hours per week) is paid at the rate of 1.5 times the guaranteed base wage. If commissions (6.75% of total sales) exceed the guaranteed base wage plus overtime, they are paid. If salary exceeds commissions, it is paid. However, salaries regularly exceeding commissions result in renegotiation of the guaranteed base wage.

12 Information in this section is based on interviews with company executives, August 1990.

13 The positive relationship between courteous salespeople and store productivity has been supported by Robert I. Sutton and Anat Rafeli, 'Untangling the Relationship Between Displayed Emotions and Organizational Sales: The Case of Convenience Stores,' *Academy of Management Journal*, 31/3 (1988): 461–487.

14 Information in this section is based on interviews with company executives conducted during February and March of 1990.

15 Certain information in this section is based on material in the case 'Fairfield Inn.' Case No. 9–689–092 (Boston, MA: Publishing Division, Harvard Business School, 1989), and interviews with company executives in March and October 1990.

16 Interview with Michael Ruffer, General Manager, Courtyard Hotels, and former General Manager of Fairfield Inn, October 1990.

17 For an analysis of the impact of multi-level hierarchies on the extent of control over employee behavior, see William G. Ouchi, 'The Relationship Between Organizational Structure and Organizational Control,' *Administrative Science Quarterly*, 22 (1977): 95–113.

18 For a similar conclusion, based on extensive exploration of the 'informing' impact of technology (particularly its ability to have an impact on learning and on the power imparted to operatives), see Shoshana Zuboff, *In the Age of the Smart Machine* (New York, NY: Basic Books, Inc., 1988), pp. 413–414. This view is reflected in an examination of various studies of the effects of pay on performance, reported by Thomas A. Mahoney, 'Multiple Pay Contingencies: Strategic Design of Compensation,' *Human Resource Management* (Fall 1989), pp. 337–347.

19 Appropriate bounds on acceptable behavior under empowerment initiatives should be clearly drawn and universally understood. While not the primary thrust of our work, it is addressed explicitly in a much broader context by Robert L. Simons, 'Beliefs and Boundaries,' a paper presented at the 1990 Strategic Management Society Annual Meeting, Stockholm, September 24–27, 1990.

20 The effect gets its name from research designed to identify determinants of employee productivity, satisfaction, and motivation carried out at the Hawthorne plant of The Western Electric Company from 1924 to 1927. For a description, see F.J. Roethlisberger in George F.F. Lombard, ed., *The Elusive Phenomena* (Boston, MA: Division of Research, Graduate School of Business Administration, Harvard University, 1977), pp. 45–48.

21 For example, in contrast to other studies, two of our cases involve companies which either have practised enfranchisement for many years (Nordstrom) or for which a business strategy was literally constructed with the concept as a major element (Fairfield Inn).

22 See, for example, the summary conclusions of the work of others by Alan S. Blinder, *op. cit.*, pp. 1–13, that participation (empowerment), if it is to improve productivity for more than short periods of time, must be bolstered in the long run by pay schemes that reward individual or group performance. But even under these conditions, only small positive long-term effects on productivity are usually observed.

23 Francine Schwadel, 'Chain Finds Incentives a Hard Sell,' *The Wall Street Journal*, July 26, 1990, pp. B1 and B4.

24 For more complete descriptions of recent events, see 'Nordstrom: Dissension in the Ranks,' Case No. 9–191–002 (Boston, MA: Publishing Division, Harvard Business School, 1990); and Charlene Mermer Soloman, 'Nightmare at Nordstrom,' *Personnel Journal* (September 1990), pp. 76–83.

---

6 DELIVERING CUSTOMER SATISFACTION

In today's marketing environment, an increasingly important source of competitive advantage is the way we service customers. While conventional marketing mix strategies have paid lip service to the role of 'place' in the '4 Ps', in reality very few companies in the past had clearly defined and articulated strategies for customer service. This state of affairs is rapidly changing as more and more companies recognize that one of the most powerful means of achieving differentiation over competitors is through the quality of customer service.[1]

In seeking competitive advantage through service quality, particular attention has to be paid to the service 'delivery system'. In just the same way that product quality is achieved through careful control of the productive process, so too is service quality determined by control of the delivery process. When we talk of a delivery process, we refer to all the service 'encounters' that affect the customer from the initial contact through to the final consumption of the product or service and beyond. The idea of the service encounter forms the centrepiece of the article by Lynn Shostack, who defines the service encounter as 'a period of time during which a customer directly interacts with a service'. In fact, all points of contact between a buyer and a supplier can be defined as 'encounters', including the physical delivery of products, the receiving of invoices, the response to after-sales service requests and so on. These are the 'moments of truth' that Carlzon[2] so powerfully brought to our attention.

The point that Shostack makes in 'Planning the service encounter' is that these encounters are often poorly managed and happen in an almost haphazard way. Instead, she advocates the 'blueprinting' or flow charting of the stages of the service process so that it might be better managed. While not specifically referring to the possibilities of re-engineering the process as a result of blueprinting it, very clearly this should be the aim wherever opportunities for simplification, quality improvement and enhanced customer value appear.

Building on the theme of quality in service, Parasuraman, Zeithaml and Berry in their pioneering article 'A conceptual model of service quality and its implications for future research' look at the problems of service performance measurement. The basic premise of their approach to service performance measurement is that the customers' perception of the service outcome should meet their (the customers') expectations. If it fails to do so then there will be a service quality 'gap'. This is a point of view that others had previously advanced. However, the contribution that Parasuraman *et al.* make is their exposition of the sources of the gap. In particular, they suggest that the overall gap between expectations and perceived performance is itself determined by four other 'gaps', i.e.

- The gap between customer expectations and management perceptions of those expectations
- The gap between management perceptions of customer expectations and the firm's service quality specifications
- The gap between service quality specifications and actual service deliveries
- The gap between actual service delivery and external communication about the service.

A different approach to service delivery is suggested by Sharma and Lambert in their paper 'Segmentation of markets based on customer service'. They argue that since customers' service needs will differ and the priorities they attach to individual service elements will also differ, then a segmented approach to service delivery should be contemplated. The framework they recommend begins with the identification of the salient service dimensions through qualitative research among the target market. A further sample of customers then rates these dimensions in order of importance and, on the basis of those importance scores, customers are placed into clusters. These clusters are then analysed by industry/demographic characteristics so that the segmentation of the market can be identified.

It is probably true to say that one of the most neglected aspects of marketing generally has been the means whereby customer value is actually 'delivered'. Yet paradoxically, as these papers suggest, delivery systems can provide a powerful source of competitive advantage. It is to be hoped that more attention will be paid to this critical issue as organizations seek to develop relationship marketing strategies.

References

1 Christopher, M.G. (1992). *The Customer Service Planner*. Butterworth-Heinemann Oxford.
2 Carlzon, J. (1987). *Moments of Truth*, Ballinger, New York.

PLANNING THE SERVICE ENCOUNTER
G. Lynn Shostack

Lynn Shostack is Chairman of the Board of Joyce International Inc., New York. Previously a director of the Coveport Group, Inc., she has also worked at Bankers Trust Co. and at Citibank, where she designed a marketing strategy that has since become a model for other banks. She is the author of many papers and articles on services management, and has been a regular columnist for the *Journal of Business Strategy.*

'Planning the service encounter' is a seminal exposition of the idea that the interaction between the provider of a service and the recipient must be carefully managed. The technique of service process 'blueprinting' is introduced and its practical application discussed.

A *service encounter* is a period of time during which a consumer directly interacts with a service. Controlling and enhancing the service encounter is a critically important task. Since service encounters are the consumer's main source of information for conclusions regarding quality and service differentiation, no marketer can afford to leave the service encounter to chance.

Service encounters have several characteristics that bear on a manager's efforts to plan and control the quality of the interaction experienced by the customer. First, a service encounter can take a number of forms, but is always experienced through one or more of the five senses. A massage is encountered through touch, food through taste and smell, a symphony through hearing, and a book through sight. All service encounters may be defined and described by isolating the senses involved in the apprehension process.

Second, a service encounter may or may not expose the consumer to the total service. Moreover, the service encounter itself is only one part of any service. From the service encounter or encounters, the consumer deduces or attempts to deduce the nature of the unencountered parts.

Third, service encounters may or may not occur at point of purchase. Often, services are purchased first and encountered later. In insurance, for example, while there is a purchase encounter, during which the consumer attempts to predict the quality and functions of the service, actual service experience does not occur until later, or perhaps never.

Fourth, a service encounter may or may not involve other human beings. We often think of service encounters as person-to-person interactions. Many services, however, are not rendered personally. Bank services, for example, can be rendered by machine. Retailing can be rendered via catalogs and mail. Many services are rendered through facilitating physical devices (for example, television or credit cards). Some services (for example, some gasoline stations) are even self-rendered. Of all service delivery mechanisms, however, people are the most complex from a quality-control point of view.

The quality and consistency of the service encounter are clearly important to the success of a service business. Unfortunately, in many service firms 'chance encounters' are the norm, especially where human interactions are concerned. Many managers who are perfectly comfortable dealing with finances, marketing, or general management, feel relatively helpless about controlling service encounters to any similar degree.

But the truth is that service encounters are manageable and controllable. Some service firms have established high levels of quality and consistency in service encounters, which have given them a high degree of perceived differentiation from their competition. This is not an accident of nature, but the result of some sort of management process, however ill documented.

When superior service firms are examined, a consistent pattern to the managerial process is evidenced. One sees a pronounced emphasis on controllable details, continuous investments in training, a concern with the customer's view, and reward systems that place value on service quality. In poor service firms, however, one sees an internal rather than external orientation, a production or throughput emphasis, a view of the customer as a transaction generator, a lack of attention to details affecting the customer, and a low priority placed on 'soft' service quality values.

In poor service firms, there is sporadic talk about service quality, and there are sporadic campaigns to induce employees to be more customer oriented. By contrast, in good service firms, the entire service structure is set up to ensure that good quality is the natural outcome, not the exception. Good service firms take a much broader view of quality than poor service firms do. It is seen as an integral part of the business, not as a 'cheerleading' exercise to improve courtesy among employees.

In this chapter, we will be examining two general hypotheses about service encounters, and the managerial implications of various service-encounter characteristics. The two broad principles which are proposed as a context for dealing with the management of service encounters are these:

1 The quality of the service encounter is a function of the quality of the total service design.
2 The nature of a service encounter is determined by the design and control of sensory input.

The importance of the overall service design

To deal with the issue of the service encounter, one must first deal with the structure and composition of services themselves. A service is basically a process; it exists in time, but not in space. A service may come with tangible trappings, but does not confer physical ownership of such intangibles as 'experience' (movies), 'time' (consultants), or 'process' (dry

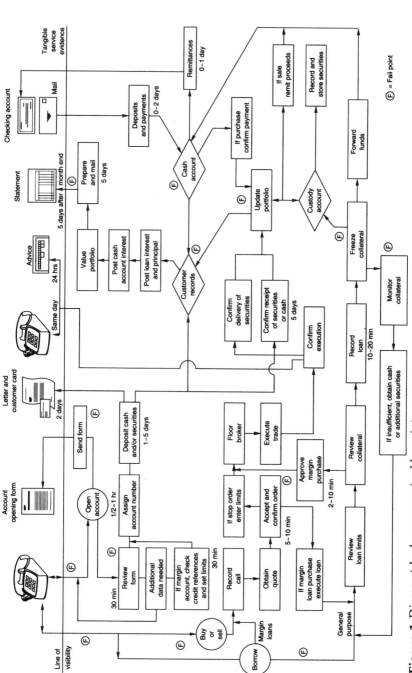

Figure 1 *Discount brokerage service blueprint*

cleaning). A service is rendered and it is experienced. A service can be observed, but not possessed (although the means for creating a service can be possessed, and so can the by-products or tangible evidence of a service). In short, services are very complex entities. And the service encounter is only the tip of the iceberg when it comes to creating and managing a service.

Figure 1 describes the fairly widespread financial service of discount brokerage. This service has been visualized through a technique called service blueprinting. As can be seen, little of the service is actually visible to the consumer. In fact, consumers have virtually no idea of the processes that underlie most services. And yet, these processes *are* the service. The tangible evidence seen by the consumer is only the visible tip.

As was stated previously, the quality of the service encounter is a function of the total service design. This section discusses how design flaws and inadequacies almost guarantee service-encounter problems.

Discount brokerage is not an especially complex service; medical or legal services are orders of magnitude more complex. Even so, the blueprint shown in Figure 1 has been considerably condensed and simplified relative to its complete form. Every step shown on the blueprint is actually a series of subprocesses. A step such as 'Prepare and Mail,' for example, requires many activities and participants, and includes over ten separate stages from operation of laser printers to stuffing and sealing envelopes. In this service blueprint, one can trace through all the components of the underlying design, and see how they culminate in various *encounter points* during which the customer interacts with the service or with the visible evidence of the service.

How design flaws affect encounters

In analyzing the functions of the service, it is easy to see how care or carelessness in the overall design can affect the service encounter. For example, if management is lax in setting standards or controlling carefully the 'Prepare and Mail' function, statements will go out late, in error, or damaged. Since the statement is one of the main encounter points for this service, a negative impression will result.

If the stock-purchase function is poorly planned and managed, accounts will not trade properly. Records will be wrong. Customers will see this through the evidence they receive. Again, the encounter will be negative.

If telephone lines are inadequate and customers cannot complete their calls, this will create negative encounters. The service representative who handles incoming phone calls will be dealing with already-disgruntled customers. Since the employee has no control over the problem, there will be little he or she can do to help guarantee to the customer that their next encounter will be better. Moreover, the constant negative input received by the employee will demoralize him or her, and lead eventually to worker indifference.

There is ample evidence of the fact that bad overall design leads to poor encounter quality. Salesclerks, whose jobs include inventory management, difficult paperwork, sales-floor maintenance, and many other operational tasks, cannot be expected to respond warmly and proactively to customers. The system does not allow them to do so, nor reward them for doing so. Speed, not interaction quality, is the prime performance criterion. Bank tellers operate under similar conditions. The design of the service, which dictates the design of the job, does not support positive encounter quality.

Every detail in the overall design is important and can affect the service encounter. I have seen corporate reputations undone by envelopes containing confidential customer data that popped open in transit due to inferior glue. I have seen computer programs changed to improve operations efficiency, with the result that statements became impossible for customers to understand.

Another example of poor design causing poor service encounters is the late-shipping practice of certain catalog companies. This is a function of an internal decision to maintain inventory at minimum levels by not stocking items unless sufficient orders are received by the firm. The design, although tolerable for one or two purchase experiences, produces a negative cumulative encounter over time. While the design might look good to the warehouse foreman, it has produced not only declining orders but poor reputations for firms that habitually ship late.

In assessing these occurrences and their causes, one of the worst errors management makes is to attribute service quality problems to its own workers. As W. Edwards Deming, the originator of Japanese quality-control techniques has stated, workers are never to blame for flaws in the design of a process. Poor process design is management's responsibility. Workers are generally trying to do their best; poor process design prevents them from doing so.

It is, of course, hypocritical for management to exhort its employees to be more service oriented, while condoning a design that works against service. This puts the employee in a double bind. If the employee functions the way management says it wishes, he or she will fail according to the real performance standards. Employees play by the real rules, not according to lofty platitudes. Their behavior is a direct function of the conditions and reward systems established by management.

The benefits of rational analysis

Clearly, management would have an easier time addressing the effects of design on service encounters if service blueprinting were a routine part of service management. With a little work, any manager can learn to break down and diagram a service. Even when a blueprint is only basic, it will begin to reveal the elements that affect service encounters and the areas that can cause encounter problems.

The first step in blueprinting is to diagram all the components of a service so that the service can be clearly and objectively seen. Many times services are imperfectly or incompletely understood even by those who manage them. Often, a service is assumed to be undocumentable simply because it has been allowed to become eccentric or so variable it cannot be captured descriptively. Without a concrete map showing all the components and functions of a service, one is left to manage in the dark.

The next important task in blueprinting is the identification of fail points – that is, the areas most likely to cause execution or consistency problems. In Figure 1 only the major fail points of the service are highlighted, but in analyzing a service, a manager may see many vulnerabilities that might affect the service encounter.

Fail points can be determined either by statistical monitoring or by hypothesis testing. Fail points can fall into several categories. Some may be internal and invisible to the customer. These may affect production efficiency or internal profitability, but will not affect customer perceptions, because they can be corrected internally. Other fail points are visible. For each fail point, a corrective or fail-safe procedure is imperative.

Setting execution standards is the third critical part of a blueprint. These represent the main production targets for the service. Execution standards not only define the costs of a service, they also define the performance criteria and tolerances for the completion of each service step. Execution standards can be set through work-measurement studies, through monitoring job performance, or through target setting. These standards provide management with a built-in warning system and a baseline standard for service quality that can be audited and adjusted over time.

Finally, the manager must identify all of the evidence that is available to the customer of the service. Each item that is visible to the customer represents an encounter point, during which interaction with the service will occur. Through this sort of rigorous analysis of the total service design, a manager can prevent many encounter problems before they happen.

Management of the service encounter

Obviously, the service encounter is only one part of a service. As stated previously, the quality of encounter is a function of the quality of the overall design, and the nature of the encounter is determined by the design and control of sensory input. This section examines the forms a service encounter can take, and how these can be managed.

There are three types of service encounters. First, there is the *remote encounter*, which involves no human interaction but rather takes place through indirect means. The second form of encounter – the *indirect personal encounter* – involves verbal interaction but no physical confrontation. The third type is the *direct personal encounter*, where the customer interacts directly with another human being. In a customer's experience with a service, he or she may engage in any or all of the three encounter forms, or combinations thereof.

The remote encounter

Many service encounters take place entirely through remote means. In financial services, for example, a customer can interact with a service entirely through the mail. Retailing through catalogs is a service rendered via remote encounter, as are credit-card services.

In financial services, the remote encounter via machine is becoming a preferred service mechanism for a significant part of the market. Many years and many millions of research dollars have gone into smoothing these encounters, to make the machines function in a user-friendly way.

When the consumer's entire encounter takes place outside a manager's purview, it would seem obvious that every piece of evidence should be carefully designed, operationally perfect, and made as functionally facilitative of a positive experience as possible. Yet how many of us have dealt with shoddy, inconsistent, hard-to-understand materials and procedures that are almost a barrier to the purchase decision and action?

Materials that are poorly printed, poorly written, or poorly designed, response mechanisms that do not work, forms that are impossible to fill out – these are all contributors to negative remote encounters. When many leaflets and brochures are stuffed into a mailed statement of account, the result is burdensome to the customer and negative in terms of the encounter. Conversely, well-planned materials and a carefully choreographed remote encounter can yield handsome business results.

The remote encounter is actually the easiest of all forms to control because it is based on some form of physical object, be it printed material or a computer terminal. These physical items can be made uniform; they can be tested, modified, and seen objectively. There is no good reason for poor quality in a remote encounter.

The materials on which a remote encounter is based communicate specific messages about a service. Engraved parchment says one thing about a service; cheap bond paper says something else. The materials used to execute the remote encounter must not contradict the positioning strategy for the service. Similarly, the content of the materials is critically important in reinforcing the type of encounter the marketer wishes to create. Literary copy makes a different impression from street slang. These issues seem trivial, yet are the essence of managing the remote service encounter.

The indirect personal encounter

The second form of encounter consists solely of verbal interaction. Although the customer deals with a human being, it is not a face-to-face interaction. A telephone company's operator services are representative of the indirect personal encounter. A more notorious example are the 'boiler rooms' that sell phony investments by telephone. In indirect personal encounters, quality control is more complex than for remote encounters because there is more potential variability in the encounter.

Nearly all service firms (and product firms) provide indirect personal encounters through their inquiry, customer-service, or error-resolution units. Often, the underlying design makes it very hard for these units to function well. Sometimes service units are not properly connected with other parts of the organization. Although the telephone representative does the job properly, he or she cannot guarantee follow-up. This causes negative customer reactions and often a backlash series of exchanges with the representatives, who are powerless to satisfy the customer and also powerless to protect themselves from the customer's ire. But even when the underlying design supports a telephone-based structure, management can improve encounter quality.

In the discount brokerage service diagramed in Figure 1, for example, telephone communication was identified as an important potential fail point. Apart from steps taken to ensure adequate mechanical operation, special care was taken to ensure as high a level of consistency and quality as possible in the actual verbal exchange. As a basic step, candidates for these positions were carefully screened for voice quality and for general articulateness. But many other steps were taken as well. Scripts for a variety of situations were written and rehearsed. Special situations were tested. Methods of handling unhappy customers were worked out (not methods of fobbing off customers, but genuine corrective measures). Execution was timed. Calls were recorded to ensure that customer instructions were accurately received.

Employee input was regularly solicited to determine whether any parts of the underlying design were hampering the verbal service encounter. Employee suggestions for improving the encounter were also solicited. The psychology of the employee's role received attention in both training and follow-up, to let employees know that management knew and appreciated the sometimes stressful conditions under which the service representatives operated.

The result of all these management steps was a smoothly running, uniformly consistent procedure which market research proved was highly satisfactory to customers. It cost no more to establish this function properly than it would have cost to hire people, put them to work without training, and then deal with the inevitable quality and image problems. These problems were prevented through front-end planning and careful attention to all the details of the indirect personal encounter.

The direct personal encounter

The direct personal encounter takes two forms: one in which a human *renders* a service; the other in which a person *represents* a service. When a person renders a service, he or she simultaneously represents it.

Professional services such as law and medicine fit this category, as well as most consultants. Barbers, tailors, repairmen, and teachers would also fit this category. However, a person may represent a service without rendering it; examples being a life-insurance agent, a travel agent, and a hotel reservation clerk.

The quality of the overall design has a material impact on the ability of both service representatives and service renderers to create satisfactory service encounters. If the underlying design is poor, it can prevent even the best-intentioned employee from fulfilling his or her function. But if we assume that the underlying design is supportive, service firms can go further to ensure positive, consistent personal encounters through the care and attention they give to sensory input received by the customer.

Many service firms understand the value of visual and verbal consistency in their human representatives. They achieve it by 'packaging' their employees in uniforms or corporate apparel. Airlines, fast-food chains, car-rental firms, even the U.S. Postal Service practice visual packaging. Doctors, too, have acquired a 'uniform' over time. It provides the client with a sense of security and familiarity. And it is no accident that lawyers are thought of in three-piece suits or that IBM, for many years, was a 'white shirt' company. For some services, a blazer or even a simple button is enough to establish visual consistency.

Because sight is the dominant sense, visual appearance is critical in the personal encounter. Customers have a difficult time trying to objectively determine service quality, particularly prior to purchase. Because they cannot a priori predict their experience, customers look to the physical evidence at hand for verification. The symbolic nature of apparel and appearance plays very heavily on both their willingness to try a service and their satisfaction with it.

The sense of hearing is the second critical type of sensory input received during a personal encounter. As in the indirect personal encounter, there is a world of difference between well- and poorly crafted verbal dialogues. Two service representatives, equally knowledgeable, can inspire totally different customer reactions and produce different sales results as a function solely of their verbal skills.

Because the verbal component of the personal encounter has so many subtleties, good service firms invest heavily in training, to ensure that the content of the exchange is at least somewhat consistent. Many go further, coaching their employees in presentation and sales skills. This is common in insurance and other direct selling businesses.

By paying close attention to what the customer sees and hears, the manager can control service-encounter quality to a much greater extent than most managers realize. Some service firms have outstanding reputations for the quality of personal encounter they render. Is this because they have discovered a whole new breed of human being? Encounter quality is not just a function of good manners. When we think of service firms such as Disney, American Express, American Airlines, H&R Block, or Tiffany's, what impresses us is that the service design supports positive encounters, instead of preventing them. Employees are considered one part of the total design, and are given the attention and care due to any function that has the power to make or break the firm.

Where many firms train only in mechanics and leave the encounter to chance, superior firms train for the encounter from philosophy through rewards, and higher esprit de corps exists in such firms. It is not a function of absolute profit or absolute pay, but rather a function of management's concern with service quality and consistency at every level.

Other forms of the encounter

Beyond the three main encounter types, there are a host of other sensory-input sources that can have a bearing on a customer's perception of a service. Stationery and signs are all visible clues to the consumer. Logos, corporate identification programs, and advertising are other forms of evidence. Though collateral evidence need not all look the same, it should provide consistent reinforcement to the market. There should be no qualitative or substantive contradictions between the sensory input the customer may get and the impression the firm is trying to create. Yet these critical forms of evidence are often assigned piecemeal, without much guidance, to creative firms whose output can literally change or redefine the service in the consumer's mind.

The environment in which the service is rendered is another powerful form of evidence. Why, then, is it left in the hands of interior designers? If the environment portrays stuffiness or intimidation, no amount of advertising will convince the market that a firm is warm and friendly. Plastic plants in a service environment convey something different about a service and the firm supplying it than living plants do; plastic plants may be perfectly consistent and appropriate for certain service environments. The point is that they should be chosen deliberately, not by default. Marketing must define the desired effects of the environment, the targeted consumer, and the overall service portrait that is being created.

Conclusion

In real estate, the three components of successful investing have always been *location*, location, location. In service-encounter management, the components for success might be stated as *details*, details, details. A service neither appears nor operates by magic. Consistently excellent encounter quality is a function of hard work. This is management's responsibility and obligation; a responsibility that cannot be delegated. With rational, thorough planning, service encounters can be everything management wishes them to be. When the service design is right and the customer input is actively controlled, positive encounters are the natural result.

Reproduced from Shostack, G.L. (1985). Planning the service encounter, in Czepiel, J.A., Solomon, M.R. and Surprenant, C.F. (eds), *The Service Encounter*, Lexington Books, pp. 243–253, by permission of Lynn Shostack.

A CONCEPTUAL MODEL OF SERVICE QUALITY AND ITS IMPLICATIONS FOR FUTURE RESEARCH
A. Parasuraman, Valerie A. Zeithaml and Leonard L. Berry

At the time this paper was written. A. Parasuraman and Valerie A. Zeithaml were Associate Professors of Marketing at Texas A&M University, USA. Leonard L. Berry is Foley's Federated Professor of Retailing and Marketing Studies also at Texas A&M University.

In this paper the authors argue that the attainment of quality in products and services has become a major concern for all organizations. While quality in tangible goods has been described and measured by marketers, quality in services is largely undefined and unresearched. The authors attempt to rectify this situation by reporting the insights obtained in an extensive exploratory investigation of quality in four service businesses and by developing a model of service quality.

'People want some wise and perceptive statement like, "Quality is ballet, not hockey?"' – Philip Crosby (1979)

Quality is an elusive and indistinct construct. Often mistaken for imprecise adjectives like 'goodness, or luxury, or shininess, or weight' (Crosby 1979), quality and its requirements are not easily articulated by consumers (Takeuchi and Quelch 1983). Explication and measurement of quality also present problems for researchers (Monroe and Krishnan 1983), who often bypass definitions and use unidimensional self-report measures to capture the concept (Jacoby, Olson, and Haddock 1973; McConnell 1968; Shapiro 1972).

While the substance and determinants of quality may be undefined, its importance to firms and consumers is unequivocal. Research has demonstrated the strategic benefits of quality in contributing to market share and return on investment (e.g., Anderson and Zeithaml 1984; Phillips, Chang, and Buzzell 1983) as well as in lowering manufacturing costs and improving productivity (Garvin 1983). The search for quality is arguably the most important consumer trend of the 1980s (Rabin 1983) as consumers are now demanding higher quality in products than ever before (Leonard and Sasser 1982, Takeuchi and Quelch 1983).

Few academic researchers have attempted to define and model quality because of the difficulties involved in delimiting and measuring the construct. Moreover, despite the phenomenal growth of the service sector, only a handful of these researchers have focused on service quality. We attempt to rectify this situation by (1) reviewing the small number of studies that have investigated service quality, (2) reporting the insights obtained in an extensive exploratory investigation of quality in four service businesses, (3) developing a model of service quality, and (4) offering propositions to stimulate future research about quality.

Existing knowledge about service quality

Efforts in defining and measuring quality have come largely from the goods sector. According to the prevailing Japanese philosophy, quality is 'zero defects – doing it right the first time.' Crosby (1979) defines quality as 'conformance to requirements'. Garvin (1983) measures quality by counting the incidence of 'internal' failures (those observed before a product leaves the factory) and 'external' failures (those incurred in the field after a unit has been installed).

Knowledge about goods quality, however, is insufficient to understand service quality. Three well-documented characteristics of services – *intangibility, heterogeneity,* and *inseparability* – must be acknowledged for a full understanding of service quality.

First, most services are intangible (Bateson 1977, Berry 1980, Lovelock 1981, Shostak 1977). Because they are performances rather than objects, precise manufacturing specifications concerning uniform quality can rarely be set. Most services cannot be counted, measured, inventoried, tested, and verified in advance of sale to assure quality. Because of intangibility, the firm may find it difficult to understand how consumers perceive their services and evaluate service quality (Zeithaml 1981).

Second, services, especially those with a high labor content, are heterogeneous: their performance often varies from producer to producer, from customer to customer, and from day to day. Consistency of behavior from service personnel (i.e., uniform quality) is difficult to assure (Booms and Bitner 1981) because what the firm intends to deliver may be entirely different from what the consumer receives.

Third, production and consumption of many services are inseparable (Carmen and Langeard 1980, Grönroos 1978, Regan 1963, Upah 1980). As a consequence, quality in services is not engineered at the manufacturing plant, then delivered intact to the consumer. In labor intensive services, for example, quality occurs during service delivery, usually in an interaction between the client and the contact person from the service firm (Lehtinen and Lehtinen 1982). The service firm may also have less managerial control over quality in services where consumer participation is intense (e.g., haircuts, doctor's visits) because the client affects the process. In these situations, the consumer's input (description of how the haircut should look, description of symptoms) becomes critical to the quality of service performance.

Service quality has been discussed in only a handful of writings (Grönroos 1982; Lehtinen and Lehtinen 1982; Lewis and Booms 1983; Sasser, Olsen, and Wyckoff 1978). Examination of these writings and other literature on services suggests three underlying themes:

● Service quality is more difficult for the consumer to evaluate than goods quality.
● Service quality perceptions result from a comparison of consumer expectations with actual service performance.

● Quality evaluations are not made solely on the outcome of a service; they also involve evaluations of the *process* of service delivery.

Service quality more difficult to evaluate

When purchasing goods, the consumer employs many tangible cues to judge quality: style, hardness, color, label, feel, package, fit. When purchasing services, fewer tangible cues exist. In most cases, tangible evidence is limited to the service provider's physical facilities, equipment, and personnel.

In the absence of tangible evidence on which to evaluate quality, consumers must depend on other cues. The nature of these other cues has not been investigated by researchers, although some authors have suggested that price becomes a pivotal quality indicator in situations where other information is not available (McConnell 1968, Olander 1970, Zeithaml 1981). Because of service intangibility, a firm may find it more difficult to understand how consumers perceive services and service quality. 'When a service provider knows how [the service] will be evaluated by the consumer, we will be able to suggest how to influence these evaluations in a desired direction' (Grönroos 1982).

Quality is a comparison between expectations and performance

Researchers and managers of service firms concur that service quality involves a comparison of expectations with performance:

> Service quality is a measure of how well the service level delivered matches customer expectations. Delivering quality service means conforming to customer expectations on a consistent basis. (Lewis and Booms 1983)

In line with this thinking, Grönroos (1982) developed a model in which he contends that consumers compare the service they expect with perceptions of the service they receive in evaluating service quality.

Smith and Houston (1982) claimed that satisfaction with services is related to confirmation or disconfirmation of expectations. They based their research on the disconfirmation paradigm, which maintains that satisfaction is related to the size and direction of the disconfirmation experience where disconfirmation is related to the person's initial expectations (Churchill and Suprenaut 1982).

Quality evaluations involve outcomes and processes

Sasser, Olsen, and Wyckoff (1978) discussed three different dimensions of service performance: levels of material, facilities, and personnel. Implied in this trichotomy is the notion that service quality involves more than outcome; it also includes the manner in which the service is delivered. This notion surfaces in other research on service quality as well.

Grönroos, for example, postulated that two types of service quality exist: *technical quality*, which involves what the customer is actually receiving from the service, and *functional quality*, which involves the manner in which the service is delivered (Grönroos 1982).

Lehtinen and Lehtinen's (1982) basic premise is that service quality is produced in the interaction between a customer and elements in the service organization. They use three quality dimensions: *physical quality*, which includes the physical aspects of the service (e.g., equipment or building); *corporate quality*, which involves the company's image or profile; and *interactive quality*, which derives from the interaction between contact personnel and customers as well as between some customers and other customers. They further differentiate between the quality associated with the process of service delivery and the quality associated with the outcome of the service.

Exploratory investigation

Because the literature on service quality is not yet rich enough to provide a sound conceptual foundation for investigating service quality, an exploratory qualitative study was undertaken to investigate the concept of service quality. Specifically, focus group interviews with consumers and in-depth interviews with executives were conducted to develop a conceptual model of service quality. The approach used is consistent with procedures recommended for marketing theory development by several scholars (Deshpande 1983; Peter and Olson 1983; Zaltman, LeMasters, and Heffring 1982).

In-depth interviews of executives in four nationally recognized service firms and a set of focus group interviews of consumers were conducted to gain insights about the following questions:

- What do managers of service firms perceive to be the key attributes of service quality? What problems and tasks are involved in providing high quality service?
- What do consumers perceive to be the key attributes of quality in services?
- Do discrepancies exist between the perceptions of consumers and service marketers?
- Can consumer and marketer perceptions be combined in a general model that explains service quality from the consumer's standpoint?

Service categories investigated

Four service categories were chosen for investigation: retail banking, credit card, securities brokerage, and product repair and maintenance. While this set of service businesses is not exhaustive, it represents a cross-section of industries which vary along key dimensions used to categorize services (Lovelock 1980, 1983). For example, retail banking and securities brokerage services are more 'high contact services' than the other two types. The nature and results of the service act are more tangible for product repair and maintenance services than for the other three types. In terms of service delivery, discrete transactions characterize credit card services and product repair and maintenance services to a greater extent than the other two types of services.

Executive interviews

A nationally recognized company from each of the four service businesses participated in the study. In-depth personal interviews composed of open-ended questions were conducted with three or four executives in each firm. The executives were selected from marketing, operations, senior management, and customer relations because each of these areas could have an impact on quality in service firms. The respondents held titles such as president, senior vice president, director of customer relations, and manager of consumer market research. Fourteen executives were interviewed about a broad range of service quality issues (e.g., what they perceived to be service quality from the consumer's perspective, what steps they took to control or improve service quality, and what problems they faced in delivering high quality services).

Focus group interviews

A total of 12 focus group interviews was conducted, three for each of the four selected services. Eight of the focus groups were held in a metropolitan area in the southwest. The remaining four were conducted in the vicinity of the participating companies' headquarters and were therefore spread across the country: one on the West Coast, one in the Midwest, and two in the East.

The focus groups were formed in accordance with guidelines tradition-ally followed in the marketing research field (Bellenger, Berhardt, and Goldstucker 1976). Respondents were screened to ensure that they were current or recent users of the service in question. To maintain homoge-neity and assure maximum participation, respondents were assigned to groups based on age and sex. Six of the twelve groups included only males and six included only females. At least one male group and one female group were interviewed for each of the four services. Consistency in age was maintained within groups; however, age diversity across groups for each service category was established to ascertain the viewpoints of a broad cross section of consumers.

Identities of participating firms were not revealed to focus group participants. Discussion about quality of a given service centered on consumer experiences and perceptions relating to that service *in general*, as opposed to the specific service of the participating firm in that service category. Questions asked by the moderator covered topics such as instances of and reasons for satisfaction and dissatisfaction with the service; descriptions of an ideal service (e.g., ideal bank or ideal credit card); the meaning of service quality; factors important in evaluating service quality; performance expectations concerning the service; and the role of price in service quality.

Insights from exploratory investigation

Executive interviews

Remarkably consistent patterns emerged from the four sets of executive interviews. While some perceptions about service quality were specific to the industries selected, commonalities among the industries prevailed. The commonalities are encouraging for they suggest that a general model of service quality can be developed.

Perhaps the most important insight obtained from analyzing the executive responses is the following:

A set of key discrepancies or gaps exists regarding executive perceptions of service quality and the tasks associated with service delivery to consumers. These gaps can be major hurdles in attempting to deliver a service which consumers would perceive as being of high quality.

The gaps revealed by the executive interviews are shown in the lower portion (i.e., the MARKETER side) of Figure 1. This figure summarizes the key insights gained (through the focus group as well as executive interviews) about the concept of service quality and factors affecting it. The remainder of this section discusses the gaps on the service marketer's side (GAP1, GAP2, GAP3, and GAP4) and presents propositions implied by those gaps. The consumer's side of the service quality model in Figure 1 is discussed in the next section.

Consumer expectation – management perception gap (GAP1)

Many of the executive perceptions about what consumers expect in a quality service were congruent with the consumer expectations revealed in the focus groups. However, discrepancies between executive perceptions and consumer expectations existed, as illustrated by the following examples:

- Privacy or confidentiality during transactions emerged as a pivotal quality attribute in every banking and securities brokerage focus group. Rarely was this consideration mentioned in the executive interviews.
- The physical and security features of credit cards (e.g., the likelihood that unauthorized people could use the cards) generated substantial discussion in the focus group interviews but did not emerge as critical in the executive interviews.

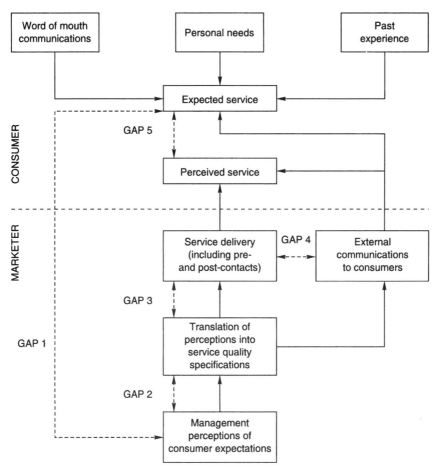

Figure 1 *Service quality model*

● The product repair and maintenance focus groups indicated that a large repair service firm was unlikely to be viewed as a high quality firm. Small independent repair firms were consistently associated with high quality. In contrast, most executive comments indicated that a firm's size would signal strength in a quality context.

In essence, service firm executives may not always understand what features connote high quality to consumers in advance, what features a service must have in order to meet consumer needs, and what levels of performance on those features are needed to deliver high quality service. This insight is consistent with previous research in services, which suggests that service marketers may not always understand what consumers expect in a service (Langeard *et al.* 1981, Parasuraman and

Zeithaml 1982). This lack of understanding may affect quality perceptions of consumers:

Proposition 1: The gap between consumer expectations and management perceptions of those expectations will have an impact on the consumer's evaluation of service quality.

Management perception – service quality specification gap (GAP2)

A recurring theme in the executive interviews in all four service firms was the difficulty experienced in attempting to match or exceed consumer expectations. Executives cited constraints which prevent them from delivering what the consumer expects. As an example, executives in the repair service firm were fully aware that consumers view quick response to appliance breakdowns as a vital ingredient of high quality service. However, they find it difficult to establish specifications to deliver quick response consistently because of a lack of trained service personnel and wide fluctuations in demand. As one executive observed, peak demand for repairing air conditioners and lawnmowers occurs during the summer months, precisely when most service personnel want to go on vacation. In this and numerous other situations, knowledge of consumer expectations exists but the perceived means to deliver to expectations apparently do not.

Apart from resource and market constraints, another reason for the gap between expectations and the actual set of specifications established for a service is the absence of total management commitment to service quality. Although the executive interviews indicated a genuine concern for quality on the part of managers interviewed, this concern may not be generalizable to all service firms. In discussing product quality, Garvin (1983) stated: '... the seriousness that management attached to quality problems [varies]. It's one thing to say you believe in defect-free products, but quite another to take time from a busy schedule to act on that belief and stay informed' (p. 68). Garvin's observations are likely to apply to service businesses as well.

In short, a variety of factors – resource constraints, market conditions, and/or management indifference – may result in a discrepancy between management perceptions of consumer expectations and the actual specifications established for a service. This discrepancy is predicted to affect quality perceptions of consumers:

Proposition 2: The gap between management perceptions of consumer expectations and the firm's service quality specifications will affect service quality from the consumer's viewpoint.

Service quality specifications – service delivery gap (GAP3)

Even when guidelines exist for performing services well and treating consumers correctly, high quality service performance may not be a certainty. Executives recognize that a service firm's employees exert a strong influence on the service quality perceived by consumers and that employee performance cannot always be standardized. When asked what causes service quality problems, executives consistently mentioned the pivotal role of contact personnel. In the repair and maintenance firm, for example, one executive's immediate response to the source of service quality problems was, 'Everything involves a person – a repair person. It's so hard to maintain standardized quality.'

Each of the four firms had formal standards or specifications for maintaining service quality (e.g., answer at least 90% of phone calls from consumers within 10 seconds; keep error rates in statement below 1%). However, each firm reported difficulty in adhering to these standards because of variability in employee performance. This problem leads to a third proposition:

Proposition 3: The gap between service quality specifications and actual service delivery will affect service quality from the consumer's standpoint.

Service delivery – external communications gap (GAP4)

Media advertising and other communications by a firm can affect consumer expectations. If expectations play a major role in consumer perceptions of service quality (as the services literature contends), the firm must be certain not to promise more in communications than it can deliver in reality. Promising more than can be delivered will raise initial expectations but lower perceptions of quality when the promises are not fulfilled.

The executive interviews suggest another perhaps more intriguing way in which external communications could influence service quality perceptions by consumers. This occurs when companies neglect to inform consumers of special efforts to assure quality that are not visible to consumers. Comments of several executives implied that consumers are not always aware of everything done behind the scenes to serve them well.

For instance, a securities brokerage executive mentioned a '48-hour rule' prohibiting employees from buying or selling securities for their personal accounts for the first 48 hours after information is supplied by the firm. The firm did not communicate this information to its customers, perhaps contributing to a perception that 'all the good deals are probably made by the brokers for themselves' (a perception which surfaced in the securities brokerage focus groups). One bank executive indicated that consumers were unaware of the bank's behind the counter, on-line teller terminals which would 'translate into visible effects on customer service'. Making consumers aware of not readily apparent service related standards such as these could improve service quality perceptions. Consumers who are aware that a firm is taking concrete steps to serve their best interests are likely *to perceive* a delivered service in a more favorable way.

In short, external communications can affect not only consumer expectations about a service but also consumer *perceptions* of the delivered service. Alternatively, discrepancies between service delivery and external communications – in the form of exaggerated promises and / or the absence of information about service delivery aspects intended to serve consumers well – can affect consumer perceptions of service quality.

Proposition 4: The gap between actual service delivery and external communications about the service will affect service quality from a consumer's standpoint.

Focus group interviews

As was true of the executive interviews, the responses of focus group participants about service quality were remarkably consistent across groups and across service businesses. While some service-specific differences were revealed, common themes emerged – themes which offer valuable insights about service quality perceptions of consumers.

Expected service – perceived service gap (GAP5)

The focus groups unambiguously supported the notion that the key to ensuring good service quality is meeting or exceeding what consumers expect from the service. One female participant described a situation when a repairman not only fixed her broken appliance but also explained what had gone wrong and how she could fix it herself if a similar problem occurred in the future. She rated the quality of this service excellent because it exceeded her expectations. A male respondent in a banking services focus group described the frustration he felt when his bank would not cash his payroll check from a nationally known employer because it was postdated by one day. When someone else in the group pointed out legal constraints preventing the bank from cashing his check, he responded, 'Well, nobody *in the bank* explained that to me!' Not receiving an explanation in the bank, this respondent perceived that the bank was *unwilling* rather than *unable* to cash the check. This in turn resulted in a perception of poor service quality.

Similar experiences, both positive and negative, were described by consumers in every focus group. It appears that judgments of high and low service quality depend on how consumers perceive the actual service performance in the context of what they expected.

Proposition 5: The quality that a consumer perceives in a service is a function of the magnitude and direction of the gap between expected service and perceived service.

A service quality model

Insights obtained from the executive interviews and the focus groups form the basis of a model summarizing the nature and determinants of service quality as perceived by consumers. The foundation of this model is the set of gaps discussed earlier and shown in Figure 1. Service quality as perceived by a consumer depends on the size and direction of GAP5 which, in turn, depends on the nature of the gaps associated with the design, marketing, and delivery of services:

Proposition 6: GAP5 = f(GAP1, GAP2, GAP3, GAP4)

It is important to note that the gaps on the marketer side of the equation can be favorable or unfavorable from a service quality perspective. That is, the magnitude *and direction* of each gap will have an impact on service quality. For instance, GAP3 will be favorable when actual service delivery exceeds specifications; it will be unfavorable when service specifications are not met. While proposition 6 suggests a relationship between service quality as perceived by consumers and the gaps occurring on the marketer's side, the functional form of the relationship needs to be investigated. This point is discussed further in the last section dealing with future research directions.

The perceived service quality component

The focus groups revealed that, regardless of the type of service, consumers used basically similar criteria in evaluating service quality. These criteria seem to fall into 10 key categories which are labeled 'service quality determinants' and described in Table 1. For each determinant, Table 1 provides examples of service specific criteria that emerged in the focus groups. Table 1 is not meant to suggest that the 10 determinants are non-overlapping. Because the research was exploratory, measurement of possible overlap across the 10 criteria (as well as determination of whether some can be combined) must await future empirical investigation.

The consumer's view of service quality is shown in the upper part of Figure 1 and further elaborated in Figure 2. Figure 2 indicates that perceived service quality is the result of the consumer's comparison of expected service with perceived service. It is quite possible that the relative importance of the 10 determinants in molding consumer expectations (prior to service delivery) may differ from their relative importance *vis-à-vis* consumer perceptions of the delivered service. However, the general comparison of expectations with perceptions was suggested in past research on service quality (Grönroos 1982, Lehtinen and Lehtinen 1982) and supported in the focus group interviews with consumers. The comparison of expected and perceived service is not unlike that performed by consumers when evaluating goods. What differs with services is the *nature* of the characteristics upon which they are evaluated.

Table 1 *Determinants of service quality*

RELIABILITY involves consistency of performance and dependability.
  It means that the firm performs the service right the first time.
  It also means that the firm honors its promises. Specifically, it involves:
  – accuracy in billing;
  – keeping records correctly;
  – performing the service at the designated time.
RESPONSIVENESS concerns the willingness or readiness of employees to provide service. It
involves timeliness of service:
  – mailing a transaction slip immediately;
  – calling the customer back quickly;
  – giving prompt service (e.g., setting up appointments quickly).
COMPETENCE means possession of the required skills and knowledge to perform the
service. It involves:
  – knowledge and skill of the contact personnel;
  – knowledge and skill of operational support personnel;
  – research capability of the organization, e.g., securities brokerage firm.
ACCESS involves approachability and ease of contact. It means:
  – the service is easily accessible by telephone (lines are not busy and they don't put
    you on hold);
  – waiting time to receive service (e.g., at a bank) is not extensive;
  – convenient hours of operation;
  – convenient location of service facility.
COURTESY involves politeness, respect, consideration, and friendliness of contact personnel
(including receptionists, telephone operators, etc.). It includes:
  – consideration for the consumer's property (e.g., no muddy shoes on the carpet);
  – clean and neat appearance of public contact personnel.
COMMUNICATION means keeping customers informed in language they can understand
and listening to them. It may mean that the company has to adjust its language for
different consumers – increasing the level of sophistication with a well-educated
customer and speaking simply and plainly with a novice. It involves:
  – explaining the service itself;
  – explaining how much the service will cost;
  – explaining the trade-offs between service and cost;
  – assuring the consumer that a problem will be handled.
CREDIBILITY involves trustworthiness, believability, honesty. It involves having the
customer's best interests at heart. Contributing to credibility are:
  – company name;
  – company reputation;
  – personal characteristics of the contact personnel;
  – the degree of hard sell involved in interactions with the customer.
SECURITY is the freedom from danger, risk, or doubt. It involves:
  – physical safety (Will I get mugged at the automatic teller machine?);
  – financial security (Does the company know where my stock certificate is?);
  – confidentiality (Are my dealings with the company private?).
UNDERSTANDING/KNOWING THE CUSTOMER involves making the effort to understand the
customer's needs. It involves:
  – learning the customer's specific requirements;
  – providing individualized attention;
  – recognizing the regular customer.
TANGIBLES include the physical evidence of the service:
  – physical facilities;
  – appearance of personnel;
  – tools or equipment used to provide the service;
  – physical representations of the service, such as a plastic credit card or a bank
    statement;
  – other customers in the service facility.

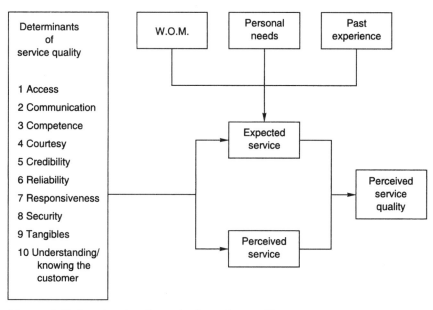

Figure 2 *Determinants of perceived service quality*

One framework for isolating differences in evaluation of quality for goods and services is the classification of properties of goods proposed by Nelson (1974) and Darby and Karni (1973). Nelson distinguished between two categories of properties of consumer goods: *search properties*, attributes which a consumer can determine prior to purchasing a product, and *experience properties*, attributes which can only be discerned after purchase or during consumption. Search properties include attributes such as color, style, price, fit, feel, hardness, and smell, while experience properties include characteristics such as taste, wearability, and dependability.

Darby and Karni (1973) added to Nelson's two-way classification system a third category, *credence properties* – characteristics which the consumer may find impossible to evaluate even after purchase and consumption. Examples of offerings high in credence properties include appendectomies and brake relinings on automobiles. Few consumers possess medical or mechanical skills sufficient to evaluate whether these services are necessary or are performed properly, even after they have been prescribed and produced by the seller.

Consumers in the focus groups mentioned search, experience, and credence properties when asked to describe and define service quality. These aspects of service quality can be categorized into the 10 service quality determinants shown in Table 1 and can be arrayed along a continuum ranging from *easy to evaluate* to *difficult to evaluate*.

In general, offerings high in search properties are easiest to evaluate, those high in experience properties more difficult to evaluate, and those high in credence properties hardest to evaluate. Most services contain few search properties and are high in experience and credence properties, making their quality more difficult to evaluate than quality of goods (Zeithaml 1981).

Only two of the ten determinants – tangibles and credibility – can be known in advance of purchase, thereby making the number of search properties few. Most of the dimensions of service quality mentioned by the focus group participants were experience properties: access, courtesy, reliability, responsiveness, understanding/knowing the customer, and communication. Each of these determinants can only be known as the customer is purchasing or consuming the service. While customers may possess some information based on their experience or on other customers' evaluations, they are likely to reevaluate these determinants each time a purchase is made because of the heterogeneity of services.

Two of the determinants that surfaced in the focus group interviews probably fall into the category of credence properties, those which consumers cannot evaluate even after purchase and consumption. These include competence (the possession of the required skills and knowledge to perform the service) and security (freedom from danger, risk, or doubt). Consumers are probably never certain of these attributes, even after consumption of the service.

Because few search properties exist with services and because credence properties are too difficult to evaluate, the following is proposed:

Proposition 7: Consumers typically rely on experience properties when evaluating service quality.

Based on insights from the present study, perceived service quality is further posited to exist along a continuum ranging from ideal quality to totally unacceptable quality, with some point along the continuum representing satisfactory quality. The position of a consumer's perception of service quality on the continuum depends on the nature of the discrepancy between the expected service (ES) and perceived service (PS):

Proposition 8: (a) When ES > PS, perceived quality is less than satisfactory and will tend toward totally unacceptable quality, with increased discrepancy between ES and PS; (b) when ES = PS, perceived quality is satisfactory; (c) when ES < PS, perceived quality is more than satisfactory and will tend toward ideal quality, with increased discrepancy between ES and PS.

Directions for future research

The proposed service quality model (Figure 1) provides a conceptual framework in an area where little prior research has been done. It is based on an interpretation of qualitative data generated through a number of in-depth executive interviews and consumer focus groups – an approach consistent with procedures recommended for marketing theory develop-ment. The conceptual model and the propositions emerging from it imply a rich agenda for further research.

First, there is a need and an opportunity to develop a standard instrument to measure consumers' service quality perceptions. The authors' exploratory research revealed 10 evaluative dimensions or criteria which transcend a variety of services (Table 1). Research is now needed to generate items or statements to flesh out the 10 dimensions, to devise appropriate rating scales to measure consumers' perceptions with respect to each statement, and to condense the set of statements to produce a reliable and comprehensive but concise instrument. Further, the statements generated should be such that with appropriate changes in wording, the same instrument can be used to measure perceived quality for a variety of services.

Second, the main thesis of the service quality model is that consumers' quality perceptions are influenced by a series of distinct gaps occurring on the marketers' side. A key challenge for researchers is to devise methods to measure these gaps accurately. Reliable and valid measures of these gaps will be necessary for empirically testing the propositions implied by the model.

Third, research is needed to examine the *nature* of the association between service quality as perceived by consumers and its determinants (GAPS 1–4). Specifically, are one or more of these gaps more critical than the others in affecting quality? Can creating one 'favorable' gap – e.g., making GAP4 favorable by employing effective external communications to create realistic consumer expectations and to enhance consumer perceptions – offset service quality problems stemming from other gaps? Are there differences across service industries regarding the relative seriousness of service quality problems and their impact on quality as perceived by consumers? In addition to offering valuable managerial insights, answers to questions like these may suggest refinements to the proposed model.

Fourth, the usefulness of segmenting consumers on the basis of their service quality expectations is worth exploring. Although the focus groups consistently revealed similar criteria for judging service quality, the group participants differed on the *relative importance* of those criteria to them, and their *expectations* along the various quality dimensions. Empirical research aimed at determining whether distinct, identifiable service quality segments exist will be valuable from a service marketer's viewpoint. In this regard, it will be useful to build into the service quality measurement instrument certain statements for ascertaining whether, and in what ways, consumer expectations differ.

Fifth, as shown by Figure 1, expected service – a critical component of perceived service quality – in addition to being influenced by a marketer's communications, is shaped by word-of-mouth communica-tions, personal needs, and past experience. Research focusing on the relative impact of these factors on consumers' service expectations, within as well as across service categories, will have useful managerial implications.

Summary

The exploratory research (focus group and in-depth executive interviews) reported in this article offers several insights and propositions concerning consumers' perceptions of service quality. Specifically, the research revealed 10 dimensions that consumers use in forming expectations about and perceptions of services, dimensions that transcend different types of services. The research also pinpointed four key discrepancies or gaps on the service provider's side that are likely to affect service quality as perceived by consumers. The major insights gained through the research suggest a conceptual service quality model that will hopefully spawn both academic and practitioner interest in service quality and serve as a framework for further empirical research in this important area.

References

Anderson, Carl and Carl P. Zeithaml (1984). 'Stage of the Product Life Cycle, Business Strategy, and Business Performance,' *Academy of Management Journal*, 27 (March), 5–24.

Bateson. John E.G. (1977). 'Do We Need Service Marketing?' in *Marketing Consumer Services: New Insights*. Cambridge, MA: Marketing Science Institute, Report #77–115.

Bellenger, Danny N., Kenneth L. Berhardt, and Jac L. Goldstucker (1976). *Qualitative Research in Marketing*. Chicago: American Marketing.

Berry, Leonard L. (1980), 'Services Marketing Is Different,' *Business*, 30 (May-June), 24–28.

Booms, Bernard H. and Mary J. Bitner (1981), 'Marketing Strategies and Organization Structures for Services Firms,' in *Marketing of Services*, J. Donnelly and W. George, eds., Chicago: American Marketing, 47–51.

Carmen, James M. and Eric Langeard (1980), 'Growth Strategies of Service Firms,' *Strategic Management Journal*, 1 (January-March), 7–22.

Churchill, G.A., Jr., and C. Suprenaut (1982), 'An Investigation into the Determinants of Customer Satisfaction,' *Journal of Marketing Research*, 19 (November), 491–504.

Crosby, Philip B. (1979), *Quality Is Free: The Art of Making Quality Certain*, New York: New American Library.

Darby, M.R. and E. Karni (1973), 'Free Competition and the Optimal Amount of Fraud,' *Journal of Law and Economics*, 16 (April), 67–86.

Deshpande, Rohit (1983), '"Paradigms Lost": On Theory and Method in Research in Marketing,' *Journal of Marketing*, 47 (Fall), 101–110.

Garvin, David A. (1983), 'Quality on the Line,' *Harvard Business Review*, 61 (September-October), 65–73.

Grönroos, Christian (1978), 'A Service-Oriented Approach to Marketing of Services,' *European Journal of Marketing*, 12 (no. 8), 588–601.

—— (1982), *Strategic Management and Marketing in the Service Sector*, Helsingfors: Swedish School of Economics and Business Administration.

Jacoby, Jacob, Jerry C. Olson, and Rafael A. Haddock (1973), 'Price, Brand Name and Product Composition Characteristics as Determinants of Perceived Quality,' *Journal of Applied Psychology*, 55 (no. 6), 570–579.

Langeard, Eric, John E.G. Bateson, Christopher H. Lovelock, and Pierre Eiglier (1981), *Service Marketing: New Insights from Consumers and Managers*, Cambridge, MA: Marketing Science Institute.

Lehtinen, Uolevi and Jarmo R. Lehtinen (1982), 'Service Quality: A Study of Quality Dimensions,' unpublished working paper, Helsinki: Service Management Institute, Finland OY.

Leonard, Frank S. and W. Earl Sasser (1982), 'The Incline of Quality,' *Harvard Business Review*, 60 (September-October), 163–171.

Lewis, Robert C. and Bernard H. Booms (1983), 'The Marketing Aspects of Service Quality,' in *Emerging Perspectives on Services Marketing*, L. Berry, G. Shostack, and G. Upah, eds., Chicago: American Marketing, 99–107.

Lovelock, Christopher H. (1980), 'Towards a Classification of Services,' in *Theoretical Developments in Marketing*, C. Lamb and P. Dunne, eds., Chicago: American Marketing, 72–76.

—— (1981), 'Why Marketing Management Needs to be Different for Services,' in *Marketing of Services*, J. Donnelly and W. George, eds., Chicago: American Marketing, 5–9.

—— (1983), 'Classifying Services to Gain Strategic Marketing Insights,' *Journal of Marketing*, 47 (Summer), 9–20.

McConnell, J.D. (1968), 'Effect of Pricing on Perception of Product Quality,' *Journal of Applied Psychology*, 52 (August), 300–303.

Monroe, Kent B. and R. Krishnan (1983). 'The Effect of Price on Subjective Product Evaluations,' Blacksburg: Virginia Polytechnic Institute, working paper.

Nelson, P. (1974), 'Advertising as Information,' *Journal of Political Economy*, 81 (July/August), 729–754.

Olander, F. (1970), 'The Influence of Price on the Consumer's Evaluation of Products,' in *Pricing Strategy*, B. Taylor and G. Wills, eds., Princeton, NJ: Brandon/Systems Press.

Parasuraman, A. and Valarie A. Zeithaml (1982), 'Differential Perceptions of Suppliers and Clients of Industrial Services,' in *Emerging Perspectives on Services Marketing*, L. Berry, G. Shostack, and G. Upah, eds., Chicago: American Marketing, 35–39.

Peter, J. Paul and Jerry C. Olson (1983), 'Is Science Marketing?,' *Journal of Marketing*, 47 (Fall), 111–125.

Phillips, Lynn W., Dae R. Chang, and Robert D. Buzzell (1983), 'Product Quality, Cost Position, and Business Performance: A Test of Some Key Hypotheses,' *Journal of Marketing*, 47 (Spring), 26–43.

Rabin, Joseph H. (1983), 'Accent Is on Quality in Consumer Services This Decade,' *Marketing News*, 17 (March 4), 12.

Regan, William J. (1963), 'The Service Revolution,' *Journal of Marketing*, 27 (July), 57–62.

Sasser, W. Earl, Jr., R. Paul Olsen, and D. Daryl Wyckoff (1978), *Management of Service Operations: Text and Cases*, Boston: Allyn & Bacon.

Shapiro, Bensen (1972), 'The Price of Consumer Goods: Theory and Practice,' Cambridge, MA: Marketing Science Institute, working paper.

Shostack, G. Lynn (1977), 'Breaking Free from Product Marketing,' *Journal of Marketing*, 41 (April), 73–80.

Smith, Ruth A. and Michael J. Houston (1982), 'Script-Based Evaluations of Satisfaction with Services,' in *Emerging Perspectives on Services Marketing*, L. Berry, G. Shostack, and G. Upah, eds., Chicago: American Marketing, 59–62.

Takeuchi, Hirotaka and John A. Quelch (1983), 'Quality Is More Than Making a Good Product,' *Harvard Business Review*, 61 (July-August), 139–145.

Upah, Gregory D. (1980), 'Mass Marketing in Service Retailing: A Review and Synthesis of Major Methods,' *Journal of Retailing*, 56 (Fall), 59–76.

Zaltman, Gerald, Karen LeMasters, and Michael Heffring (1982), *Theory Construction in Marketing: Some Thought on Thinking*, New York: Wiley.

Zeithaml, Valarie A. (1981), 'How Consumer Evaluation Processes Differ between Goods and Services,' in *Marketing of Services* J. Donnelly and W. George, eds., Chicago: American Marketing, 186–190.

SEGMENTATION OF MARKETS BASED ON CUSTOMER SERVICE

Arun Sharma and Douglas M. Lambert

Arun Sharma is Associate Professor of Marketing at the University of Miami, and Douglas M. Lambert is Professor of Marketing and Logistics at the University of North Florida, USA.

Market segmentation has long been recognized by marketing theorists and practitioners as a powerful tool for categorizing customers and for tailoring marketing strategies. However, in the past it has typically relied upon conventional criteria for characterizing these groupings e.g. demographic, or socio-economic or industrial classifications. More recently marketers have come to recognize the opportunities that service preferences offer for creative segmentation. In this article the authors suggest a practical means for segmenting markets by customer service.

Customer service can be viewed as the output of the logistics system and the place component of the marketing mix.[1] Also, customer service may represent the best opportunity for a firm to gain a sustainable competitive advantage in the marketplace.[2,3] Webster[4] has suggested that, to prosper, organisations need to move from a production orientation to a marketing orientation. Customer service can be the most cost-effective component of the marketing mix on which management can build a differential advantage for firms.

Generally, customer service has not received sufficient attention from marketers. One of the areas where additional research is needed is the segmentation of markets based on customer service requirements. There are clear benefits from segmenting markets, the major advantage being the ability to target the marketing mix for a specific group of customers. This article suggests that customers have differing customer service needs which can be used to segment markets and target marketing strategy.

The objectives of this research are threefold:

1 To review the conceptual issues associated with segmenting industrial markets on the basis of customer service needs;
2 To develop a method of classifying a market into segments with different customer service needs when *a priori* segments do not exist;
3 To report the findings of empirical research in a segment of a high technology industry.

While the role of customer service in mature industries[5] has been recognised, emerging or high technology industries have not been studied. The empirical study identifies segments of an emerging or high technology industry which have differing customer service requirements.

It further describes the segments based upon demographic data and logistics performance information.

The article is divided into five sections: first, discussion of the importance of customer service; second, a review of the issues in industrial market segmentation and the appropriateness of customer service as a segmentation base. The third section introduces the research and provides a brief overview of the methodology, followed by a report on the segmentation of a high technology market. The final section presents the implications for managers and ideas for further research.

Importance of customer service

Customer service is important because it can be used to differentiate a firm's products, keep customers loyal and increase sales and profits.[6] Bennion[7] asked buyers in the forging industry to identify the importance of various factors in the evaluation of a supplier. Customer service-oriented factors accounted for 40 per cent of the variance. It is expected that emerging industries will also consider customer service issues to be important. Given the importance of customer service in the development of a successful marketing strategy, it is somewhat surprising that only a handful of studies have discussed the importance of segmenting markets on the basis of customer service.[2,8,9,10] Also, of the studies mentioned earlier, the only empirical study was by Gilmour[8] who showed that customer service should be altered for different segments of customers. However, the industry studied had *a priori* segments which had different needs. When a high technology industry is studied, these *a priori* segments may not exist. The next section reviews segmentation issues which helps develop a segmentation scheme that emphasises customer service.

Industrial market segmentation

Frederick[11] was one of the first researchers to recognise segments in industrial markets: 'The first step in analysing an industrial market is to divide the whole market into its component parts. Any particular group of prospective or present users of a product to whom a concentrated advertising and sales appeal may be made should be considered as a component market.'

The first formal definition of segmentation was by Smith[12] who said: 'Segmentation is based on the development of the demand side of the market and represents a rational and more precise adjustment of products and marketing efforts to consumer or user requirements. In the language of the economist, segmentation is disaggregative in its effect and tends to bring about recognition of several demand schedules, where only one was recognised before.'

Segmentation has been used extensively in consumer marketing over the last 30 years. It is recognised that effective segmentation requires that the segments are measurable, accessible, substantial and homogeneous.[13,14] Also, segmentation should have strong links with the competitive strategy of the organisation.[15,19] Although the application of segmentation techniques has been less frequent in industrial marketing[20,23] there has been a significant amount of segmentation research in industrial marketing.

The literature on industrial market segmentation can be classified into three major categories.[13,23] First are studies dealing with the un-ordered base selection. These studies normally deal with specific situations with no normative models for the selection of segmentation bases.[24] The second category of studies consists of two-stage models that were first proposed by Frank et al.[25]. They suggest that two levels of segmentation be developed for industrial markets based on organisational characteristics and decision-making characteristics. The framework has been used by Wind and Cardozo,[20] Webster[27] and Choffray and Lilien.[26,38] The third major category is multi-step segmentation. Bonoma and Shapiro[22] suggest a nesting approach which allows the marketer to choose specific segmentation bases subject to the target market. The nested approach has the following bases from the outermost nest to the innermost: demographics, operating variables, purchasing approaches, situational factors and personal characteristics of decision makers.

Segmentation bases

Researchers have suggested a number of bases for segmenting industrial markets. These can be divided into two groups, the identifiable/accessible group and the needs/benefits group.[22,28] The identifiable/accessible approach, the more popular of the two approaches, is based on variables which are easy to access and identify (normally demographic variables). It is easy to classify and target organisations based on demographic characteristics since these data are readily available.

The needs/benefits orientation is based on underlying needs and benefits sought by the buying organisation.[22,38] This segmentation approach suggests that the vendor must implement a separate marketing strategy for each segment selected as a target market including products or services that deliver benefits uniquely sought by members of each market segment.[29]

Issues in industrial market segmentation

Only a few of the numerous industrial market segmentation studies have developed bases of market segmentation which were translated into application-oriented strategies for practitioners.[13,20,22] This is because there are a number of problems associated with the selection of segmentation bases that are comprised of demographic variables as well as needs/benefits.

The segmentation bases that are most useful for marketing strategy formulation such as the decision-making units or buying centre characteristics are not easy to analyse.[13,20] Therefore other 'second choice' bases such as size of purchase and location are used. The most prevalent segmentation bases are demographic which are the easiest to analyse but are less useful and less actionable. There are two major problems with the segmentation based on demographic variables.[13] First, these buying characteristics (size, location) are assumed to reflect certain underlying buying needs and uniformities in organisations. The major problem is that these underlying buying need uniformities may not exist. For example, buyers at a trade show can be identified as one segment even though their buying needs and the benefits sought by them may be heterogeneous.

The second problem which is related to the first issue is the implementation of segmentation strategies.[13] Wind[30] was among the first researchers to note the absence of a crucial requirement, 'actionability' (i.e. does the segmentation base give an indication of marketing strategy) in segmentation schemes based on demographic variables. This view was supported by Winter[31] who characterised the segmentation practice as '15 years of regression' referring to the lack of actionability in a majority of market segmentation studies. These studies had segmented markets based on demographic variables. Although these researchers were commenting on the segmentation of consumer markets, similar criticisms were directed at industrial segmentation research.[23,28,38] For example, segmentation of markets based on size or location of firm does not suggest any marketing strategies.

There are problems with segmentation studies that exclusively use underlying needs and benefits to segment markets.[13] The major problem with this approach is that for classification of organisations the data that are needed are not easily available outside the organisation. An example is a manufacturer of high technology products who wants to develop a segmentation approach based on customer service requirements. This is a very good segmentation approach but would require the marketer to research every new or prospective customer to know their customer service requirements in order to assign them to segments. Thus, when segmentation is an ongoing process the high costs of classifying each new or prospective organisation, and assigning them to segments by studying them closely, makes this an expensive segmentation strategy to follow.[28] The difficulty in segment classification may be a reason that most industrial market segmentation studies based on the needs/benefits approach are one-shot studies with little emphasis on implementation and ongoing segmentation.[23,38]

Research methodology

The importance of customer service in competitive strategy has been established. There has also been a recognition that markets should be segmented based on customer service requirements of the customers.[2,8,10] Customer service may be more critical for high technology industries since it differentiates between competing vendors, particularly for companies implementing just-in-time production. Since the products are not standardised, the amount of post-sale logistics support is an important factor in the choice of a vendor (e.g. fill rate, on-time delivery). This article presents the results of research that segmented a high technology market on the basis of customer service requirements and the segments were described using variables that can be easily accessed (demographic data). The segments were classified on the basis of externally available information making identification, evaluation and ongoing segmentation easy to implement.

Overview of the methodology

Christopher[9] and Sterling and Lambert[2] have presented methodologies for collecting information and segmenting markets. Sterling and Lambert[2] have suggested that an external audit be used to collect information on customers' criteria for selecting and evaluating vendors. Christopher[9] has suggested a methodology to segment the market, but his paper did not address the ongoing external identification of segments. The authors propose a methodology which combines past frameworks and enables the segmentation of a market and the identification of segments.

The methodology is presented in Figure 1 and is based on Christopher,[9] Sterling and Lambert[2] and Sharma.[13] The steps are:

1 *Identification of customer service elements.* The elements of customer service used by buyers in selecting and evaluating suppliers can be obtained by studying the elements suggested by earlier researchers, and since every industry has different requirements, conducting in-depth interviews with a range of buyers to verify the service elements, to add elements which are specific to the industry, and reword questions to industry-specific norms.
2 *Survey of customers.* Once the elements of customer service are known, buyers of the product need to be surveyed to determine the importance of these elements in their decision to select and evaluate suppliers.
3 *Data analysis: dimensions of customer service.* There are a large number of individual elements of customer service. To make the importance weights of customers more understandable, the dimensions of customer service need to be extracted. Factor analysis can provide the managers with these understandable dimensions.
4 *Data analysis: cluster customers with similar needs.* Once the dimensions of customer service are established, the importance scores of the dimensions can be clustered to form segments with similar customer service needs. Customer service is a need-based segmentation base. Specific customer service packages can be targeted to these segments.

5 *Data analysis: identification of segments.* The final stage of the analysis is the identification of the segments based on the organisations' characteristics. These can be demographic or logistics-related variables. This suggests that there should be an easy and inexpensive method of classifying customers not classified in the initial study. Discriminant analysis can be used in classifying these organisations.

The sample

The research was conducted in a product segment of a high technology industry. The attributes or measures of customer service and other marketing mix elements were developed using the dimensions of service suggested by earlier studies.[2,3] These measures were refined and additional customer service attributes were generated through personal in-depth interviews with 30 buyers of the high technology product under study. Firms from a range of geographic locations, sizes, types of industry served, and vendors were contacted. Buyers were asked to evaluate the attributes in terms of their importance in the selection and evaluation of suppliers. Demographic data and logistics policy information were also collected.

A mailing list of buyers in the industry was used for initial screening. Phone calls confirmed that 775 of the firms bought the product and their names and addresses were accurate. Follow-up telephone calls were made to non-respondents followed by a second and third mailing of the questionnaire. A total of 246 completed questionnaires were received which represented a response rate of 31 per cent.

In order to test for the existence of non-response bias two analyses were performed. First, the respondents were divided into groups; early respondents (respondents from first mailing) and late respondents (respondents from second and third mailing). There were no statistical differences among the respondents ($p < 0.05$). Second, a two-page questionnaire which measured the importance of 21 randomly selected attributes from the 128 attributes on the original questionnaire were sent to a random sub-sample of the non-respondents. The response of this sub-sample was compared to the respondents of the first three mailings and found not to be significantly different. Therefore, non-response bias is not a problem in this research.[32]

Research findings

The data were analysed on the basis of the methodology suggested in Figure 1.

Dimensions of customer service

Buyers were asked to rate the importance of 48 customer service attributes. Sample measures are presented in Table 1. Since 48 importance

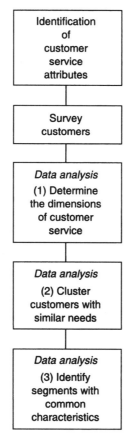

Figure 1 *Methodology for segmenting markets based on customer service*

measures cannot be easily represented, these were factor analysed to reduce the data to understandable dimensions[13]. The expectations were that five factors: logistics information system capability, product availability, miscellaneous logistics services, order servicing and leadtime[33] would emerge. However, there were eleven factors with eigenvalues greater than one and the rotated factor loadings could not be interpreted. On closer examination one dominant principal factor emerged from the analysis which had significant loadings on 42 of the 48 customer service attributes (please see Appendix for details of the procedure). Using the 'break-in-eigenvalue' and interpretability criteria this was the only factor retained.[34] This result of a single factor can be attributed to the industry. The Lambert and Harrington[3] study was conducted in a commodity segment of the chemical industry, where the customer service dimensions are well defined. However, in an emerging industry, these customer service dimensions may not be well defined.

Table 1 *Customer service attributes*

Information is provided when order is placed: projected shipping date; inventory availability; and projected delivery date

Accuracy in filling orders (correct product is shipped)

Consistent lead times (vendor consistently meets promised delivery date)

Damage-free shipments

Ability to expedite emergency orders in a fast, responsive manner

Availability of status information on orders

High fill rate (% of order included in initial shipment)

Supplier will automatically backorder out-of-stock items

Length of promised lead times (from order submission to delivery)

Adequate identification/labelling of package contents

Supplier absorbs cost of freight and handling

Supplier absorbs cost of expedited freight and handling

Adequate availability (ability to order) of newly introduced products

Low or no minimum order quantity requirements

Service backup if salesperson is not available

Frequency of deliveries (ability of supplier to consolidate orders)

Computer-to-computer order entry

Palletised and utilised loads where possible for handling efficiency

Ability of supplier to change requested delivery dates on custom products

Bar-coded products

Order processing personnel located in customer area

Ability of supplier to meet specific and/or unique customer service needs

Assistance from supplier in handling carrier loss and damage claims

Freight pickup allowances for pickup of orders at the suppliers' warehouses

Availability of blanket orders

Ability to select delivering carriers

Documentation of temperature protection *en route* from vendor

Suppliers' warehouse is located in customers' immediate area

Free WATS line (800 number) provided for entering orders

Willingness of supplier to stock a custom slit product that the customer regularly orders.

The results suggest that respondents thought that overall customer service was important in their decision to purchase the product, and they did not discriminate on the individual dimensions of customer service. Put another way, customers evaluated the entire bundle of customer service attributes, rather than individual dimensions.

The standardised factor scores of the 246 buyers were calculated and saved for cluster analysis. The factor scores which were standardised (mean of 0, and a standard deviation of 1) represented the importance of customer service. If the factor was positive then the specific buyer regarded customer service as more important than the average buyer. However, if the score was negative then the buyer regarded customer service as less important than the average buyer.

Cluster customers with similar needs

The purpose of cluster analysis was to group buyers who had rated the importance of customer service attributes similarly. Factor scores for each case were generated on the customer service dimension. These scores were used to cluster buyers with similar needs (please see Appendix for the procedure). The final cluster centres are presented in Table 2.

Table 2 *Cluster analysis*

	Cluster 1	Cluster 2
Final cluster centres: importance of customer service	0.7317[a]	−0.5958[a]
Number of cases in each cluster	128	118

[a] The factor scores are standardised – the average score of the buyers is 0.

The two clusters represented segments which rated the importance of customer service differently. Cluster 1 (labelled segment A; 128 firms) considered customer service to be important in their decision to choose a vendor (customer service factor score positive). Cluster 2 (labelled segment B; 118 firms) did not find the customer service to be as important in the decision to buy the product (customer service factor score negative). The importance factor scores are presented in Table 2. The segments were significantly different across the customer service dimensions.

How the segments respond to marketing mix variables

The segments also differed on all marketing mix importance scores (Table 3). The first marketing mix element examined was the product component. There were 30 product attributes which were factor analysed. Using

Table 3 *Segment characteristics*

	Segment A	Segment B
Product:		
Product quality	0.28	−0.20[a]
Range of products offered	0.41	−0.43[a]
Product innovation	0.31	−0.27[a]
Promotion:		
Sales support	0.31	−0.36[a]
Mass media and direct mail	0.50	−0.44[a]
General assistance	0.25	−0.23[a]
Promotional activities (gifts, entertainment, trade shows)	0.14	−0.13
Price:		
Price sensitivity	0.52	−0.44[a]

[a] Significantly different at $p < 0.01$.

Note: The factor scores are standardised and the average score of the buyers is 0.

a scree test, three factors emerged. These factors were: product quality; range of products offered; and, product innovation. Group A found all three product dimensions to be more important than Group B. There were 34 promotion or communication attributes which were factor analysed and using the scree test four factors were retained. These were labelled: sales support; mass media and direct mail advertising; general assistance; and promotional activities (gifts, entertainment, trade shows). Group A considered promotional factors to be more important than Group B. The final marketing mix element was price. There were 16 price attributes and on factor analysis, one factor was retained using the break-in- eigenvalue and interpretability criteria.[34] Group A was seen to be more price sensitive than Group B. The marketing mix factors were similar to the factors obtained by Lambert and Harrington[3] which would validate the results of this study.

Identification of segments

When market planning is an ongoing process, the high costs of classifying each new customer organisation by studying it closely makes classification based on decision characteristics an expensive strategy to follow.[13,22] This suggests that there should be an inexpensive method of classifying customers that were not classified in the initial research.[13] This article suggests that segments can be identified based on a composite of demographic variables (organisational demographics and materials management policy), making on-going implementation of the segmentation scheme easier.

The objective of the discriminant analysis was the establishment of a procedure for classifying segments based on the buying organisation characteristics.[13] Data were collected in two major areas. The first was the demographic information of the company and the second the materials management policy. The specific variables are listed in Table 4. Of these, gross annual sales, percentage of products sold to external customers, percentage of products sold to specific industries, and annual purchases of the product under study were used in the analysis. These were selected because these variables discriminated between groups (please see Appendix for details on the discriminant analysis).

Table 4 *Demographic and logistics policy attributes*

Demographic data
Gross annual sales
Age of business
Growth of company
Number of manufacturing locations
Percentage of products sold to external customers
Percentage of products sold to large and small customers
Typical production mix
Percentage of products sold to specific industries

Logistics policy
Annual purchases of the product under study
Average number of days of supply of the product
Addition/deletion of suppliers
Amount of purchases of standard size

The discriminant analysis was done in two stages. In the first stage, all cases were included. These were 246 cases which had no missing data on the demographic characteristics. The classification rate of the analysis was 66.67 per cent. In the second stage the sample was randomly split and 75 per cent of the sample was used to generate the discriminant functions. Based on the discriminant functions, the remaining 25 per cent of the cases were classified. In this analysis, the classification rate of the group included in the analysis was 66.5 per cent. The classification rate of the group excluded from the analysis was 63.27 per cent. These results are presented in Table 5.

All the analyses provided classification rates which were stable at around 65 per cent and significantly higher than the 50 per cent expected by chance alone. It would seem that other variables can increase this classification rate. As examples, we did not have data on the purchase of

Table 5 *Discriminant analysis*

Analysis	Classification rate for cases included in the analysis (%)	Classification rate for cases excluded from the analysis (%)
All cases included	66.67	–
Split sample	66.50	63.27

the product studied as a percentage of the total purchases of the company, or the percentage of total sales that used the specific product under study. We expect that variables such as these could significantly improve the classification rates.

Managerial implications: developing customer service strategy for segments

Segment A is composed of companies that are small but have larger purchase requirements when compared to segment B (see Table 6). The market is dominated by two major competitors (labelled Firm X and its major competitor Firm Y). Interestingly, segment A is dominated by Firm

Table 6 *Demographic characteristics*

	Segment A	Segment B
Average gross sales volume (in million $)	78.96	113.22
Average annual purchase of product under study (in thousand $)[a]	326.35	291.43
Percentage of products sold externally each year	87.84	94.01
Percentage of products sold to:[a]		
Major accounts	54.35	46.02
Small accounts	20.41	25.15
Production mix:[a]		
Product A	7.80	11.99
Product B	27.39	22.25
Percentage of products sold to:[a]		
Computer manufacturers	29.92	24.21
Government/defence	5.61	1.38

[a] Significantly different at $p<0.05$.

X (48 per cent of the respondents selected Firm X as their primary vendor; 32 per cent for Firm Y) whereas segment B is dominated by Firm Y (49 per cent for Firm Y; 35 per cent for Firm X). Also, the overall vendor evaluations are different across segments (overall performance evaluated on a seven-point scale). Firm Y has similar evaluations from segment A and segment B (5.14 and 5.16). In contrast, Firm X has a higher evaluation in segment A (5.72) than in segment B (5.03).

Segment A bought more of the product under study and the proportion of purchases to sales volume was higher than for segment B. This suggests that the purchases were more important to segment A. It is understandable, then, that segment A considered the product important and was more sensitive to customer service offerings. Segment B, on the other hand, regarded the purchase of this product as regular purchase. In targeting segment A, customer service needs to be emphasised. In marketing terms, intensive marketing (intensive customer service) needs to be practised for segment A and regular marketing for segment B.

Based on the share and evaluation data, it is clear that Firm X has been able to create a preference for its products in segment A. Segment A is more sensitive to customer service offerings and Firm X has been able to differentiate itself by meeting the needs of the segment. However, segment B evaluates Firm X lower than Firm Y. This may be because the service that Firm X provides is more suited for segment A and may not fit the needs of segment B. As an example, if a customer does not want sales support but is called on by the salesperson very often it may be seen as a negative aspect of a company.

Since Firm X is strong in segment A, it should continue its present customer service strategy for that segment. For segment B, Firm X should initiate a two-stage marketing approach. The first stage is to convince customers that they should be more sensitive to customer service considerations. This can be done by salespeople showing customers how better vendor customer service can help customers better manage their inventories, lower costs and improve service to their customers. The second stage is to convince customers that Firm X provides better customer service than its competitors.

Summary

The importance of customer service in mature industries is well understood. However, this article emphasises the importance of segmenting markets in emerging industries based on customer service. A method of classifying a market into segments with different customer service needs when *a priori* segments do not exist was developed. Two aspects of the segmentation process are critical. First, the segmentation method should be needs-based. Second, the segments should be externally identifiable making segmentation an inexpensive strategy to follow. Finally, the article reported on the application of the methodology in a segment of a high technology industry. Two market segments were identified, each with differing customer service needs. The methodology developed is easy to use and can be used by practising managers.

Notes and References

1 This definition is based on Stock, J.R. and Lambert, D.M., *Strategic Logistics Management*, 2nd ed., Irwin, Homewood, IL., 1987. The use of the term 'customer service' for the attributes under study is well established.
  Some of the references are Hutchinson, W.M. Jr., and Stolle, J.F., 'How to Manage Customer Service', *Harvard Business Review*, November-December 1968; LaLonde, B.J. and Zinszer, P.H., *Customer Service: Meaning and Measurement*, National Council of Physical Distribution Management, Chicago, 1976; LaLonde, B.J., Cooper, M.C., and Noordeweir, T.G., *Customer Service: A Management Perspective*, Council of Logistics Management, 1989; Sterling, J.U., and Lambert, D.N., 'Customer Service Research: Past, Present and Future', *International Journal of Physical Distribution & Materials Management*, Vol. 19 No. 2, 1989.
  These attributes have most recently been used within the 'customer service' framework by Lambert, D.M. and Sharma, A., 'A Customer-based Competitive Analysis for Logistics Decisions', *International Journal of Physical Distribution & Logistics Management*, Vol. 20 No. 1, 1990, pp. 17–24, Lambert, D.M. and Harrington, T.C., 'Establishing Customer Service Strategies within the Marketing Mix: More Empirical Evidence', *Journal of Business Logistics*, Vol. 10 No. 2, 1989, pp. 44–60; and Sterling, J.U., and Lambert, D.M., 'Establishing Customer Service Strategies within the Marketing Mix', *Journal of Business Logistics*, Vol. 8 No. 1., 1987, pp. 1–30.
  However, researchers have also suggested that these attributes be labelled 'Physical Distribution Service'. For a review see Mentzner, J.T., Gomes, R. and Robert E. Kraphel, R.E. Jr., 'Physical Distribution Service: A Fundamental Marketing Concept?' *Journal of the Academy of Marketing Science*, Vol. 17 No. 1, 1989, pp. 53–62.
2 Sterling, J.U., and Lambert, D.M., 'Establishing Customer Service Strategies within the Marketing Mix', *Journal of Business Logistics*, Vol. 8 No. 1, 1987, pp. 1–30.
3 Lambert, D.M. and Harrington, T.C., 'Establishing Customer Service Strategies within the Marketing Mix: More Empirical Evidence', *Journal of Business Logistics*, Vol. 10 No. 2, 1989, pp. 44–60.
4 Webster, F.E., 'Top Management Concerns about Marketing Issues for the 1980s' *Journal of Marketing*, Vol. 45, 1981, pp. 6–19.
5 For an example see reference 3 above.
6 Tucker, F.G., *Customer Service in a Channel of Distribution: The Case of the Manufacturer – Wholesaler – Chain Drug Retailer Channel in a Prescription Industry*, PhD Dissertation, The Ohio State University, 1980.

7 Bennion, M.L., 'Segmenting and Positioning in a Basic Industry', *Industrial Marketing Management,* Vol. 16, 1987, pp. 9–19.

8 Gilmour, P., 'Customer Service: Differentiating by Market Segment', *International Journal of Physical Distribution & Materials Management,* Vol. 12 No. 3, 1982, pp. 37–44.

9 Christopher, M., 'Creating Effective Policies for Customer Service', *International Journal of Physical Distribution & Materials Management,* Vol. 13 No. 2, 1983, pp. 3–24.

10 Webster, C., 'Can Customers be Segmented on the Basis of their Customer Service Quality Expectations', *The Journal of Services Marketing,* Vol. 3 No. 2, Spring, 1989, pp. 35–53.

11 Frederick, J., *Industrial Marketing,* Prentice-Hall, New York, 1934.

12 Smith, W.R. 'Product Differentiation and Market Segmentation as Alternative Marketing Strategies', *Journal of Marketing,* Vol. 21, July 1956, pp. 3–8.

13 For a review please see Sharma, A., *Organizational Decision-Making as a Segmentation Base for Industrial Markets,* Doctoral Dissertation, University of Illinois at Urbana-Champaign, University Microfilms International, Ann Arbor, 1988.

14 Kotler, P., *Marketing Management: Analysis, Planning and Control,* 4th ed., Prentice-Hall, New York, 1980 and Young, S.L., Ott, L., and Feigin, B., 'Some Practical Considerations in Market Segmentation', *Journal of Marketing Research,* Vol. 15, 1978, pp. 405–12.

15 Foote, N.N., 'Market Segmentation as a Competitive Strategy', in Leo Bogart, L. (Ed.), *Current Controversies in Marketing Research,* Markham, Chicago, 1969, pp. 129–39.

16 Johnson, R.M., 'Market Segmentation: A Strategic Management Tool', *Journal of Marketing Research,* Vol. 8, February, 1971, pp. 13–18.

17 Anderson, W.T., Jr., Cox, E.P. and Fulcher, D.G., 'Bank Selection Decisions and Market Segmentation', *Journal of Marketing,* Vol. 40, January 1976, pp. 40–5.

18 Johnson, H.G. and Flodhammer, A., 'Some Factors in Industrial Market Segmentation', *Industrial Marketing Management,* Vol. 9, 1980, pp. 201–5.

19 Winter, F. and Thomas, H., 'An Extension of Market Segmentation: Strategic Segmentation', in Thomas, H., and Gardner, D. (Eds.), *Strategic Marketing and Management,* John Wiley, New York, 1985.

20 Wind, Y. and Cardozo, R., 'Industrial Market Segmentation', *Industrial Marketing Management,* Vol. 3, 1974, pp. 153–66.

21 Choffray, J.M., and Lilien, G.L., 'A New Approach to Industrial Market Segmentation', *Sloan Management Review,* Vol. 3, 1978, pp. 17–30.

22 Bonoma, T.V. and Shapiro, B.P., *Segmenting the Industrial Market,* Lexington Books, Lexington, Ma., 1983.

23 Plank, R.E., 'A Critical Review of Industrial Market Segmentation', *Industrial Marketing Management,* Vol. 14, 1985, pp. 79–91.

24 For example see Assael, H. and A. Marvin Roscoe, A.M., 'Approaches to Market Segmentation Analysis', *Journal of Marketing,* Vol. 40, October, 1976, pp. 67–76.

25 Frank, R.E., Massy, W.F. and Wind, Y., *Market Segmentation*, Prentice-Hall, Englewood Cliffs, NJ, 1972.
26 Choffray, J.M. and Lilien, G.L., 'Industrial Market Segmentation by the Structure of the Purchasing Process', *Industrial Marketing Management*, Vol. 9, 1980, pp. 331–42.
27 Webster, F.E., *Industrial Marketing Strategy*, John Wiley & Sons, New York, 1979.
28 Bonoma, T.V. and Shapiro, B.P., 'Evaluating Marketing Segmentation Approaches', *Industrial Marketing Management*, Vol. 13, 1984, pp.257–68.
29 Corey, R.E., 'Key Options in Market Selection and Product Planning', *Harvard Business Review*, September-October 1973, pp. 119–26.
30 Wind, Y., 'Issues and Advances in Segmentation Research', *Journal of Marketing Research*, Vol. 15, August 1978, pp. 319–37.
31 Winter, F., 'Market Segmentation: A Review of its Problems and Promise', in Gardner, D. and Winter, F.W. (Eds.), *Proceedings of the 1981 Converse Symposium*, American Marketing Association, Chicago, 1982.
32 If non-response bias is a major problem, early respondents should be different from late respondents with respect to their answers to questions. The assumption of this time-trend extrapolation test is that non-respondents are more like late respondents than early respondents. Similarly, non-respondents should be different from respondents if non-response bias is a major problem. See Armstrong, J.S. and Overton, T.S., 'Estimating Non-response Bias in Mail Surveys', *Journal of Marketing Research*, Vol. 14 No. 3, August 1977, pp. 396–402.
33 We have adopted the framework suggested by reference 3; this can be referred to for a detailed explanation of this procedure. In addition a majority of the researchers in this area agree that the importance of the various dimensions change depending upon the product.
34 Spiro, R.L. and Weitz, B.A., 'Adaptive Selling: Conceptualisation, Measurement and Nomological Validity', *Journal of Marketing Research*, Vol. 17, February 1990, pp. 61–9.
35 Anderberg, M.R., *Cluster Analysis for Applications*, Academic Press, New York, 1973.
36 Hair, J.E. Jr., Anderson, R.E., and Tatham, R.L., *Multivariate Data Analysis*, 2nd ed., Macmillan, New York, 1987.
37 Frank, R.E., Massy, W.F., and Morrison, D.G., 'Bias in Multiple Discriminant Analysis', *Journal of Marketing Research*, Volume II, August 1965, pp. 250–58.
38 Choffray, J.M. and Lilien, G.L., *Market Planning for New Industrial Products*, John Wiley & Sons, New York, 1980.

Appendix: Glossary of analytical terms and details of analysis

Factor analysis

An analysis to uncover factors. Factors are a linear combination of the original variables. Factors also represent the underlying dimensions in the original set of variables.[36]

Eigenvalue: Accounts for the amount of variance accounted for by a factor. An eigenvalue of 1 suggests that the factor explains the variance of a single variable.

Break in eigenvalue: When there is a large break in eigenvalue between the first and second factor and the first factor represents a large number of variables, then this criterion can be used in the selection of the number of factors.[34]

Factor scores: 'Factor analysis reduces the original set of variables to a new smaller set of variables, or factors. When this new smaller set of variables (factors) is used in subsequent analysis, some measure or score must be included to represent the newly derived variables. This measure (score) is a composite of all the original variables important in making the new factor. The composite measure is referred to as *factor score*.'[36]

Standardised data: When data is on differing scales (e.g. age, height), then to increase the comparison of data categories the data is standardised. The data is standardised by changing the relative value of each case so that the mean is equal to 0 and the standard deviation is equal to 1.

Cluster analysis

'Cluster Analysis is a technique for grouping individuals or objects into clusters so that objects in the same cluster are more like each other than they are like objects in other clusters'.[36]

Method: The Ward's minimum variance was used as the primary clustering technique. The Ward's method suggested a two cluster solution. Based on a two cluster solution, the algorithm used for determining clusters was based on nearest centroid sorting.[35] The case is assigned to the cluster for which the distance between the case and the centre of the cluster (centroid) is the smallest. The cluster centres are selected by choosing cases which have a large distance between them and using their values as initial estimates of cluster centres. The cluster centres are changed as new cases are added to clusters. Once all cases are classified, the cases are reclassified using the classification cluster centres as initial cluster centres. This procedure was repeated but the cluster centres were stable. The results of clustering were similar to the results of the Ward's method.

Discriminant analysis

Discriminant analysis uncovers the relationship between a categorical dependent variable (e.g. group or segment membership) and several metric independent variables (e.g. organisational demographic and materials management policy data).

Method: The validation of the discriminant analysis can be done by reclassifying all cases included and excluded from the analysis. It has been suggested that if the proportion of cases correctly classified is more than that obtained by pure chance (proportional chance criterion) alone, then that is a good algorithm.[36] The formula for proportional change criterion is: C proportional = p_a^2, + p_b^2, where p_a = proportion of cases of group a in the sample. In the present analysis are two groups in a sample of 246 with sizes 128 and 118. The value of C proportional for the sample is 0.50. Thus a classification rate which is substantially higher than 50 per cent will suggest good discriminant functions.

Another issue in discriminant analysis is the inflated estimate of the correct classification if the entire group is used for both the generation of discriminant functions and the classification matrix. Frank *et al.*[37] have suggested the split sample approach. The process consists of randomly splitting the sample and using the discriminant function used in the first group to validate the membership of the second group. This reduces the bias due to the sampling errors and gives better estimates.

7 GENERATING CUSTOMER COMMITMENT

Much of the literature on generating customer commitment draws on the philosophy of relationship marketing[1,2] and focuses primarily on the impact of retention marketing on company profitability and on proposing various strategies and plans to improve customer retention rates. The pioneers in the field of customer retention are Bain & Company, a US strategy consulting firm whose primary focus has been on customer retention economics. They have developed approaches for both measuring customer retention and modelling the impact of retention on company profitability. This chapter contains two articles from the partners of Bain & Company and a third by David Maister, a consultant and former professor at the Harvard Business School.

The first article, by Frederick Reichheld, examines the key issues related to managing loyalty. In his paper he argues that if marketing is to be restored to its rightful position within the company, then marketing professionals must embrace loyalty-based strategies and tools, and create a scientific measurement system that links loyalty to profitability. He goes on to describe four basic tools to managing loyalty, namely: measurement systems based on retention economics; customer targeting based on lifetime value; defection analysis and value proposition revision and renewal.

The second Bain article is by Bain & Company partners Robin Buchanan and Crawford Gillies and looks at the importance of Value Managed Relationships (VMRs) in building partnerships between suppliers and suppliers' customers. They point to some specific examples within British industry where VMRs have been very beneficial and suggest that improving customer satisfaction and retention in these industries has greatly improved company profitability and competitiveness.

The client retention strategies detailed in David Maister's article 'Marketing to existing clients', are intended specifically for professional service firms. However, we consider that the three basic stages he outlines are pertinent to all business sectors and provide useful guidelines to reducing defection in other forms of organization. Like the previous two articles, Maister outlines why existing clients are more profitable than new ones. However, he also provides an interesting explanation as to why so many companies devote a disproportionate amount of time to chasing new customers, especially in professional service firms. Unlike the other two articles, Maister is less concerned with the measurement of customer retention or even undertaking defection analysis; his focus is on designing successful marketing strategies for existing clients.

These papers on generating customer commitment emphasize the importance of understanding the impact of customer retention on company profitability. They all propose various strategies aimed at improving customer commitment, either through the use of Value Managed Relationships between suppliers and the supplier's customers; marketing to existing clients in professional service firms; or managing loyalty using a structured approach. The key message is that all companies could be doing more to cultivate business from their existing customers and, by focusing on customer retention issues and loyalty-based management, the company will be able to gain competitive advantage and improved profitability.

References

1 Heskett, J.L. (1987). Lessons from the service sector. *Harvard Business Review,* March/April, 118–125.
2 Berry, L.L. and Gresham, L.G. (1986). Relationship retailing: transforming customers into clients, *Business Horizons,* November/December, 43–47.

LOYALTY AND THE RENAISSANCE OF MARKETING
Frederick F. Reichheld

Frederick Reichheld is a director of Bain & Company, Boston, and leads its Loyalty/Retention Practice. His pioneering work in the area of customer and employee retention has quantified the linkage between loyalty and profits. His publications include articles in the *Wall Street Journal* and *Harvard Business Review* ('Zero defections: quality comes to service', September 1990 and 'Loyalty-based management', March 1993).

Reichheld's paper provides a very comprehensive account of the key issues relating to managing loyalty. He explains that loyalty can provide the basis of a new management science which can lead the way to a rejuvenation of marketing to its previously preeminent position. He argues that long-term, corporate success depends on cultivating loyalty from three key constituencies of a business: customers, employees and investors. Creating value for these three groups should be the true mission of the company and not maximizing shareholder value, which has been the traditional approach.

Once upon a time, there was a discipline called Marketing, and it was the undisputed king in the Land of Business. King Marketing's power and importance were extolled throughout the land. In recent times, alas, King Marketing has been overthrown by other disciplines, including Finance,

Strategic Planning (once a loyal subject of Marketing) and Manufacturing. These usurpers now rule the Land of Business, and Marketing's loyalists have been forced into subservient roles. Those who still pledge fealty to King Marketing ask the question far and wide, 'What has led to the decline and fall of the king, and how might he be restored to his previous glory?'

This short fable describes a remarkable development that has taken place in the past 25 years. Unfortunately, it is a story all too real, as any marketing professional can tell you. Not long ago, marketing was clearly seen as the engine propelling business forward, the discipline that integrated the functional areas of the firm to serve the needs of the customer. It was understood that marketing played a key role in the success of the enterprise. Today, marketing departments around the world are struggling with diminished stature and thinning ranks as layoffs target those who cannot justify their contribution to corporate profits.

The status of the marketing profession has been diminished for one simple reason: It has failed to keep pace with advances in other disciplines and has not defined for itself a meaningful and measurable role that is critical to the mission of the firm.

Finance has jumped ahead of marketing by innovating new capital structures, such as partial spinouts of divisions, and through powerful advances in measurement/information systems, such as activity-based costing. Leveraged buyouts and the strong influence of Wall Street also have elevated the importance of finance in the minds of corporate CEOs: involuntary turnover in the CEO's office has come about largely because of poor financial results.

Manufacturing has rescued itself from relative obscurity through the development and application of total quality management (TQM) principles. Defect tracking systems and a new understanding of the economics of quality have revolutionized business processes around the world, and innovative vendor partnerships have helped create powerful strategic opportunities.

Meanwhile, marketing has been spinning its wheels, fascinated with quick fixes such as price promotions and reluctant to let go of the easy '80s, when markets boomed and marketing's problems were much less obvious. Some elements of marketing, such as the advertising and public relations functions, have grown in importance but are performed primarily by outside agencies.

What, then, is marketing's role? Some marketing departments have latched on to customer service as their function, some have developed customer satisfaction surveys, and others focus on promotional gimmicks or direct mail programs. Still, the layoffs and budget cuts continue.

The decline of marketing is unfortunate because marketing really is at the core of the forces that drive business success and profits.

We have studied hundreds of firms operating in a variety of industries as part of a continuing effort to understand what factors really do make a difference in a company's success or failure in the marketplace. Our work has revealed that the most successful companies are those that care about and cultivate loyalty – from customers, employees, and investors. The real enemy of profits is churn, which manifests itself in the form of price-sensitive customers, job-hopping employees, and fast-buck speculators.

From this perspective the fundamental task of the marketing function should be managing customer loyalty, with a clear understanding of the relationship between customer, employee, and investor loyalty. To manage loyalty effectively, marketers must view it within the context of the firm's mission.

The true mission

Traditional thinking has it that the purpose of the corporation is to maximize share-holder value. However, this simplistic view is tragically incomplete – and pursuit of this single goal can destroy a business, particularly when measurement systems focus on short-term rather than long-term shareholder needs. This flawed perspective is behind the accelerating downward spiral of layoffs and downsizings. It has resulted in a pursuit of profits at the expense of employees and customers – and it will backfire. In the words of Henry Ford, 'Business must be run at a profit . . . else it will die. But when anyone tries to run a business solely for profit . . . then also the business must die for it no longer has a reason for existence.'

The true mission of the firm is to *create value* for the three key constituencies of a business system: customers, employees, and investors. The value-creation process for this trilogy of stakeholders is at the core of any successful enterprise enabling its very existence.

Each member of the trilogy contributes some combination of time, money, energy, and expertise; and, to succeed, a business must deliver even more value in return. Returns will be maximized by creating and allocating value in such a manner as to minimize churn in the business system because the learning and trust required to sustain value creation cannot exist in an unstable, high-churn system.

The loyal employee learns, over time, how to serve the customer, and the loyal customer learns how to access the business system in a way that makes it easier to be well-served. The loyal stockholder learns how to anticipate ups and downs in the business and doesn't induce behaviours that destroy long-term value in order to ensure short-term accounting profits. A successful business is really a partnership that includes customer, employee, and investor. Like any partnership, the activities of the business must be mutually beneficial, or it will eventually fail. When any one participant overreaches, the system will collapse.

First among equals

Even though all three constituencies must be well-served, it is the customers who must be considered 'first among equals' because customer loyalty has to be earned each and every day. Of the three groups, the customers' loyalty is the most mobile: they generally have the least emotional and financial capital invested in the company and usually can go somewhere else with minimal effort. Even though accountants, cash flow statements overlook this fact, all cash flow originates in the customer's wallet. It is marketing's challenge to manage this life-giving wellspring of customer loyalty by ensuring that the firm attracts the right customers – customers whose loyalty the firm is able to earn *and* keep – and that they consistently receive superior value from the firm. It is this task that places marketing at the heart of the value creation process and at the source of all cash flow.

However, marketers currently do not have the tools required to do this job. Their measurement systems ignore cash flow and focus instead on variables such as market share or satisfaction scores. These are no match for the financial accounting systems that track the value created for investors. The accountant's measures influence most business decisions and, because accounting misses many of the economic consequences of loyalty, (for example, long-term customers are less costly to serve) it has been systematically undervalued and undermanaged. Accountants report on quarterly and yearly periods, and have not yet developed a balance sheet that recognizes the value of loyal customers and employees, even though these are the firm's most important assets. As a result, customers and employees have become second-class citizens.

While corporate mission statements trumpet lofty goals such as 'delivering the best value to customers' or 'being the best place to work', existing measurement systems are inadequate to manage the value being delivered to customers and employees. The quarterly earnings demands from shareholders, the only constituency with a system to measure results relevant to its concerns, prevail over the needs of customers or employees.

The irony is that pension fund managers pick investment managers on the basis of their quarterly investment performance, encouraging the latter to pursue incredibly shortsighted strategies in hopes of elevating their short-term rankings. The result: Capital markets, which clearly should be governed by long-term interests, are driven by precisely the opposite forces.

Satisfaction a beginning

Some marketers saw what zero defects did to transform manufacturing and realized that 'measurable equals manageable'. It was natural for them to latch on to satisfaction surveys. These activities provide measurable results and are based on familiar market research techniques. However, merely measuring satisfaction eventually produces unsatisfying results.

Today, many firms are busily measuring customer satisfaction, and well they should because a dissatisfied customer is unlikely to remain loyal to the firm or buy into its value proposition. However, the corollary is not true: customers who describe themselves as satisfied are not necessarily loyal.

How can this be? The answer is that the link between a customer's words and his or her actions in this area is only tenuous. In most businesses, 60%-80% of customer defectors said that they were 'satisfied' or 'very satisfied' on the last satisfaction survey prior to their defection! In the interim, anything can happen, and often does. Competitors change their offerings, the customer develops new requirements and begins to look for alternatives or other unknowns intervene.

The point is that those who are measuring satisfaction should be commended – and urged not to stop there! Measuring satisfaction is tricky because it's an effort to measure state of mind, when behavior is what really counts. Retention measurements, such as annual retention rate, frequency of purchases, and share of wallet, aim directly at the real target: Does customers behaviour show that they are being convinced to maintain their stake in the firm? Do they buy the value proposition of the company, i.e., are they coming back for more?

Even in an industrial setting with fewer customers, valuable early warnings can be detected by studying defections. For example, when a customer fails to renew a service contract with an office equipment manufacturer, this can be a sign that the company is in danger of losing the next equipment purchase: satisfaction scores are not nearly as reliable an indicator. One major office equipment supplier reports repurchase rates are mired at 40% while its satisfaction scores are skyrocketing.

As Dave Illingsworth, the first general manager of Lexus USA, said, 'The only meaningful measure of satisfaction is repeat purchases'. Illingsworth knows whereof he speaks. Lexus USA has become a loyalty leader, setting new standards of performance in terms of owner repurchase retention in the American automobile market, according to its own and other car companies' internal research.

A new management science

Just as manufacturing began to transform itself when it focused on the quality goal of zero defects, marketing will regain its former stature and become a different discipline by embracing the mission of managing toward zero defections.

Loyalty can be the basis for a new management science because it is measurable as retention or persistence first of customers, but then also of employees and even investors. The 'forces of loyalty' are measurable in cash flow terms because of the link between loyalty, value and profits. As a first-order effect, loyalty reliably measures whether superior value has been created because they do or don't come back for more (see Figure 1). It then initiates a series of second-order effects that cascade through a business system as follows:

● Revenues and market share grow as the best customers are swept into the company's book of business, building repeat sales and referrals. The best customers are those who have the highest inherent loyalty

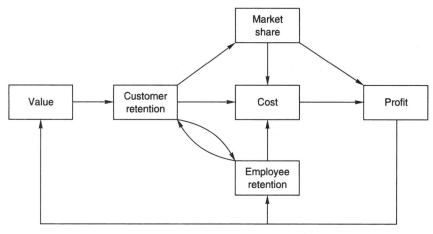

Figure 1 *Loyalty-based business system*

because they understand and buy into the company's value proposition. They are the company's best assets because of how long they stay and how profitable they will become.

- Costs shrink as the expense associated with acquiring and establishing relationships with new customers and replacing old ones declines. The long-term customers are much easier to serve because they know the system and how to use it and have built up good working relationships with loyal employees.
- Employee retention increases because job pride and job satisfaction increase, in turn creating a loop that reinforces customer retention through better service. Increased productivity results from longer employee tenure because of continued learning by the employees as they gather experience in creating value for customers.

As costs go down and revenues go up, profits increase as a third-order effect of loyalty. This provides the resources to invest in better employee compensation and in new activities that further enhance the value delivered to customers. Profits and growth drive shareholder value and reduce the cost of capital, further enhancing the company's ability to deliver value.

Whereas loyalty is a noble behavior pattern in most domains of human life, its relevance to business transcends altruism. Our analyses show that profits soar in response to loyalty: in fact, we have found that a decrease in defection rates of five percentage points can increase profits by 25%–100%. These results are generated by comparing the net present values of the profit streams for the average customer life, given current defection rates with the same figures at the lower defection rate. Moreover, these results are consistent across industries as diverse as

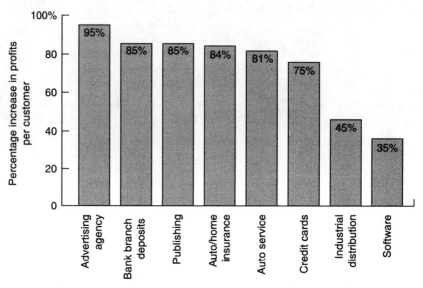

Figure 2 *Profit impact of 5% increase in retention rate*

software (35%), industrial distribution (45%), and branch bank deposits (85%). (See Figure 2.)

Managing loyalty

Marketing – acting alone – cannot create sustainable loyalty. Customers remain loyal, not because of promotions and marketing programs, but because of the value they receive. Value is driven by a full array of features, such as product quality, service, sales support, and availability. The sales force controls customer acquisition, manufacturing is responsible for quality, the service department manages direct interactions with the customer, and so forth.

Marketing's job is to ensure that the efforts of each department are coordinated into effective delivery of a unique value proposition, which will provide superior value and thus, earn customer loyalty. Marketing conceptualizes the value proposition and envisions how to present it in terms that the customer will understand, but bringing it to life requires the efforts of all the other company functions.

Indirect influence does not imply lack of impact, however. Consider the indirect, but significant power exerted by the finance department on profit, through its measurement systems, budgeting, target setting, and other analytical tools. Acting on its own, finance cannot generate sustainable profits, but its measurement tools give it enormous influence.

Marketing can be as powerful as finance and even more effective, by using four basic tools to manage loyalty:

● Measurement systems based on retention economics.
● Customer targeting based on lifetime value.
● Defection analysis.
● Value proposition revision and renewal.

Measurement systems

If you can't measure it, you can't manage it. However, most companies today have not defined loyalty nor established effective measures of it. Even when measures do exist, they have not been linked to compensation decisions because the measures are still much too vague.

For example, one insurance company claimed to track customer retention to the decimal point. However, probing further, we found different executives at the firm claimed current performance that ranged from 82%–90% (quite a range when 5 percentage points equals a 25%–100% profit increase). Some were using six-month numbers others were using annual figures and still others included involuntary cancellations. Some ignored policies written and terminated within six months. Because they weren't considered critical to the day-to-day functioning of the business, retention measures were seen by the organization as irrelevant.

Another example: General Motors claims very high owner loyalty, but does its definition of loyalty encompass Chevrolet owners switching to a Pontiac dealership? What's the right definition? What drives the economics of the business? Honda doesn't make minivans – should its marketers be as concerned about a customer who defects to minivans as they are about one who trades in an Accord for a new Toyota Camry?

If marketing is going to take on a new level of responsibility for corporate success, it must develop consensus on the most relevant definitions and auditable measurement processes. These measures then must be linked to cash flows and profits in such a clear manner that investment decisions can be made based on them.

Once retention economics have been quantified, it is finally possible to determine how much it is worth investing to increase loyalty and retention. Even though no one can say what effect an increase of customer satisfaction from 70% to 80% would have, increasing retention from 70% to 80% has a precise calculable net present value. (See 'Calculating the value of a customer' below.)

Customer targeting

The first job of a loyalty-based marketing effort is to enable the firm to find and keep the right customers. The right customers are those to whom the best value can be delivered by the firm over a sustained period of time.

Calculating the value of a customer

Profits from loyal customers increase over time, and this pattern repeats itself in many industries (see Figure 3). Applying this general model specifically to the credit card industry produces the results shown in Figure 4. In the beginning, acquiring the new customer typically involves a cost of $50–$100. The largest cost component is mailing thousands of solicitations to generate a 2%-3% response rate of new applications. Also included in acquisition costs are credit evaluation, card issuance, and other expenses of setting up a new account on the data processing system.

Newly acquired customers use the card sparingly at first, representing only a small profit during year one. However, if the cardholder remains for a second year, profits improve significantly. As customers use the card more, balances grow, and profits continue to increase.

To calculate the net present value of a customer, you must know how long he or she will remain with the company. If a typical credit card customer stays for five years, it is a simple matter of adding up the expected life cycle profits for the first five years and applying a reasonable discount rate of, say, 15%. Thus, the customer who stays for the average duration is worth $134 (see Figure 5).

Notice how retention rate and average customer duration are related. When a company lowers its defection rate, the average customer relationship lasts longer and profits go up. For example, 90% retention implies a 10-year average customer duration and a customer value of $300, more than twice the value at 5 years duration and 80% retention.

Although these results are significant, the credit card business is not unique. The shape of retention/defection curves and net present value of customers will vary by industry, but profits generally will rise as defection rates fall.

Fred Reichheld

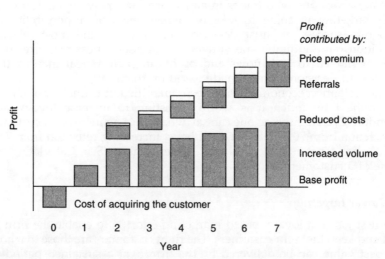

Figure 3 *Keeping customers pays off*

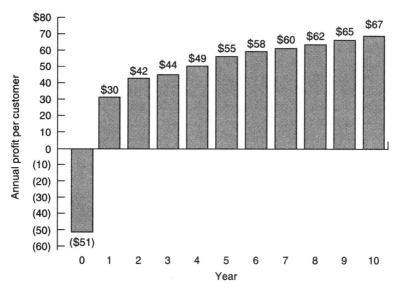

Figure 4 *Customer lifecycle profits: credit cards*

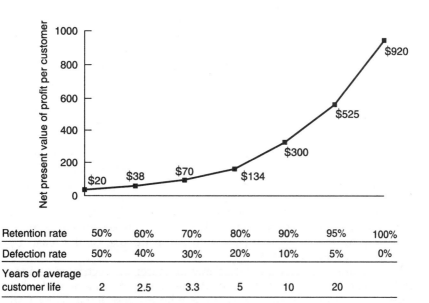

Retention rate	50%	60%	70%	80%	90%	95%	100%
Defection rate	50%	40%	30%	20%	10%	5%	0%
Years of average customer life	2	2.5	3.3	5	10	20	

Figure 5 *How retention drives customer value in credit cards*

Consider for example the approach taken by MBNA in the credit card business. MBNA, which began life as the credit card subsidiary of Maryland National Bank in the 1980s, avoided the new account feeding frenzy during the industry's early years and focused on marketing cards only through affinity groups such as the American Dental Association. MBNA was one of the first credit card companies to measure retention, enabling the company to learn which affinity organizations had members with high inherent loyalty.

These measurements allowed MBNA to concentrate its marketing on systematically attracting the groups that had highly loyal members, thereby building a portfolio of customers who behaved like long-term annuities. The benefits of customer loyalty have turbo-charged MBNA's profits and growth. Earnings have increased dramatically, and the company has rocketed to No. 2 in balances among bank card competitors.

MBNA's success also demonstrates that loyalty-based management does not imply reducing value to shareholders so that customers can get a better deal. Rather, it means that long-term shareholder value will be maximized only through superior customer loyalty. The value of this company to shareholders has grown by $2 billion over the past several years.

State Farm, the nation's leading personal insurance carrier, is another example of effective customer selection. State Farm focuses on attracting better-than-average drivers who will stay loyal for many years. State Farm agents work from neighborhood offices, allowing them to build long-lasting relationships with their customers and provide the personal service that is the cornerstone of the corporate philosophy.

When agents are rooted in their communities they usually know who the best customers will be. They know families and even generations and they are aware of what is happening in the community because they are part of it. They can scan the local newspaper for the high school honor role for example, and make sure their young customers' good grades are recognized with premium discounts. The most powerful computer and most brilliant underwriter at headquarters can't compete with the insight that comes from direct experience and personal relationships built at the local level.

Great-West Life Assurance Co is an example of a company that motivates salespeople to locate exactly the right kinds of customers for its own value proposition. Great-West pays a 50% premium to group-health insurance brokers who hit customer retention targets.

GM's new Saturn division is another example. By establishing a non-negotiable list price as the standard within its dealer system, Saturn is discouraging the price shoppers who make up one of the least loyal customer segments.

In an industrial setting a major manufacturer of electric components and connectors has studied its customer base and segmented it into those who are highly loyal and those who are less loyal. They found that, in the case of the loyal customers, their purchasing departments bought on service and quality and the purchasing agents stayed in their own jobs for a long time. Among the less loyal customers, purchasing agents had shorter tenures and bought on price. In response to these findings, the company focused all its product development on the loyal customer segment and directed new account activity toward similar companies.

Defection analysis

At first glance, it may seem paradoxical that a business system so concerned with loyalty would spend significant time and resources on studying its defectors. However, that is what must happen in a company dedicated to pursuing zero defections. Defection analysis borrows from the principles that produce zero defects in TQM. Because defection is a failure for a loyalty-based enterprise, we can study it by adapting the highly sophisticated tools of failure analysis.

In a loyalty-based business system, failure is a problem only if the root causes are not analyzed and used for organizational learning. Japanese manufacturers for example view a defect as a 'gift' and use failure analysis to improve operations. Airlines, operating in an extremely complex and dangerous environment exceed the highest standards of quality control by spending millions retrieving and analyzing the flight recorder ('black box') carried on every airplane to determine what caused a crash.

Although it is more pleasant to experience success than failure, success does not provide as many learning opportunities to an organization. Success flows from a complex interplay of factors that cannot be dismantled easily to learn new lessons. When a system is working, and you try to ask which components are making it work the answer is 'all of them'.

Failure by contrast shows us which link in the chain has been broken. A defect stands out as a clear understandable message telling an organization exactly where improvements are needed. In the words of Warren Buffett, one of the most successful investors in the world, 'In my business we try to study where things go astray and why things don't work .... [We] start out with failure and then engineer its removal.'

The MicroScan division of Baxter Diagnostics Inc. is a good example of intelligent use of failure analysis. MicroScan makes the sophisticated instruments used by medical laboratories to identify microbes in patient cultures and determine which antibiotics will eliminate these 'bugs' most effectively at the lowest cost.

In mid-1990 MicroScan was neck-and-neck with Vitek Systems Inc. in a race for market leadership. MicroScan was succeeding, but its managers knew they needed to do more to win the struggle against Vitek. Microscan analyzed its customer base highlighting accounts that had been lost as well as those that remained active but showed a declining volume of testing. MicroScan interviewed all of the lost customers and a large number of the 'decliners', probing deeply for the root causes underlying their change in behavior, especially when they defected to alternative testing methods.

The results were clear and somewhat painful for MicroScan managers to accept – these customers had concerns about the company's instrument features, reliability, and responsiveness to their problems. The management team overcame natural feelings of denial and acted decisively. The team shifted R&D priorities to address specific shortcomings customers had identified such as test accuracy and time-to-result. The company then accelerated development of a low-end model and brought it to market in record time. It also redesigned customer service protocols to ensure that immediate attention was given to equipment faults and delivery glitches.

MicroScan's willingness to learn from failure paid off. Two years later the company had pulled away from Vitek to achieve clear market leadership. Tracking and responding to customer defections became a central part of MicroScan's approach and a model for other Baxter divisions.

MicroScan would not have been so successful in understanding its failures without a religious devotion to root-cause analysis which is a far more detailed methodology than standard market research. Traditional closed-account research is to root-cause analysis as the stethoscope is to the CAT-scan. Defector surveys are relatively common but without root-cause analysis the knowledge needed to correct the underlying reasons for defection is limited.

Root-cause analysis may require dealing with more than 300 endpoints rather than the 25 common with traditional research methods. It delves much more deeply into the sequence of interactions leading up to a particular behavior. For example when defectors from an insurance company are asked why they left they may say, 'Because of my claims experience'. However, there may be 15 different reasons underlying a poor claims experience ranging from 'The amount was insufficient' to 'The amount was what I expected but the check came three weeks late'.

In addition, a detailed root-cause analysis will determine whether the defector is a customer the company wanted to keep in the first place. This type of analysis requires a computer-assisted procedure because of its inherent complexity. A typical interview will take 20 minutes using a computer but may take as long as 1½ hours without it.

Learning about defections helps the company revise and improve all of its procedures for the long haul. However, as the foundation for developing recovery systems, it also can have short-term value. As the tactical arm of defection analysis, recovery systems should not become more important than the organizational learning itself. It's easy to get excited about bringing defectors back into the fold, because of the obvious economic benefits connected with success in this area. Depending on the size of the original customer base, recovery systems can yield significant profits. Experience to date has shown, for example, that credit card companies can recover 10%–50% of their defecting customers.

However, some customers shouldn't be saved because they do not fit the loyalty profile that will benefit the organization in the long term. Only if defectors are good customers with economically soluble root causes for leaving is it worth the effort to get them back.

Value proposition renewal

Customers are loyal because they get the best value, not because a company does the best job in promoting its product or service. Therefore, if a company really wants to keep customers loyal, it must be willing to monitor and revise the fundamental value proposition that brought customers into the system in the first place. Even though the customer who initially signs onto a company's product line may have the same name and social security number five years later, he or she will not be the same person from a marketing point of view.

One of the most important strategic decisions any company can make is how long to try to keep a particular customer – how long into the life cycle should the company extend itself to serve a customer well?

Entenmann's, an extremely successful baking company, discovered the usefulness of using this loyalty tool when it interviewed its customer base and detected a concern from its traditional target about cholesterol and high-fat foods. In response, the company brought out a new line of fat-free products that gained immediate acceptance and boosted profits as well.

Staples, the highly successful chain of office-supply stores, not only tracks defections among its small business customers zealously, it constantly revises and updates product lines in response to customer feedback. The company's unique database of customer purchase histories allows telemarketers to probe into changes in purchase patterns to understand what improvements must be made. The company uses this information to change its services and target its catalogs and coupons more effectively. For example, Staples recently added delivery service in response to findings about customer needs that had been developed through research. As many of Staples' small business customers grew larger, they had been defecting to competitors with delivery services.

USAA insurance company is another example of an organization that provides a range of products that conform with customers' evolving needs. USAA tracks 'share of wallet' by life cycle stage and has added retirement-oriented investment products to its initial auto insurance offerings to serve the growing businesses that make up its customer base.

When a company considers revising its value proposition it must distinguish between a system that is not living up to its own managers' expectations and a system that is not competitive with that of other companies. The value proposition may have been excellent, the system may work as designed, and the products may make some customers happy, but they still may not be competitive.

For example, the Honda product line and dealer system did a good job of earning customer loyalty by delivering an excellent value proposition, but customer loyalty declined when it failed to redesign the Accord to compete with the Camry and the Taurus. Now that the redesign has taken place, Honda may become competitive once again.

Sometimes managers need to consider fundamental change in their systems rather than incremental adjustments. For example, insurance marketing departments while trying to develop cross-selling programs to help agents increase their incomes are ignoring the fact that life insurance is a seriously flawed value proposition. Currently 80% of customers cancel a typical universal life policy before year nine. That's how long it typically takes before customers finally begin to achieve a fair market return on their investment. Before then most would have been better off simply buying a term policy and investing the rest in a mutual fund. Sometimes, they are prematurely enticed into another policy and often they don't even realize that they will reduce the value of their investment if they cancel. As a result 80% of customers get a below-market rate value from their policy.

Agents can't make a good living from a defecting customer base, and 80% of new hires leave within four years. Meanwhile, investors are facing capital shortages as the companies are forced to live off their old book of business or customer base. In the life insurance business, the basic value proposition is flawed and must be completely overhauled for the industry to prosper.

Revising the value proposition ultimately is linked with defection analysis. If a company honestly invests in finding out why defections occur, defecting customers will tell the organization exactly where its value proposition is deficient. Because value is the key to loyalty, defections eventually lead back to that fundamental concern.

Mid-life crisis

When Mark Twain heard that his obituary mistakenly had been published in the newspapers he remarked. 'Recent reports of my death have been greatly exaggerated'. The marketing function has something in common with the famous humorist in that it has been written off as dead by some when it is, in fact only suffering a mid-life crisis.

Marketing can emerge from this crisis with new strength if it begins to see its role through the lens of loyalty and understands that managing the value of the firm is really managing loyalty. Marketing must become the center of corporate learning, working not only as the heart of the organization but also as its brain.

If marketing is to be restored to its previously preeminent position, marketing professionals must go beyond the service quality and satisfaction movements and embrace loyalty-based strategies and tools. Marketers can only become managers of loyalty for their firms if they create a scientific measurement system that links loyalty with the bottom line.

At the same time marketing should seek and receive the support of senior management in carrying out this newly defined mission. Marketing's success in restoring its former glory is in the interest not only of the marketing profession but of the business enterprise itself.

Loyalty-based management not only will exalt the marketing function, it also will drive the firm and entire industries to create greater success and wealth for all. King Marketing's restoration is really a goal to be supported by everyone in the Land of Business – customers, employees and investors alike.

Reproduced from Reichheld, F.A. (1994). Loyalty and the renaissance of marketing. *Marketing Management*, **2**, (4) 10–21. Reprinted with permission from *Journal of Marketing Management*, published by the American Marketing Association.

VALUE MANAGED RELATIONSHIPS: THE KEY TO CUSTOMER RETENTION AND PROFITABILITY
Robin Buchanan and Crawford Gillies

Robin Buchanan is Managing Partner of the London office of Bain & Company Inc., the business strategy consulting firm. He is a Chartered Accountant with an MBA from the Harvard Business School. His work experience included positions in international banking, venture capital and accounting, with client assignments covering all major manufacturing and service industries. Crawford Gillies is also a partner in Bain & Company's London Office and is Head of the firm's Re-Engineering Practice in the UK. During his consulting career he has worked throughout Europe and the USA on a wide range of topics concerning strategy, acquisitions, re-engineering and organizational capability. His industry expertise included financial services, information services and retailing, and he has lectured on the topic of customer loyalty at conferences and business schools throughout the UK.

The authors of this paper argue that Value Managed Relationships (VMRs) play a vital role in improving customer satisfaction and retention between suppliers and suppliers' customers. They describe VMRs as a collaborative and communicative partnership, which works by reducing systems costs and enhancing profitability and competitiveness. Buchanan and Gillies describe four areas where typically the largest benefits arise: integrated design, manufacturing, quality control and inventory systems.

During the 1980s British industry was dramatically revitalised. Employee productivity rose sharply and there was a marked improvement in both product quality and industrial relations. Entrepreneurial drive, once such a feature of the UK economy, has returned. As a result British companies are more competitive and more profitable than they have been for a very long time.

But if these advances are to be sustained through the 1990s, British industry cannot afford to rest on its laurels: new ways of satisfying customers and reducing costs will have to be found.

One of the key elements of business success and profitability is customer satisfaction. As a rule, the more satisfied the customer, the more durable the relationship. And the longer this lasts, the more money the company stands to make. At first sight this might appear so blindingly obvious as to be hardly worth saying. But not everybody seems to have got the message.

While many companies spend a great deal of effort, time and money wooing new customers, surprisingly few take equal trouble to retain existing customers – even though the rewards, as we shall show, can be considerable. We have found that only a very small number of organisations, while paying ritual lip service to the concept, actually go to the trouble of regularly measuring customer satisfaction in any systematic way, partly because they are obsessed by a perceived need to win new business and partly because they fail to understand the very real and demonstrable relationship between customer retention and profitability.

By chasing new customers at the expense of retaining existing ones, companies are, quite literally, missing a golden opportunity. Our clients have found that if they increase the rate at which customers are retained by as little as five percent, profitability can move in some cases, by over 100%. In other words: Customer Retention adds profit to the bottom line.

Customer satisfaction – the Customer Retention concept

Companies have little difficulty in perceiving the theoretical virtues of this exercise. What they find more difficult is putting it into practice, largely because the systems needed to quantify and analyse customer satisfaction are missing. There need be no real difficulty here. Just as the concept of 'zero defects' has become a standard objective in many manufacturing quality systems, so what might be called 'zero defections' is an equally valid and useful target when dealing with customers. Once this is in place, companies have something tangible at which to aim, which in turn leads them to refocus their entire operation – often with dramatic results.

Bain & Company has developed a number of techniques for measuring customer satisfaction and linking them directly to corporate profitability. The simplest and most powerful of these is 'Customer Retention' where satisfaction is measured by the rate at which customers are kept – the 'Customer Retention Rate'.

This is expressed as the percentage of customers at the beginning of the year that still remain at the end of the year. The more satisfied the customers are, the longer they stay and thus the higher the retention rate.

A retention rate of 80% means that, on average, customers remain loyal for five years whereas one of 90% pushes the average loyalty up to ten years. And as the average 'life' of a customer increases, so does the profitability of that customer to the firm.

Established customers are more profitable

Long-term customers are more profitable for six reasons:

- regular customers place frequent, consistent orders and, therefore, usually cost less to serve;
- longer-established customers tend to buy more;
- satisfied customers may sometimes pay premium prices;
- retaining customers makes it difficult for competitors to enter a market or increase their share;
- satisfied customers often refer new customers to the supplier at virtually no cost;
- the cost of acquiring and serving new customers can be substantial. A higher retention rate implies that fewer new customers need be acquired, and that they can be acquired more cheaply.

As the retention rate goes up, so too does overall profitability. Bain's clients have experienced profit increases of anything from 30% to 125%. This latter result was achieved by a financial services client which succeeded in increasing its retention rate from an industry average of 90% to 95%. Over a period of six years, its market position rose from 38th to fourth in its industry.

But established customers are not only more profitable, retaining customers can help you grow your business. Even in low growth businesses, there is generally a regular churn of customers – 20% of customers may defect each year to your competition. The most powerful, yet often overlooked, way to grow is to increase your retention.

Improving Customer Retention

For a Customer Retention programme to achieve maximum effect, companies must not only measure their retention rates but they must communicate the results – and their importance – to all employees.

In a recent survey where managers were asked about their most important corporate objective nearly all indicated it was achieving set goals or, as they put it, 'Hitting Plan'. In other words, what gets measured, gets done. This applies irrespective of whether the aim is to reach sales targets or short term profit goals. But as customer satisfaction is difficult to quantify and, therefore, measure, it has seldom been a top priority – either with managers or employees.

One way of underlining to employees the importance of keeping customers is for management to stress the cash value of each customer. Domino's, a US fast food chain, has calculated that a single customer who comes back regularly over a period of ten years is worth $5000 to the firm. Employees there now recognise that what they do or say can have far-reaching financial consequences beyond the profit of one pizza. Everybody at the store, from the telephone operator to the delivery person, now knows how important it is to ensure that the customer is satisfied.

Attitudes to customer satisfaction vary from firm to firm and, even more, from industry to industry. With their large customer base, companies in the service sector have, with exceptions like Domino's, traditionally not placed great importance on Customer Retention. Manufacturing companies, on the other hand, have always been concerned about losing large clients. But in neither case have companies made radical and determined efforts to increase or even measure their retention rates. And while there is no single magic formula, in our experience one of the most radical and effective techniques is to build what we call a Value Managed Relationship (VMR).

Value Managed Relationships

What are VMRs?

VMRs are collaborative, communicative partnerships between suppliers and the supplier's customers. These partnerships are radically different from traditional supplier/customer relationships in the following ways:

Traditional approach	VMR Approach
Multiple suppliers	Few suppliers
Regular price quotes	Long term relationship, mutual investment
Adversarial negotiations	Partnership
Sporadic communication	Frequent, planned communication
Little cooperation	Integrated operations
Quality and timeliness to meet lowest threshold	Quality and timeliness 'designed in'
Emphasis on lowest unit price	Emphasis on lowest overall cost

One of the best places to observe what benefits a VMR can bring and how it works in practice is Japan. Japanese automobile component companies supply, on average, 24 times more value per vehicle than their US counterparts. Japanese vehicle manufacturers tend to buy more than twice as many components yet use one tenth of the number of suppliers as their American counterparts. Consequently, their suppliers obtain a lot more business, and are rewarded with long term contracts. Thus we can say that these suppliers have developed VMRs with their customers.

During the 1980s British industry too increased its use of VMRs. However, it has been the purchasing managers of customers who have led the way. We believe that now is the time for the marketing and sales departments of suppliers to use VMRs as a tool to attract and retain customers.

The long-term nature of VMRs makes them the ideal Customer Retention tool.

How do VMRs work?

Instead of focusing on the lowest unit price, VMRs are aimed at reducing system costs – i.e. the total cost of all functions incurred by both the supplier and customer in relation to a specific product or service. For example, two suppliers working closely with a healthcare manufacturer, a Bain client, were able to help the manufacturer move from having eleven suppliers for a particular product to just the two of them. These remaining suppliers passed on a 17% price cut to the manufacturer. But the benefits were not only one way. In return, the suppliers secured long term contracts, their business increased in volume by between 200% and 400%, and they were able to cut their own costs by the amount of the price reduction. Furthermore, the efficiency of the suppliers in handling orders increased markedly. These two suppliers had attained a notable victory over the competition.

Although each step in the process can often be improved, the largest benefits typically arise from four areas: integrated design, manufacturing, quality control, and inventory systems.

Design for lower cost: Integrated design enables both parties to reduce costs – lower manufacturing costs for the supplier and lower assembly costs for the customer. For instance, a food packaging supplier, a Bain client, and a food manufacturer were recently able to save 17.4% of total costs by integrating the design function. The savings were found in two areas. Cheaper, more effective raw materials were substituted and the product itself was redesigned to make it easier to manufacture.

Improve manufacturing efficiency: The consolidation of the supply base allows the supplier to schedule production over longer, higher-volume runs. Fewer schedule changes and machine change-overs result in lower costs and improved quality. The supplier is able to move down the experience cost curve faster and investment planning becomes less risky. A supplier to a large car manufacturer, a Bain client, moved from being one of twelve suppliers for a component, to one of three, and saw quality improve by 15% and its manufacturing costs decrease by 6%.

Improve quality: This same supplier helped save £150 per car by working closely with the manufacturer on quality control. The supplier was able to design and manufacture components exactly to specification. Therefore, the need for incoming inspection at the customer plant was eliminated. As a result the supplier was able to increase its prices without increasing the total costs to the customer.

Slash inventories: Further large savings can arise from inventory costs. Suppliers typically hold excess inventory of finished products to satisfy erratic customer demand. Customers also hold component inventory to smooth out supplier shipments. 'Just-in-Time' deliveries and close cooperation between supplier and customer can minimise the aggregate inventory level. As a result of closer liaison between customer and supplier, a Continental European computer manufacturer was able to cut total inventory costs by 90%.

Risks

However valuable the VMR-building exercise might be, it is not entirely risk-free. Dependence on a large customer and the exchange of confidential information could represent risks which many suppliers feel they cannot afford to take. To reduce the risks they must build a relationship of mutual trust over a number of years. But start now, as the risks of losing business to a competitor greatly outweigh the risks of developing a VMR.

VMRs – Results

An example of a supplier-driven VMR is that of a toiletries manufacturer and a large retail chain. The toiletries manufacturer, a Bain client, recognised the opportunity to increase sales and profitability of both parties by entering into a VMR with one of its large customers. The toiletries company assembled a package of benefits and approached the customer at senior executive level. A joint taskforce was set up which achieved substantial improvements for the retailer. During the first two years of the VMR the retailer's toiletries sales grew by 40% and his gross margin by 83%.

How does the supplier benefit?

The supplier who developed the VMR obtained even more dramatic results. Sales to the retailer increased 62% over two years and margins improved from 4.9% to 17.4%. Overall, the supplier's operating profit jumped more than fivefold.

In general, VMRs provide five major benefits to the supplier:

- retained customers
- increased sales volume
- improved margins through cost reduction
- higher quality output
- locked-out competitors, both domestic and foreign

Summary

Customer retention must become an essential element of British companies' drive to become world-class competitors. Improving customer satisfaction, and hence Customer Retention, can greatly enhance profitability and competitiveness. Supplier-driven Value Managed Relationships are in essence the ultimate tool for retaining customers. VMRs represent an exciting opportunity to improve performance and assist in the continued revitalisation of British industry.

Reproduced from Buchanan, Robin, W.T. and Gillier, Crawford, S. (1990) Value managed relationships: the key to customer retention and profitability. *European Management Journal*, **8** (4), 523–526. Copyright 1990, with kind permission from Elsevier Science Ltd, The Boulevard, Langford Lane, Kidlington OX5 1GB, UK.

MARKETING TO EXISTING CLIENTS
David Maister

David Maister is an author, teacher and consultant and is recognized as an authority on the management of professional service firms. He taught for six years on the MBA and Executive programmes as a professor at Harvard Business School and is with Maister Associates, a Boston-based consulting firm. His views have been quoted in leading journals and magazines, including *Time, Newsweek, Business Week* and *The Economist*.

Although writing about professional service firms, Maister's article has obvious applicability to other sectors. The article starts with an explanation of why existing clients are good prospects and why there is a relative neglect of existing clients in professional firms. Maister continues with a detailed account of how to design a client-specific retention strategy. He outlines three basic stages to the strategy which include: making the client disposed to use the firm again; increasing the firm's capabilities to serve the client; and finding and pursuing the next engagement. He argues that a final and critical step in capturing these opportunities is to ensure that the reward systems are tailored in such a way that the pursuit of existing clients is a legitimate part of the professionals' business activities.

Most firms that advise on professional services say that their existing clients represent the most probable (and often the most profitable) source of new business. However, when one examines their behavior, one finds that while they usually have well-established and organized programs for developing 'new clients', they make little, if any, *organized* effort to obtain new business from existing clients. Similarly, most firms' expenditures for getting business (either out-of-pocket expenses or the allocation of the people's time) are overwhelmingly spent trying to get new clients, with only a small fraction of the total devoted to winning new business from existing clients.

Simply put, firms say they believe one thing, but appear to be doing another. What's going on here?

Why existing clients are good prospects

The best place to begin our exploration of this apparent paradox is to examine the reasons why existing clients are said to represent the 'best' source of new business. The possible explanations are many.

First and foremost, it is most firms' experience that time spent marketing to existing clients is more likely to result in new business: existing clients represent *higher probability* prospects.

This is so because the ability to win the client's trust and confidence is a dominant influence in the sales process of professional services. Often, this single criterion is the deciding factor in competitive situations. Accordingly, where the firm is already working for the client, it has a headstart on the single most important purchasing influence, resulting in a higher probability of success. Other aspects of the sales process, such as discovering the real (often unstated) client concerns and needs are far easier to do in an existing client setting. A third factor which increases the probability of winning new business in existing client situations is the basic fact that such new-business opportunities are usually non-competitive: if the firm uncovers a new need in the course of its current work, it can often win permission to proceed with the new work without going through a competitive proposal process.

A second attraction in targeting existing clients is that, in most situations, marketing costs to win a given volume of new business are lower. The firm does not have to spend as much (unbilled) time researching the client and its industry, since that will already have been done to win the existing account. There will be less need to conduct a wide variety of activities that are a major part of the new prospect sales process: awareness building, qualifying activities, 'comfort building' or 'investigatory' interviews, competitive proposals and presentations, and so on.

A third advantage in targeting existing clients is that 'follow-on' engagements from existing clients often are more profitable than first-time engagements from new clients. There is less risk of 'write-offs' of time spent getting up to speed on the client or the client's industry. There is less risk of false starts or misspecification of the project dimensions, which also lead to written-off time. Being noncompetitive, the existing client situation usually implies less pressure on fees, and a greater ability to charge full rates because the client has already been exposed to the firm and its ability to deliver value for money. In new-client situations, where the firm and its capabilities are unknown, prospects will always be more skeptical and fee-sensitive.

Another factor contributing to greater potential profitability on existing clients is that there is a higher probability that the firm can work, over time, to integrate more juniors into the delivery of services to client, by building up the client's acceptance of, and comfort with, the juniors. This is in contrast to the new-client situation, where, due to the lack of full comfort with this 'new' provider, there is often a pressure from the client to ensure extensive senior-professional involvement. Thus new-client opportunities may be less leveraged than is possible on existing clients, and the higher profitability that comes with greater leverage is more difficult to achieve.

A fourth reason to give priority to existing clients is that, if firms are to expand their capabilities and strengthen their position in the marketplace, then they must conscientiously pay attention to the *types* of work they bring in. They must seek new types of work that give the firm the opportunity to stretch and build its skills. By very definition, the firm does not have an established track record of performing this work, and it is work that is hard to market to a new prospect. However, once existing clients have developed an appropriate level of trust and confidence in their providers, they are more likely to 'give them the chance' to work on more challenging matters. It is therefore in the existing client base that firms are most likely to find the opportunity to conduct the type of work that not only contributes to this year's bottom line, but adds to its capability to earn more (and higher) fees in the future – to make a contribution to the firm's intellectual capital and not just exploit its existing capabilities.

The importance of winning new clients

If existing clients offer such attractions, why do so many professional firms devote the vast bulk of their nonbillable marketing time (and budget) to the pursuit of new clients?

Part of the answer, of course, is that a steady flow of new clients is important to any professional firm. New clients are needed to 'reseed the gene pool', i.e., provide new environments for the professionals to work in and thus build skills. New clients provide a 'freshness', a 'reinvigoration' that can be motivating to professionals who might have become overly familiar with existing client situations. There is thus somewhat of a link between the volume and variety of new clients and the motivation, morale, dynamisms, and enthusiasms of the professional staff.

If firms *are* active in nurturing existing client relations, existing clients can and do become 'saturated', creating the need for new clients. Even before this state is achieved, some firms are more comfortable pursuing new clients for fear that if they target existing clients too vigorously, they may be perceived by existing clients as too 'leech-like', putting the firm's need for additional revenues ahead of the client's interests.

Many firms give great priority to getting new clients on the grounds that new clients are worth more to the firm than the value of the initial engagement, because they offer the potential for additional future revenues. This simple insight leads to an important conclusion about the relationship between new-client marketing efforts and marketing to existing clients. If the firm is weak (or neglectful) at developing new business from existing client relationships, the lower is the value (and hence the 'return on marketing investment') of getting new clients. The better the firm is at marketing to existing clients, the higher will be the value of its new-client marketing activities.

The issue then is not whether firms should pursue one or the other, but rather, what the appropriate balance should be in expending the marketing effort and budget. As noted above, my researches suggest that the balance today is excessively tilted toward new clients and away from organized attention to generating new business from existing clients. We must now try to understand why this is so.

Why is there a relative neglect of existing clients?

I have learned from numerous conversations on this topic with consultants, lawyers, accountants, actuaries, and other professionals that primary among all the reasons for the relative overemphasis on new clients is the simple fact that pursuing and getting a new client is more *fun*. New clients provide the thrill of the chase, in a way that nurturing existing relationships does not. Pursuing a new-client proposal opportunity usually has the characteristics of a well-defined, finite project with relatively clear tasks and specific deadlines. Nurturing an existing relationship often has few inherent deadlines, little obvious structure, and more ambiguous tasks. Consequently, it is reported to me, it is a less 'satisfying' activity: it doesn't provide the same 'rush of adrenaline'.

If this is indeed a basic human proclivity ('we always give more love and attention to those we're trying to seduce than those we're married to'), then it is unfortunate that firm management practices *reinforce* rather than try to counteract this natural bias. In most firms, I have learned, there is a tendency to overreward the bringing in of new clients and underreward bringing in new business from existing clients. As one consultant expressed it to me: 'When a new client is brought in, rockets go off, bells sound, your name gets in the firm newsletter, and you can bank on a good bonus. If you bring in an equivalent amount of business from existing clients, the management yawns and says "at least s/he's doing his/her job".'

In similar spirit, obtaining new business from existing clients is often taken for granted: 'If we do good work they'll give us the new business, so we don't need to spend nonbillable time on it.' A related attitude is: 'If it's an existing client, everything we do is or should be, billable. Our marketing takes place on billable time.' As might be expected, this posture frequently leads to the result that good marketing activities don't get done.

Accounting practices at some firms compound this problem. If all time spent on existing clients must be accounted for, then things done in the name of pursuing more business from existing clients often show up in the accounts as extra costs (and hence lower profitability) on the existing engagement. Hence desirable marketing activities are not done.

There is something strange in such environments. In the pursuit of a new prospect, often in competition, firms appear willing to spend hundreds of nonbillable hours pursuing opportunities that have lower probability, happily 'giving away' time to bring in new revenue. But they don't or won't invest an equivalent (or smaller) amount of nonbillable time to bring in an equivalent volume of new business from existing clients. Existing clients are charged for what is readily given away to prospects.

Further explaining why firms tend to overallocate time to new prospects and underinvest in existing-client marketing, is the fact that the types of marketing activities necessary to get the two types of new business are fundamentally different. As we shall see below, the pursuit of new business from existing clients requires an 'intimate' involvement with the client and his/her business: It requires getting 'close' to the client and developing a high level of interpersonal trust. By contrast, the activities that make up a campaign to pursue new prospects are less 'high-touch', less intimate, more detached: doing research on the prospect (rather than dealing with him or her), writing proposals, giving seminars, making structured presentations. For better or for worse, I have learned that many professionals are more *comfortable* pursuing new clients.

Another key explanation, I have found, is that at many firms, marketing is reactive, i.e., responds to an external impetus such as an RFP. Accordingly, available marketing time is quickly filled with activities initiated by these external stimuli. Since existing client opportunities must be actively sought out and brought to the surface often before the client is aware of the need, a reactive posture inevitably results in underexploitation of existing client opportunities.

How to make it happen

It is clear that there are strong forces biasing individuals and firms away from the targeting of existing clients. Many, if not most, professional firms could benefit substantially from a studious look at how they are allocating their nonbillable marketing time between new and existing clients, and deciding whether they could benefit from an explicit program of targeting existing clients more than at present. It is equally clear that if such a program is to be implemented, firm management must take some concrete steps to make it happen. Fortunately, once a firm has resolved to go in this direction, the management process necessary to make it happen is relatively easy to describe and to implement.

The process begins with the identification of the key client prospects in the existing client base. As with all aspects of marketing, the fundamental rule is to focus and target one's efforts on the best opportunities. Accordingly, it is not wise to launch a program of marketing to *all* existing clients, but only to those carefully selected prospects where the firm concludes that (a) there are additional client needs that the firm can serve and (b) the relationship is good enough to raise the probability that a marketing effort will pay off.

This review should be conducted by the head of the firm (or office) with the senior professionals responsible for each client relationship. From this process should come a ranking or prioritization of the best opportunities.

Next, it is necessary to establish a budget for each target account, including both out-of-pocket expenses and, more importantly, the allocated amount of time that should be spent on this opportunity, given the likelihood of generating the business and, of course, the attractiveness of that business.

This budgeting should be done on an 'equivalency' principle: First, figure out how much nonbillable marketing time the firm spends to obtain a given volume of revenue. For example, the firm may discover that, on average, 100 person hours are spent to obtain a $200,000 engagement. If there are prospects of obtaining a $200,000 engagement at an existing client, then the firm should be prepared to establish a marketing budget for the existing client which approximates this amount, usually being a little less because marketing to existing clients should be more cost-effective. So, as an illustration, the firm might conclude that the situation warrants 50 to 75 hours in nonbillable marketing time for the designated existing client.

Because of the accounting problem described above (confusion between chargeable activities for the current engagement and non-chargeable time to get the next engagement), it is wise to establish this 'Marketing to Client X' budget as a separate, formal 'charge number' in the firm's accounts. Now that there is a budget, the firm should assign responsibility to the senior professional on the engagement. S/he is now responsible for two budgets – running the current engagement for quality and profitability and using the marketing budget to maximum effectiveness.

An advantage of this approach is that it provides a vehicle for each member of the client service team to get involved with the business development effort. Junior members of the team can (subject to approval of the team leader) charge time to the marketing budget when they engage in activities directly targeted at 'developing the account'. Without such accounts, it is often difficult to get junior staff members, subject to personal billability targets, to engage in these 'nonbillable' tasks. Since there is only a finite, predesignated amount in the marketing budget, there is little chance that excessive, unproductive nonbillable activities will result.

The potential role of junior members of the engagement team in the marketing effort needs to be stressed. They often have more frequent and direct client contact (especially in the research and interview stages of the project) than more senior professionals and are in a better position to pick up the signals and clues that the client organization has additional needs. One major consulting firm makes it a regular practice to hold meetings of the client service team every two weeks, not to discuss the current engagement but to ask each team member, from the most junior to the most senior, 'what have you learned about what is going on in the client organization since last we met two weeks ago?' Naturally, this practice forces each team member to keep eyes and ears open and to operate continuously with two agendas: performing the current engagement and finding the next.

Once the budget has been agreed to, firm management should require of those senior professionals who are responsible for the 'target accounts' that they formally develop a written marketing plan for obtaining the target client's additional business. As with all marketing, a written, specific plan (with target dates) provides the structure and discipline to ensure that the desired activities are actually carried out. Once the plan has been developed (by the account team), it should be reviewed and approved by the head of the firm (or office) and become a concrete commitment against which subsequent activity can be reviewed and appraised. While this may sound excessively bureaucratic, I have learned that only in this way can the firm ensure that execution follows. As noted above, there is an inherent bias against this sort of activity, and the (hopefully) continued arrival of RFP's will continually work to distract senior professionals from execution of the existing client marketing plans.

Designing the client-specific marketing campaign

If a client service team has, as a rough approximation, 50 to 75 hours to spend trying to get more business from an organization and an executive with whom they already work and have access to, what should they do with the time to maximize the chances that additional revenues will be obtained?

Successful marketing to existing clients, I have learned, has three basic stages, none of which may be omitted. They are (a) making the client disposed to use the firm again, (b) increasing the firm's capabilities to serve the client, and (c) finding and pursuing the next engagement.

Making the client disposed to use the firm again

This first element is probably the most critical stage of the process. If the firm is to win new business from an existing client then that client must not only be 'satisfied' with the firm's services but 'superpleased'. The pursuit of new business thus requires that time and energy be expended on the current engagement in order to lay the groundwork for the subsequent 'selling' effort.

The activities involved here are those that most professionals would acknowledge as good client relations on *any* engagement, but which most professionals would also acknowledge are often neglected or performed less than fully. They include going the extra mile on the current engagement, increasing the amount of client contact, building the business relationship and the personal relationship. Some specific tactics for this stage are shown in Table 1. None of these tactics are new: what may be new is providing the budget, the incentive and the specific plan to ensure that these activities actually take place. There is a profound difference between acknowledging the wisdom of the tactics listed in Table 1 and having an organized plan of action to ensure their execution.

One or two of these activities deserve some elaboration. 'Volunteering to attend client's internal meetings' is a particularly powerful tactic. As an illustration, suppose that a client service team learns that its client is holding a national meeting of, say, all of its branch managers on a topic that is not covered by the team's current engagement. The team leader

Table 1 *Making the client disposed to use firm again*

1 *Going the extra mile on the current engagement*
Use new business budget to fund extra analysis
Use budget to improve turnaround time, service
Improve quality of presentations
More documentation, explanations, accessibility

2 *Increasing the amount of client contact*
Telephone regularly
Visit at every opportunity
Schedule business meetings near mealtime
Invite to firm offices
Introduce one's partners
Get firm leaders involved

3 *Building the business relationship*
Help him with contacts
Put on special seminars for his staff
Volunteer to attend client's internal meetings
Offer free day of counselling on non-project matters
Send him useful articles
If possible, refer him business

4 *Building the personal relationship*
Social activities
Remember personal, family anniversaries
Obtain scarce tickets
Provide home telephone number
Offer use of firm's facilities

could approach the client and say: 'Would you like me (or one of my partners) to attend the meeting, *free of charge*, to be a resource to you?' Many, if not most, clients would accept such an offer, putting the firm in position to accomplish two important marketing tasks: first, sit in on a client meeting where the client's problems, issues, and needs are being discussed and, second, have the opportunity to demonstrate expertise and be helpful on a new issue. In terms of getting new business, there is perhaps no other tactic which has as great a return on time invested.

The list of tactics in Table 1 includes building both the business relationship and the personal relationship. There is no better way to build a relationship than to find some way to be helpful or useful to the other person. To get a favor (the next engagement) one must first give a favor (do something *for* the client, free of charge, that demonstrates both caring and a commitment). It should be stressed that, in terms of impact, building the *business* relationship takes precedence over the personal relationship. Making a friend of the client is helpful, but only as a supplement to, not a substitute for, a strong business relationship.

Increasing the firm's capabilities

The second stage of marketing to existing clients is the investment of time in increasing the firm's capabilities to serve the client. The goal here is to do those things that persuade the client that the firm's knowledge and

Table 2 *Increasing firm's capabilities to serve the client*

1 *Increasing knowledge of client's industry*
  Study industry magazines/newsletters thoroughly
  Attend industry meetings *with* client
  Conduct proprietary studies

2 *Increasing knowledge of client's business*
  Read all his brochures, annual reports, other public documents
  Ask to see his strategic plan
  Volunteer to critique internal studies
  Reverse Seminar

3 *Increasing knowledge of client's organization*
  Ask for organization chart
  Ask who he deals with most
  Ask him about his boss
  Ask about power structure
  Arrange to meet other executives
  Spend time with his juniors

4 *Increasing knowledge of client*
  Find out precisely how he's evaluated
  Find out what he's unhappy with

talent not only *can be* but *are* customized to the specific client situation. As in all marketing, new business from existing clients must be *earned*. As Table 2 suggests, some of the nonbillable marketing budget should be dedicated to encouraging and performing the familiar tasks of increasing the firm's knowledge of the client's industry, business, organization, and the client himself or herself.

The performance of these activities are not just symbolic ways of pleasing the client and demonstrating interest. If done thoroughly and well in a planned, systematic fashion (i.e., as part of a structured marketing plan), they will serve to uncover new client needs, reveal areas where the client is dissatisfied with the current state of affairs (a critical condition for him/her to commit to a new project), and also provide the documentation and evidence to persuade the client to proceed in new areas. In essence, the firm is 'preparing the proposal' as it simultaneously improves its capability to be of value to the client.

Finding and pursuing the next engagement

The third and final category for which the nonbillable marketing budget can be used is the explicit process of selling the client on the new project. As should be clear, this task has not been neglected in the first two stages, which have included the traditional sales tasks of building trust and confidence, discovering client needs, and demonstrating specialized capabilities. If well done, the third stage often requires little time.

If not yet done, activities in this stage involve creating opportunities to demonstrate initiative and competence (rather than waiting for them to arise). It requires a planned program of digging out intelligence on new needs and assembling this evidence, and crafting opportunities to make the client aware of the new need. Table 3 lists some of the tactics that can be employed.

It should be clear that few existing client opportunities would warrant the application of all of the tactics described in Table 1 through 3. Rather, they should be seen as a 'menu' from which the best selected set of tactics can be chosen which (a) fit what has been deemed to be the appropriate level of effort in each specific case (i.e., what the budget is) and (b) are most likely to be effective in the specific client situation. In all cases, however, some time must be spent on each of the stages. As a matter of effectiveness, one cannot skip stages 1 and 2 entirely and hope to be productive with marketing efforts solely from category 3.

What I hope is also clear is that the time spent designing and executing a targeted marketing campaign for a specific client along the lines described above would indeed be more likely to result in new work than the same amount of time spent trying to generate new leads and convert those leads into new clients. As we have seen, both need to be done, but firms should not forego the ripe opportunities available in the existing client base.

A final, mandatory step in capturing these opportunities is to modify the reward systems of the firm so that each line professional perceives

Table 3 *Finding and pursuing the next engagement*

1 *Creating opportunities to demonstrate initiative and competence*
   Volunteer services of one's partners
   Arrange meetings with one's partners

2 *Digging out new intelligence on new needs*
   Use entire project team to gather info.
   Get invited to their meetings
   Arrange to meet other executives
   Spend time with client staff at all levels

3 *Assembling evidence of new need*
   Conduct additional analysis
   If possible, conduct additional interviews
   Conduct special studies

4 *Creating awareness of new need*
   Bring problem areas to his attention early. (Find ways to worry him)
   Document evidence of problems
   Compare his company's statistics to others
   Share results of work done for others

5 *Finding sponsor/friend/coach in client organization*
   Figure out who wants change

6 *Asking for the new engagement* **at the right time**
   'Point out' opportunities early and often, with no 'hard sell'
   Concrete proposal only when we're confident it will be accepted

that time spent on this activity is valued by the firm at least as much as pursuing new clients. 'Rewards', here, must be taken to mean not just financial compensation, but the rewards of celebration, status, strokes, and hoopla. If firms wish to capitalize on the new business opportunities available to them in their existing client base, they must ensure that the management's practices and behavior actively encourage and reward this activity. As we have noted, there is no, or little, argument in professional circles of the desirability of the activities described above. There is, however, significant room for firms to move in creating the environment in which they will actually take place. If professional firms' management want the substantial benefits that flow from developing existing client relationships, they can have them. But they seem not to occur automatically: they must be explicitly managed for.

Reproduced from Maister, D. (1989). Marketing to existing clients, *Journal of Management Consultancy*, **5**, (2), 25–32. With kind permission from Elsevier Science B.V., Amsterdam, The Netherlands.

PART THREE
Implementing
Relationship Marketing

8   PLANNING AND DEVELOPING RELATIONSHIP STRATEGIES

A review of the relationship marketing literature suggests that greater emphasis has been directed towards relationship marketing *strategy* than its implementation. This final chapter includes three articles relating to the planning and implementation of relationship strategies.

The first article, by Rosenberg and Czepiel, develops a marketing approach for customer retention. This article is one of the first to discuss a distinct marketing mix for *keeping* customers. They propose a 'customer keeping marketing mix' consisting of five elements: product extras, reinforcing promotions, salesforce connections, specialized distribution and post-purchase communication. The article examines how each of these five elements can be developed to improve customer retention and long-term profitability. The approaches taken by a number of organizations are provided as examples.

This article suggests that lack of organizational coordination and control frequently contributes to the loss of customers. It advocates the improvement of crossfunctional integration and assigning specific executive accountability for customer keeping as a means of reducing defection. The article concludes by emphasizing the need to distinguish between getting and keeping customers and to rigorously identify the balance of effort needed in both of these activities. It also highlights the need for management to develop special ways of treating customers to keep them coming back.

The second article, by Keith Fletcher, Colin Wheeler and Julia Wright of Strathclyde Business School, explores recent development in database marketing (DBM). Database marketing will continue to have an increasing impact on relationship building as it harnesses the capability of computer and telecommunications technologies. The article includes an overview of what database marketing is, its history and development, its information requirements and how database marketing differs from other approaches to marketing. It emphasizes a number of means by which database marketing could be used as a competitive tool to strengthen customer relationships. While the entire article does not focus on relationship marketing, it does give an excellent overview of

DBM and its role in developing and enhancing relationships with precisely targeted customers. It has obvious application in mass-customization.[1] DBM has enormous potential to develop and enhance relationships[2] and will increasingly be used to help implement relationship marketing strategies.

The final paper by Glenn De Souza, President of Strategic Quality Systems Inc., emphasizes the value of developing a customer retention plan. He suggests a customer retention plan with four major elements: measuring customer retention, interviewing former customers, analysing complaint and service data, and identifying switching barriers. This paper places emphasis on three key aspects of customer retention. First, it illustrates the reasons customers defect and categorizes them into: price defectors, products defectors, service defectors, market defectors, technological defectors and organizational defectors. Second, it acknowledges the need for rigorous complaint analysis – an issue that is recognized by the Malcolm Baldridge National Quality Award. (The award criteria examine not only the extent to which entrants resolve complaints quickly but also how they analyse complaints and translate the findings into systemic improvement.) Third, the article suggests a number of ways of building in switching barriers through activities such as electronic data interchange, strategic bundling and improved account management activities.

These three articles provide an overview of some of the current thinking regarding implementation of relationship marketing strategies. Much of what has been written identifies the strategic importance of relationship marketing. Effort now needs to be directed towards developing implementation approaches for these strategies. Much of the research effort now being undertaken is starting to focus on this issue.

References

1 Pine, B. (1993). *Mass Customisation: The New Frontier in Business Competition*, The Free Press, New York.
2 Davies, J.M. (1993). *The Essential Guide to Database Marketing*, McGraw-Hill, New York.

A MARKETING APPROACH FOR CUSTOMER RETENTION
Larry J. Rosenberg and John A. Czepiel

At the time of writing Larry J. Rosenberg was an Associate Professor of Marketing at the University of Massachusetts at Amherst. His research interests include the future of marketing, non-store retailing, marketing for entrepreneurs and Japanese marketing. John A. Czepiel was an Associate Professor of Marketing at the Graduate School of Business Administration, New York University. His research interests are focused on the issues of consumer satisfaction and the marketing of services.

This article emphasizes the importance of implementing two marketing mixes – one aimed at catching customers and the other at keeping them. It examines five key elements involved in developing a customer retention marketing mix. It then focuses on the need for internal restructuring and reorganization of both marketing and operations activities to emphasize customer retention.

'The way many companies relate to customers is akin to looking for a needle in a haystack, finding it, and then throwing it back to look for it once again.' 'It is not worth the time and money to get customers if you don't keep them.' Two marketing executives.

Because of the growth mentality that pervades consumer marketing, most of its efforts have been geared toward attracting a stream of new customers. As a result, the front-end function of customer getting commands a substantial portion of budgets, top management attention, and talented marketing personnel. The back-end efforts of customer retaining generally are neglected.[2,7,11]

The customer retention area deserves more attention on two counts:

1 *Effectiveness*. In more cases than is assumed, marketing can succeed in building a loyal following of repeat buyers rather than constantly wooing new recruits. This activity can ensure a defensible and growing market share.
2 *Efficiency*. It is estimated that the average company spends six times more to get a new customer than it does to hold a current one. A lost customer reduces company profits by $118, compared with a $20 cost to keep a customer satisfied.[10]

These dual advantages are being enjoyed by those consumer marketers who are acutely aware of the potential of holding onto customers – packaged-food producers, automobile dealers, banks, and telephone companies.

A passive approach to customer keeping may prove harmful to companies. A marketing strategy that goes after both new and old customers is generally not effectively addressing the existing customer.

Some companies seem hooked on steady doses of fresh customers to cover up regular losses of existing ones. Some life insurance companies and supermarket chains fall into this trap.

Our discussion applies to a wide range of consumer marketers, although not every customer-retaining approach will fit all firms and products. For example, some organizations know or at least meet their customers as individuals (durables, major services), while others must settle for knowing them statistically (packaged goods, fast services).

A time for customer retention

Customer retention is taking on a greater importance as forces reshape the environment in which consumer marketing operates. Simply winning new customers becomes a riskier way to prosper; at the same time, the yields increase from holding onto customers – including getting more business from them. Here is why customers today must be kept for tomorrow:

- Lower growth of population and income in the decade ahead appreciates the 'asset' of existing customers.
- New-product opportunities – always limited by technological development – are harder to find and hold on to as more firms pounce on the attractive new products available.[5]
- Pressure to reduce consumer dissatisfaction creates a need to better care for customers, especially after the sale.[8]
- Customer loyalty erodes when there is a wide range of similar nationwide products and retailers.
- A conservation ethic regarding limited resources, especially energy, is paralleled by the notion of customers as finite human resources and as part of the larger community of the corporation.

The upshot of these trends is that the aggressive growth philosophy of most corporations is questionable because it cannot be sustained. Most marketing managers today grew up (and prospered) in an era when marketing's principal job was getting new customers. Now, however, the need is to conserve a firm's customer base and to enlarge its buying activity. Marketing managers must start asking: 'What are we doing to keep customers?'

Ways to retain customers

More and bolder initiatives in holding onto customers are occurring among firms of various sizes and industries. Although the buying situations differ for consumer goods versus services and for durables versus nondurables, customer-keeping approaches can be tailored to these diverse products.

Companies can benefit more from their current customers through customer portfolio analysis, a customer-retaining marketing mix, and reorganization for customer retention.

Customer portfolio analysis

The first strategic customer-keeping consideration involves knowing the purchasing history of a product's or company's customers. For each product there is what we call a *customer portfolio* – a combination of customer types that generate sales and resulting profit. An *optimal* customer portfolio consists of a balance of new and repeat buyers yielding target sales and profits.

The construction of a customer portfolio begins with determining meaningful customer classifications based on market research of actual purchase patterns. Kodak monitors six camera customer categories: current customers, new customers, brand switchers, trial users, customers who upgrade their purchases, and those obtaining equipment by trade-in. Maytag uses three appliance customer segments: new purchasers, repeat buyers, and those who switched from Maytag to a competitor and then returned.

The portfolio segments can be measured in terms of number of customers, number of purchases, demographic and psychographic profiles, and contributions to sales and profits. Assume that a given company discovers through market research what its four customer categories contributed to actual 1983 sales as shown in Table 1. In order to raise profits, management desires to attract a different customer mix for 1984. This can be achieved by aiming specific marketing efforts toward the customer segments targeted for expansion, and monitoring through research all the categories several times throughout the year (such as quarterly).

Three basic factors must be considered in seeking the optimal balance in a customer portfolio. First, products vary according to how readily product differences can be perceived by consumers. When products are selected on the basis of 'objective' superiorities after consumers have tried

Table 1 *How the customer portfolio contributes to sales for a hypothetical company*

Customers categories	Actual sales 1983	Target sales 1984
First time	25%	25%
Repeat	40	45
Switched away, then returned	15	20
Last time	20	10
	100%	100%

them, keeping these customers is relatively easy – witness the strong repeat rates of foreign automobiles. When product characteristics are experienced largely on a 'subjective' basis, as are cosmetics and beer, brand switching usually results more from the consumer's need for variety than from product dissatisfaction. Hair shampoos exhibit a high rate of brand switching because of the desire for sensual variety and the difficulty in objectively evaluating product performance.

Second, product category volume growth affects the balancing of a customer portfolio. Having too large a proportion of repeat purchases in the rapid-growth stage of a market may indicate insufficient attention to the getting function. Continually generating a large proportion of new buyers in the maturity stage may signify an underdeveloped keeping function.

Third, the relative costs and benefits of attracting and retaining customers must be gauged. This requires the calculation of costs involved in winning new customers and holding onto present ones, against benefits in terms of revenues contributed by each of these groups. These figures can be estimated from data generated in test market experiments.

The customer portfolio must be based on sound *customer feedback research*. Most marketing research is project-oriented: it addresses known or assumed problems, or it evaluates specific market opportunities. The customer feedback survey is geared to monitor marketing performance by periodically measuring how satisfied (or dissatisfied) customers are.[3] Quantifying customer feedback over time provides a revealing indicator of changes and of marketing's effectiveness. It also can flag trouble spots. The amount and content of unsolicited customer complaints reflect a biased sample, but the survey puts them into proper perspective. Both General Electric and AT & T have relied heavily on asking for systematic feedback from customers for several years.

Customer-retaining marketing mix

The *'marketing mix'* is a central concept in devising a marketing strategy. Because of the company bias favoring customer getting, specific actions to retain customers receive less planning attention than they deserve.

One remedy is to conceive of two separate marketing mixes, one for customer getting and the other for customer keeping. Several major elements should be part of the new marketing mix for customer retention: product extras, reinforcing promotions, sales force connections, specialized distribution, and post-purchase communication.

Product extras

Keeping customers frequently requires giving them more than the basic product that initially attracted them. *Product extras* for individual customers over time can play a sales-expansive role.[6]

The main approach is to create a total *product service* system. Whatever the customers purchased initially, the company can then present them with related benefits provided by other items in the product line. In this way, they come to realize the existence and value of a *total consumption system*. McDonalds no longer just sells hamburgers, but complete meals, also for different times of the day (breakfast, lunch, snack), and different services (eat-in or take-out). The customer gets involved in the system rather than focusing solely on the basic product, which might be subject to aggressive competition.

A crisis with customers occurs when the product breaks down or the service goes unperformed. In anticipation, the product extra of *easy-to-remedy features* can rescue a displeased customer. General Electric has touted this approach for its small electric appliances. For physical products, that can mean a design system of modular parts, so the malfunction of any one can be repaired with ease and speed. Mailing a replacement part to a customer has proven to be cheaper than maintaining large service centers. Newer residential telephone models can be fixed this way, thus cutting down on expensive repair visits.

An approach to anticipating the product breakdown crisis is making *preventive maintenance* items and services available. Tape recorders will work best after long usage when a demagnetizer attachment cleans the machine's heads. The manufacturer indifferent to marketing this attachment not only loses an aftermarket sale but increases the risk that the tape recorder owner will become dissatisfied with the product's performance. At a fairly predictable date after purchase, certain items can be offered as replacements for parts of the product that get used up – vacuum dust bags, drill bits, and auto engine components. The sale of a service contract can secure similar advantages, as has been shown by several producers of large appliances.

Reinforcing promotions

Product promotion works better when aimed at existing customers. If a marketer knows who these customers are, benefits can be obtained by giving them reinforcing communications.

First, tuning-in to customers makes it possible for the company to advance their levels of knowledge and loyalty on products already purchased. To some firms, advertising and couponing to keep customers involves a defensive approach to play up product quality and preempt rival new entries. Second, this type of promotion can introduce customers to the firm's other products, especially through cross-sampling – a *Vicks 44* coupon on *Vicks Vap-O-Rub*.

A list of actual customers makes possible direct communication with them. A firm can build such a list through sales receipts, warranty cards, credit account records, and marketing research surveys.

One promotional device for reinforcing customers involves *customer-only publications*. These are targeted to buyers who have already exhibited some degree of commitment to the product or company by one or more purchases. The vehicles can take the form of periodic newsletters, special reports, exclusive catalogs, and even the annual report. The *Apple* magazine has proved to be a valuable link with the firm's personal computer owners.

A prime moment to add to the customer's momentum is after the purchase act. Any consumer doubts or confusion concerning the purchase can be reduced at that time. *Direct mail* is an effective way to do this. A letter can ask about satisfaction with the previous purchase, furnish further product or usage information, present offers for other products, or suggest a time to buy the new model. Mercury Marine, through warranty card records, reaches its boat-engine buyers via mail prior to the three-year mark when they are ready to abandon boating or trade up to a larger boat and engine.

Increasingly, *telemarketing* is being used to follow up purchases. Telephone calls are a more personal and immediate approach than the mail. This technique has been used by automobile dealers after the car has been driven for a while or when it needs major maintenance.

Sales force connections

The sales force can play a decisive role in the customer-retention function. At a retail or service counter the salesperson is the focal point of the company's strategy and is the firm to the customer.[4]

A sales force must be oriented to serving a *long-term relationship* with the customer. Salespeople who lack preparation and knowledge about the product line, and who try to sell a product rather than solve customer problems, usually do not keep customers for long. The roots of such a situation lie with sales management as much as with the salesperson. Selection, training, and compensation that foster short-run goal achievement gear a sales force to today's results at the expense of tomorrow's. Department stores and specialty stores, which want to attract a loyal customer following, tend to hire better qualified salespeople, train them more, and pay them above-average wages.

The *account executive system* goes a long way to permitting the salesperson to effectively cater to the needs of specific clients over time. Some retail banks have scored with customers through the *personal banker* arrangement. Customers are assigned one-on-one to a staff member who handles their multi-service business on a continuing basis. As banking services become more and more alike, this client relationship should grow in popularity.

The sales force's ability to help customers is enhanced by *supportive expertise*. When customer problems arise, the salesperson can call upon a team of specialists (engineers or nutritionists, for example). Another source of expertise can come from a computerized databank, which provides routine information (costs, inventory stocked, delivery time).

Specialized distribution

To make products available to the buyer, distribution systems generally focus on where the ultimate transaction takes place. In considering getting and retaining as separate functions, the possibility exists for arranging distribution along these two lines.

The first method calls for *separate distribution channels* for the getting and keeping functions. One channel is designed to entice, welcome, and complete purchases by new customers. The other serves the needs of repeat customers. No particular channel or retail type lends itself to this distinction; instead it depends on how the distribution strategy is formulated. Trade-book publisher Grosset and Dunlap regards book stores as places where people visit for a specific book or browse and buy on impulse. Many of its books contain return cards describing related book topics which become the start of a mail-order channel. Once the publisher identifies a person's book category preferences, they receive pre-publication announcements of appropriate titles.

In many cases, both roles are played by one distribution unit, especially a retail outlet. Yet even in a single location, *layout of facilities* can separately handle attracting and retaining customers. For example, large bank branches can locate various functions in specific physical areas. One designated counter is where accounts are opened and services arranged for the first time. In another corner is found the automated-teller center where convenience-minded customers use a computer terminal at any hour of the day for a variety of banking transactions.

Vital to a manufacturer's distribution strategy is having *dealer support* to foster repeat buying of its brands. While this is assumed to happen when outlets carry a single brand in a merchandise category, it becomes more challenging when the retailer sells several competing brands. Through an exclusive or selective distribution network, retailers develop a commitment to the brand when they receive adequate attention from the manufacturer. Maytag, with its line of expensive and long-lasting home appliances, grants franchises only to those dealers who share its philosophy of conscientious customer service and have solid reputations in their community. This has meant mainly taking on conservative mom-and-pop appliance stores and linking up with quality department stores.

Post-purchase communication

A company must anticipate that some customers will encounter either minor or serious problems after purchasing. If the firm is not ready to hear and correct these difficulties, the customer may not repurchase (cake mix or auto) or may cancel the arrangement (magazine subscription or insurance policy). Whether company or customer is at fault, standby post-purchase activities can be instrumental in saving these customers.

The front line for customer complaints and inquiries should be *assertive customer relations*.[9,12] This can consist of a separate department or the function can be assigned to those personnel already dealing with customers. At best it should be a blend of the two. The firm should encourage customers to initiate contact whenever the need arises – to clarify instructions, to request further information, to point out a problem, or to seek a remedy. Information hot lines based on *800* numbers,[1] response cards, and service desks can facilitate this process.

Reorganization for customer retention

The lack of organizational coordination and control frequently contributes to the loss of customers. This problem takes two basic forms: a lack of sensitivity to customer turnover rates, and insufficient linkage between the marketing function and the operations group (manufacturing or service).

Because customer turnover is an accepted fact of life, it often goes unmeasured. Thus, marketers should set acceptable *target turnover rates* for evaluating market performance. In the absence of clearly defined limits on customer turnover, organizations find it easy to rely on promotions to recruit new batches of customers. In consumer goods companies, the prized assignments are on new products (with their promising growth potential), while established brands (unless very large ones) are favored less.

Another approach is to assign *executive accountability* for customer keeping. Establishing a management post for taking care of *old business* may make as much sense as one for prospecting new business or for developing *new products*. In some companies, consumer affairs directors have taken on this role.

Inadequate coordination between marketing and the operations group characterizes many types of firms. This lack applies especially to service businesses where marketing has done less to determine product attributes and where customers find product quality difficult to measure. Coordination problems frequently result in overselling, where marketing sees its task solely as attracting customers by promising virtually anything. Expectations of the product or service benefits generated by such an approach become so inflated that the customer will invariably be disappointed by the actual performance.

To improve the coordination between marketing and operations, clearly specifying the *interdependency* of both functions should help. This can mean targeting some promotional strategies toward repeat usage while others pursue trial purchases. For the operations group it entails accepting the primacy of the customer as arbiter of product quality and service. This should be followed up with setting and periodically reevaluating quality and service standards.[13] As a result of this process, New York's Citibank upgraded its service capability between 1976 and 1981 by augmenting the service staff over 20% and by increasing its training budget tenfold.

Conclusion

To achieve better sales and profits, most companies could be doing more to cultivate business from their existing customers. However, enthusiasm for customer-retaining strategies must not endanger sound customer-getting efforts. How companies balance the two is the big question. To intensify reaching old customers while still seeking new ones, for many firms, will mean changes in market analysis, planning systems, management incentives, and marketing and/or operations organization.

In the rush toward growth, consumer marketers have tended to regard success as stemming from obtaining new customers while unwittingly minimizing the importance of satisfying old ones. It is time for more companies to distinguish between their getting and retaining functions, to assess the balance between them, and to remedy any deficiencies in customer retention. This process requires management to value the potential of current customers and to treat them in special ways to get them to keep coming back.

References

1 Abrams, Bill (1983), 'More Firms Use "800" Numbers to Keep Consumers Satisfied,' *Wall Street Journal* (April 7), p. 31.
2 Bender, Paul S. (1976), *Design and Operation of Customer Service Systems*. New York: AMACOM.
3 Czepiel, John A., and Albert Aiella, Jr., (1979). 'Consumer Satisfaction in a Catalog Type Retail Outlet: Exploring the Effect of Product and Price Attributes,' in R.L. Day and H.K. Hunt (eds.), *New Dimensions in Consumer Satisfaction*. Bloomington, Ind.: Graduate School of Business Administration. Indiana University, pp. 129–135.
4 Czepiel, John A. (1980). 'Managing Consumer Satisfaction in Consumer Service Businesses,' Cambridge Mass.: *Marketing Science Institute, Report* pp. 80–107.
5 Day, George S. (1977). 'Diagnosing the Product Portfolio,' *Journal of Marketing*, 41 (April), pp. 29–38.
6 Farr, George L. (1983). 'Developing New Game Strategies,' presented at the American Marketing Association 1983 Strategic Marketing Conference, Chicago, April 19.
7 Fenvessy, Stanley J. (1976). *Keep Your Customers (and Keep Them Happy)*. Homewood, Ill.: Dow Jones-Irwin.
8 Kotler, Philip (1972). 'What Consumerism Means for Marketers,' *Harvard Business Review*, 50 (May-June), pp. 48–57.
9 LaBarbera, Priscilla A., and Larry J. Rosenberg (1980). 'How Marketing Can Better Understand Consumers,' *MSU Business Topics*, 28 (Winter), pp. 29–36.
10 O'Boyle, James (1983). 'Telemarketing Turns Customer Service into a Profit Center,' *Telemarketing*, 2 (September), pp. 12–15.

11 Peters, Thomas J., and Robert H. Waterman, Jr. (1982). *In Search of Excellence: Lessons from America's Best-Run Companies.* New York: Harper & Row.
12 Rosenberg, Larry J., John A. Czepiel, and Lewis C. Cohen (1977). 'Consumer Affairs Audits: Evaluation and Analysis,' *California Management Review,* 19 (Spring), pp. 12–20.
13 Takeuchi, Hirotaka, and John A. Quelch (1983). 'Quality Is More Than Making Good Product,' *Harvard Business Review,* 61 (July-August), pp. 139–145.

THE ROLE AND STATUS OF UK DATABASE MARKETING
Keith Fletcher, Colin Wheeler and Julia Wright

Keith Fletcher, Colin Wheeler and Julia Wright are academics and researchers at the Strathclyde Business School with a special interest in database marketing (DBM).

This article highlights one of the key benefits of database marketing: the development of long-term customer relationships as a means of increasing customer loyalty, reducing brand switching and enhancing cross-selling opportunities. The article provides a very clear review of DBM, its benefits, and how it differs from other forms of marketing.

What is database marketing?

While no universal definition of database marketing (DBM) exists, new versions are produced with monotonous regularity (Jenkinson 1987, Seaton 1988, Direct Response 1987). Rather than reviewing all of these definitions at this point, attention is focused on authors who have written about DBM in depth.

According to Stan Rapp (1989), database marketing is 'the ability of a company to use the vast potential of today's computer and telecommunications technology in driving customer-orientated programmes in a personalised, articulated and cost-effective manner.'

Shaw and Stone (1987) provide a more specific definition: Database marketing is an interactive approach to marketing communication, which uses individually addressable communications media (such as mail, telephone, and the sales force):

● To extend help to a company's target audience
● To stimulate their demand, and
● To stay close to them by recording and keeping an electronic database memory of customer, prospect and all communications and commercial contacts, to help improve all future contracts.

These definitions are both illustrative of a general agreement that DBM is a customer-orientated approach to marketing, and that its special power lies in the techniques it uses to harness the capabilities of computer and telecommunications technology.

As Shaw and Stone imply, a key tool of DBM is a marketing database: an organised set of files providing a common store of all historic customer data.

The aim of DBM is to use this database to promote three main benefits, namely:

1 strategic improvements through the better use of marketing information internally, leading to increased efficiency and effectiveness.
2 identification of strategic advantage through better use of customer and market information leading to the development of new and unique products and services.
3 the development of long-term customer relationships to increase customer loyalty, reduce brand switching, and enhance cross-selling opportunities.

A database marketing strategy provides the framework for the delivery of these benefits through the creative use of information in a company's marketing and sales activities. To achieve this requires a study of the existing information base of a company, and its capability to support existing marketing activities. It also requires an identification of innovative opportunities to use information to match market needs, by a study of potential market opportunities, and the identification of information required to allow marketing to capitalise on the opportunity.

Information requirements of DBM

The type of information required for DBM to operate can easily be obtained from both internal and external sources, and will include customer, market and competitor information. A large amount of this data is often already collected for invoicing or control purposes, but is frequently not in a format suitable for use by the marketing department. Alternatively its value is often not recognised and records of such things as customer enquiries, complaints and other communications are not held after the query has been dealt with.

Information on the firm's existing customers will form the core of the data base, with the sales invoice being perhaps the most valuable input. While the invoice is created for financial purposes it contains a considerable amount of customer data which can be made immediately available to marketers. Among the data recorded on a sales invoice might be:

INFORMATION	MARKETING USE
customer title	(sex, job description identification)
customer first name	(sex coding, discriminates households)
customer surname	(ethnic coding)
customer address	(geodemographic profiling & census data)
date of sale	(tracking of purchase rates, repurchase identification)
items ordered	(benefit/needs analysis, product clusters)
quantities ordered	(heavy/light user, crude segmentation)
price	(life time value calculation of profitability)
discount (if any)	(price sensitivity)
terms & conditions	(customer service needs, special requirements)

The specific information held may vary by type of market. For example an industrial database will hold data on key purchases, and influencers, organisation structure, industry classification, business size; while a sophisticated consumer database may use the postcode to overlay specialist geodemographic data or include lifestyle information allowing customer profiles to be developed.

As the sophistication of the information collection increases the need for ad hoc external market research projects decreases. The firm builds its own database of existing and potential customers which allows the use of sophisticated targeting and segmentation strategies, through its understanding of the market's purchasing behaviour.

Clearly the information held in the marketing database is potentially an invaluable aid in decision-making. However, a database built for marketing purposes must, like the marketing function itself, be future orientated. It must be possible to exploit the database to drive future marketing programmes and DBM provides a strategy to do this.

The marketing database required to use DBM must be at the *centre* of an organisation's MkIS (Marketing Information System), since it can provide information for all levels of marketing decision-making. However, DBM also provides techniques for exploiting the information held to drive marketing programmes and, eventually, marketing strategy. Conceptually, then, it is a specialised form of marketing; physically, it is a specialised subset of the corporate information system.

How does DBM differ from other approaches to marketing?

DBM can be differentiated from other forms of marketing in several ways. Firstly, it communicates directly with customers through a variety of media, including direct mail, telemarketing and direct response advertising. Secondly, it usually requires the customer to provide a response which will allow the company to take some form of appropriate action (such as contact by phone, sending out literature and arranging sales visits). In all cases however, it must be possible to trace the response back to the original communication, something not always available in other marketing approaches.

The concept of DBM is often confused with that of Direct Marketing, defined as 'an interactive system of marketing which uses one or more advertising media to effect a measurable response and or transaction at any location'.

Indeed, while DBM has been stimulated by the increased interest in direct marketing, many direct marketing professionals have questioned the validity of the DBM concept. Bryan Halsey of HLY Grey Direct, for example, has argued: 'I feel strongly that the word (Database) does our industry a disservice – I prefer customer knowledge'. Paul Hawkes of Abram-Hawkes went even further when he declared that 'there is no such thing as Database Marketing', continuing that 'just when our business leaders were becoming convinced of the simple truth of consumer supremacy we had to muddy the water and re-mystify the whole process by introducing a new generation of techno-babble and gobbledegook'!

Unfortunately, these broad pronouncements are fairly common-place in the direct marketing press. Such attitudes are, neverthless, revealing. The general dislike of the term 'database marketing' may be due to a lack of understanding of the conceptual nature of DBM; some marketers may therefore still be convinced that 'database marketing is direct marketing done properly' while other comments often reflect a common mistrust of the computer technology required to practise DBM.

There are then, similarities between the two disciplines: both are *interactive* disciplines and both seek a measurable response. Indeed, although direct marketing has been recognised as a discipline for several decades, the recent growth of DM has coincided with the development of DBM.

Indeed, statements such as 'Direct Marketing will evolve into database marketing' are becoming increasingly common. They are nevertheless misleading. As Roberts and Berger (1989) point out, marketing programmes designed to capitalise on the information available in the customer database will often involve direct marketing elements simply because the database allows for analysis and identification of individual customers, prospects or distributors. Targets can then be reached with individualised direct marketing. DBM and DM nevertheless remain separate disciplines. It is possible to distinguish between the two by saying that DBM shows how to use market data to the best advantage through whatever medium; while DM shows how to use direct media whatever the target market. Also database marketing, unlike direct marketing, extends beyond communications into marketing planning and strategy.

History and development of DBM

The origins of database marketing can be found in two relatively recent trends: developments in technology; and socio-economic changes which, in turn, have resulted in a change in marketing attitudes and approaches.

1 Developments in technology

It is widely agreed that database marketing owes its existence to the sophistication of today's computer and telecommunications technology. While in theory, it would be possible to practise DBM manually, the realities of manipulating thousands of customers records would make it a time consuming and ineffective process. If the database is to contribute fully to marketing operations then, according to Shaw and Stone (1988) it should have the following characteristics:

1 Each actual or potential customer is identified as an individual record on the marketing database.
2 Each customer record contains not only identification and access information (e.g. name and address) but also a range of marketing information (such as the data already listed in this section).
3 The information is available to the company during the process of each transaction with the customer to enable it to decide how to respond to the customer's needs.
4 The database is used to record responses of customers to company initiatives.
5 The information is also available to marketing policy makers to enable them to make decisions about the product and marketing mix most suitable for each target market identified.
6 In large corporations, selling many products to each customer, the database is used to ensure that the approach to the customer is co-ordinated and a consistent approach developed.
7 The information built up, over time, on the database will gradually reduce the need for market research. Marketing campaigns are derived such that the response of customers to the campaign provides the information which the company is looking for.
8 Marketing management automation is developed to handle the vast volume of information generated by DBM. Although no company has yet achieved this level of sophistication, many are adopting it as their goal.

In today's markets, basic DBM requirements would consist of:

i   a relational database (usually), which can draw information from different files linked by a common field
ii a query language to access the database
iii a high quality output device (usually) such as a laser printer
iv additional software packages for market segmentation analysis, forecasting, the overlying of geodemographic psychographic data, merge/purge etc.

The technological developments which have made DBM a feasible option for many companies could be categorised as follows:

i   *Hardware developments* The developments in computer capability have resulted in much faster instruction execution, giving greater through-put and faster access times. This is combined with greatly increased on-line storage which makes more data immediately accessible. On the other hand, the machine related computing costs have been falling dramatically. According to Courtheoux (1988) computer hardware costs have declined 20% to 25% per year for about a generation and this trend is likely to continue indefinitely. Low cost mini and supermicro systems with rigid high speed drives now make invest-ment feasible for the smaller companies.

ii   *Communications developments* – advances in data communication techniques, coupled with decreased costs have made remote site computers (and databases) easily accessible, and networks of com-puters feasible. Since data integration and accessibility are key advantages of DBM, communications developments have served to enhance its effectiveness.

iii *Software developments* – if the full potential of the hardware is to be realised each user needs customised software. The most significant improvement for DBM in this area has been in database management systems (DBMS), which have become increasingly flexible and can also allow non-programmers to access and manipulate data. Because of this marketers can be closely involved in the DBM process which, in turn, may enhance marketing effectiveness.

iv   *Other technologies* – improvements in, for example, printing technol-ogy (where personalised mailshots and customised catalogues are now possible); and telephone communications have increased DBM's potential as an integrator of communications strategies, since the marketing database can greatly enhance their effectiveness.

Clearly then, technological development has not only made possible the practice of database marketing, but has also enhanced its original effectiveness and extended its range.

2 Marketing developments

These technological developments come at a time when several social and economic factors which support the adoption of database marketing have also been active. There would appear to be general agreement in the literature on the identifiable trends and their relevance to DBM.

The demassification of markets has led to the emergence of new distinct buying segments; DBM techniques can target these segments more effectively. Consumer markets have seen the decline of brand loyalty and the proliferation of new products. Together with the rise of the service economy, it has consequently become more important to establish relationships with customers in order to maintain their loyalty.

Indeed, Shaw and Stone (1988) point out that these trends have particularly affected corporate marketing. Often dominated by the idea of the Unique Selling Proposition, corporate marketing is now being forced to practise the small business philosophy of staying close to customers, understanding and meeting their needs and treating them well after the sale. A computerised customer database allows messages to be targeted at very specific segments of the market; customer responses are recorded and then taken into account in future campaigns. This is equally true in industrial markets, where buyers' increased expenditure has led them to be more discerning and seek information from a wider variety of sources.

There is a general agreement in the marketing press that marketing in the 1990s must emphasise the building of long-term relationships with customers. Indeed in the industrial marketing literature a whole new theory of relationship marketing has developed. Clearly database marketing techniques provide a means of putting this theory into practice.

At the same time, economic factors have conspired to promote the cause of DBM. The huge increase in television advertising costs have been followed by increases in the cost of other mass media such as television and the national press. In view of the clear trend towards market

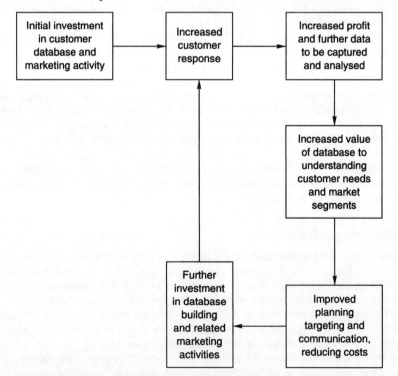

Figure 1 *The DBM cycle of investment and profit*

fragmentation, this means that while costs have risen, effectiveness has declined. Using DBM, however, more precise targeting allows more relevant information to be provided for many small segments of customers.

Brenda Sharp (1989) gives an example of DBM in use and argues that effective niche marketing has only been made possible through the use of computers, and believes that in the business-to-business marketplace database marketing is an absolute must if resources are not to be wasted.

Potential applications of DBM

Some of DBM's potential applications have already emerged in this discussion. However, before adopting DBM, a company must be able to assess specifically the ways in which it can use a computerised customer database. The main applications are summarised as follows and are divided into two broad categories: tactical applications and more long-term, strategic uses.

i Tactical applications

Companies can use DBM for many different purposes, although the typical tactical application might be in customer loyalty and care programmes, generating and qualifying sales leads, cross selling and price/promotion testing.

A relational database allows data capture of customer responses to a number of promotional activities on a number of variables. This allows segments of customers to be drawn together by whatever variable is seen as having relevance. After analysing the most suitable and potentially profitable customer profile for a particular product, the marketer can then pull out of the database a list of customers/prospects with the required characteristics. Promotional material can then be targeted specifically to the needs of the identified group of customers, reducing marketing costs while improving response rates.

The database allows tests on the effectiveness of different elements of the approach (product, medium, offer, target market), to be carried out quickly so that prompt corrective action can be taken. The activities of sales force, telemarketing, direct mail etc can be co-ordinated by DBM techniques which select the contact strategy most suitable for different groups of customers, allowing better matching of mix and customer.

Finally, since all customer contacts are recorded on the database, opportunities for repeat sales and cross-selling of other company products are maximised. In this way, customer loyalty may be built up over time. The diagram opposite indicates how DBM allows the original promotional investment to be recycled, achieving a closed loop of customer sales and loyalty as well as helping to define new customers more accurately.

ii Marketing strategy

The strategic implications of database marketing are often under-valued; however, marketers are gradually realising that 'building and maintaining relationships have significant long-term implications and therefore affect the strategic and long-range planning of the firm's marketing' (Evert Gummerson 1987). If, as generally agreed, DBM builds up long-term relationships, then these relationships will necessarily take time to evolve; they thus become central in strategic planning.

In addition to this however, DBM could itself be seen as a marketing planning resource for several reasons. Firstly, it generates a huge amount of market and customer data, thereby reducing the need for market research. Secondly, it allows campaigns to be designed to obtain the required information. At its most sophisticated, DBM has the potential to drive marketing policy.

The way in which information technology can be used to gain competitive advantage has been stressed by many authors and Porter's (1985) framework provides a useful guide for identifying competitive opportunity areas. DBM can be seen to be operating strategically if the information it holds is used to

- change the basis of competition
- strengthen customer relationships
- strengthen position with supplier
- build barriers to new entrants
- generate new or substitute products.

This is shown in Table 1.

1 Changing competitive basis

An example of how database marketing was used to change the basis of competition can be seen in the strategy followed by U.S. cigarette giants RJR Nabisco and Philip Morris Cos. In 1982 RJR began to build a large scale database of consumer behaviour, mailing 80 million questionnaires a year asking consumers about their purchasing habits and lifestyle. Careful testing showed RJR how to use the information to segment its market, to cross sell, and to gain 'conquest sales' – sales won from competitors. By 1986 their direct mail activity had increased to cover their entire product line and RJR knew exactly what was needed to attract different types of smokers. Rival Philip Morris was forced to counter-attack, using an innovative direct response advertisement which allowed consumers to send for two packs of an unnamed cigarette. The request card also asked for information on their present smoking habits, which was later followed by a mailing asking for their evaluation of the product and other information.

Two million smokers responded to the campaign which was repeated in 1988 at a cost of 15 million dollars. Both companies have continued to

Table 1 *The role of database marketing as a competitive tool*

Competitive opportunity	Marketing strategy	Role of information
1 Change competitive basis	Market development or penetration Increased effectiveness/Better margins Alternative sales channels Reducing cost structure	Prospect/customer information Targeted marketing Better control
2 Strengthen customer relationships	Tailored customer service Providing value to customer Product differentiation Create switching costs	Know customer needs 'Individual' promotions Response handling, identify potential needs Customers as 'users' of your systems
3 Strengthen buyer/supplier position	Superior market information Decreased cost of sales Providing value to supplier Pass stockholding onto supplier	Internal/external data capture Optimisation of sales channels Measure supplier performance Identify areas of inefficiency
4 Build barriers	Unique distribution channels Unique valued services Create entry costs	Knowledge of market allows improved service/value 'Lock in' customers, suppliers and intermediaries Immediate responses to threats
5 Generate new products	Market-led product development Alliance opportunities New products/services	Market gap analysis Customer dialogue, user-innovation Information as a product

build their databases but the nature of their strategy makes it difficult for either to track the other's actions, or estimate the marketing spend. Similar techniques have been used in the airline industry and financial services market with great success.

2 Customer relationship

A detailed knowledge of customers' needs and past purchasing habits helps a firm in building long term customer relationships ensuring customer loyalty and increasing the possibility of cross-selling. In 1988 De Vere Hotels (part of the Greenhall Whitley Group) recognised the benefits to be gained from DBM and developed a sophisticated marketing database in a move to create a structured customer communication programme.

While individual quality hotels already use information on regular customers to improve service De Vere took a more structured approach to the information held by its 30 hotels. By combining data the names and addresses of 30,000 individual active De Vere customers were obtained, plus by analysis of type of booking etc, the information to allow targeting by age, geographic area, lifestyle, leisure interests and previous usage. Club De Vere was then launched with the specific aim of both keeping existing customer relationships, increasing loyalty, and allowing the personalisation of services. The club is a communication channel by which members give details about themselves and their needs, as well as lifestyle and other information such as the type of incentives that would attract them. A telephone hot-line is planned so customers can enquire about special offers or suitable De Vere hotels. Computerised registration updates the database and allows revenue streams to be tracked. While developed as a strategic plan to deal with traditional dip periods in demand the database can be used also as a tactical weapon that can increase occupancy rates at any period, with very little lead-time. It is also possible to identify which of De Vere's customers are interested in other Greenhall Whitley offerings, such as wine and spirits, restaurants etc.

3 Supplier links

A similar approach can be applied to suppliers. By building up relationships, typically by improving information flows on stock requirements, delivery needs etc, the quality of supply can be improved and costs reduced. These benefits can be passed down the value chain in the form of improved value or benefits to the ultimate customers.

Channels of supply to the market can also be changed by the use of telesales, mail order etc. to reduce the costs associated with dealing with particular customer segments.

4 Barriers to market entry

Many industries are realising that a customer database can give a major competitive advantage over competitors who do not have such information. The ability to contact past, present and potential customers with personalised messages makes it simple to respond to a new competitor using traditional above-the-line advertising techniques. The newcomer must use a 'mass-market' approach with common appeals until the segmentation knowledge is gained, and even then the new entrant's cost per sale will be much higher than existing companies. The high costs for the attacking new entrant, always more than the cost of defending a position, will therefore remain high, even before considering the investment required in building an equivalent customer database. While the potential entrant is attempting this the defending firm is counter-attacking with spoiling tactics aimed at encouraging brand loyalty and reminding customers of the switching costs involved in changing supplier or brand.

Conversely, the knowledge held about a customer's life-style and needs may allow firms to jump industry barriers, such as with the sale of complementary services as banking, life and house insurance, mortgages, estate agent services etc.

5 *New products and services*

Products and services are seen increasingly as being augmented products, i.e. a bundle of tangible core and peripheral benefits of both a physical and psychological nature. For many products, such as cars, drink, perfume, etc., the image is often more important than the reality, and for others the services associated with the basic offering are the main differentiating feature. Information can frequently be built into the product offering to enhance its appeal, as with automatic teller machines which allow constant information on bank account details etc., or direct telephone banking and insurance services which offer immediate transactions. These services could not exist without a sophisticated database system, both in technological and customer information terms.

Overview of the current status of DBM in British industry

Juliet Williams of Christian Brann reflects the views of a growing section of the direct marketing world in describing the marketing database as 'a critical corporate asset' (*Direct Marketing* 28th June 1989). However, it is debatable how far this growing awareness of DBM has been translated into practice. Two measures are applied here in assessing the relative sophistication of DBM usage: firstly, the types of customer information held in the database and secondly, the sophistication of the overall marketing information system.

i *The sophistication of customer information*

The vital importance of customer and prospect records as a source of market research has been highlighted. Despite this most surveys have reported a low level of sophistication of customer information held within information systems. In an early study (Fletcher 1983) it was found that while the vast majority of systems could supply information about customers and sales, customer and competitive analysis was seldom reported as the reason. The development of sales targets being often the only use made of the data.

Doyle *et al* (1985) also report that a significant proportion of British companies were unclear about their customers' needs and while paying lip service to a customer orientation, only half of those interviewed could state with any degree of precision who their customers were, whereas fewer still understood how buying decisions were taken.

A recent Oasis survey (1989) of 193 companies indicated that although the types of information held on information systems varied, quantitative data was the most commonly possessed. 82% held information on value of sales; 74% on industry classification and 73% on product usage. The more qualitative kind of information was generally less common; 51% held demographic information and only 30% information on personal interests. However, it is this type of information which can help the vendor organisation to gain a more in-depth understanding of its marketplace. Relationships with customer companies – vital to industrial marketing – were also found to be given a relatively low priority. Information about purchase influences within the buying unit was held by only 57% of respondents.

Two further surveys appear to substantiate these findings. A survey carried out for Market Information Surveys found computerisation low in 'softer' data areas: Competition (32%), Prospects (52%), Client Service (46%); 'harder' data had been computerised to a greater extent; Sales records (75%), Client data (66%).

David M. Reid (1989), in a survey of 100 Scottish CEOs found 'pervasive low levels' of information pertaining to the interactive aspects of customer buyer behaviour.

Reid concludes that, while companies seem aware of the existence of their customers, 'there is little evidence that they form discriminating views of the customer types they are serving based on the selection of target customers'.

Several possible causes of these findings could be hazarded. Firstly, the computerisation of 'softer' data is more difficult and requires substantial

Table 2 *Percentage of companies having low to medium knowledge*

	Percentage
Customer characteristics	48%
Who takes buying decision	59%
Key influences on buying decision	77%
Why customer buys from them	79%

investment in new software and training. However, perhaps more significant is a continuing lack of understanding of the concept and applications of DBM. A Direct Response survey in 1988 made several interesting discoveries. Although 75% of companies said they used DBM, many did not know what the term meant! Companies were also found to be under-exploiting their current databases: although nearly all involved in DBM had a computer system which was able to store, sort and extract customer information, only 40% could perform any sophisticated analysis of marketing campaigns, and less than 50% kept information on *potential* customers. These findings are corroborated by another Direct Response survey in June 1988 which found that 54% of companies did not know and could not guess roughly at how much of their business was due to DM efforts. Since one of DBM's greatest assets is 'The ability to trace back the response to the original communication', then clearly DBM techniques are not being used effectively.

Although indications are of an increasing trend towards customer service and greater segmentation and targeting, the facts available clearly indicate that problems do exist in the adoption of DBM techniques.

ii *The sophistication of marketing information systems*

If DBM is seen as a specialised subset of the corporate information system, then problems in DBM adoption should be traced back to the computerisation of marketing information in the company as a whole.

The Fletcher (1983) study of top UK firms reported a low level of sophistication. While half the sample claimed to have marketing information systems, approximately 37% of these were extremely limited, capable only of simple arithmetic and statistical tasks and used for retrieval and monitoring of data for the development of sales targets. Fletcher commented that management still seem reluctant to use the new technology for a number of reasons, some of them rather suspect, and that a lack of market or customer orientation shown by some firms was a cause for concern.

The Oasis report seems to support these comments as it found that only a quarter of respondents expressed positive satisfaction with the performance of the systems which they currently used to manage their marketing information. One possible reason for this is the lack of integrated MkIS. Indeed, the Martech survey revealed that, while the majority of marketing functions have access to computerised data, less than 50% have any form of dedicated marketing information system designed to meet their specific requirements. The report concludes that much of the recent growth in marketing computerisation 'has been on fragmented, packaged productivity tools which have brought reasonable short-term benefits'. They are however 'no longer consistent with the clear trend towards integrated marketing systems with the ability to support operational and strategic decisions'.

Clearly, the natural evolution in systems strategy will be to adopt an efficient MkIS as an essential component of successful information management. In the face of increasing environmental pressures, many organisations do not seem to be moving along this path fast enough. As a result, they are failing to analyse and fully exploit available data.

Conclusion

It is likely that the present growth in direct marketing will continue which will encourage the use of DBM to improve the targeting and tactical application of mix elements. Equally, as computer hardware and software costs decline, more and more firms are likely to utilise computerised information systems at a strategic level.

The final element which is needed to ensure these enabling conditions to develop into a database marketing system, is a recognition of the importance of a market and customer orientation and the creation of a database marketing strategy.

DBM will soon become not a way of gaining competitive advantage but an essential element of business practice to be ignored at a firm's peril. If DBM is to be implemented effectively by marketers then research is required to identify the constraints upon its adoption and the necessary evolutionary stages which may exist. This will help the company identify the type and level of sophistication of customer information required so as to match it with the necessary technical and marketing skills necessary to exploit this knowledge.

References

Courtheoux, R., (1984) 'Database Techniques: How to tap a key company source' *Direct Marketing (USA)* vol. 47 pt 4, pp. 38–48.

Direct Response, (1987) 'The year of the database – or was it?' December pp. 36–38.

Doyle, P., Saunders, J. and Wong, V., (1985) 'A comparative Investigation of Japanese Marketing Strategies in the British Market' *Working Paper*: Bradford Management Centre.

Fletcher, K., (1983) 'Information Systems in British Industry' *Management Decision* vol. 21, no. 2, pp. 25–36.

Gummerson, E., (1987) 'The new marketing–Developing long-term interactive relationships' *Long Range Planning* vol. 20, no. 4, pp. 10–20.

Hawkes, P., (1988) Practical Database Planning, *Direct Response*, July 1988, p. 25.

Halsey, B., (1988) *'Marketing'* 6th October 1988, pp. 41–43.

Jenkinson, (1987) 'Is it database marketing or mailing list management?' *Direct Response* May, pp. 49–54.

Martech, (1989) *Marketing Information Systems* June, Martech Information Systems, London.

Oasis, (1989) *A Report on the Management of Information*: Organisation & System Innovations Ltd. in association with the Institute of Marketing.

Reid, D., (1989) 'Data Access and Issue Analysis in Strategic Planning' *Marketing Intelligence Planning* vol. 7, ½, pp. 14–18.

Roberts, M. and Berger, P., (1989) *Direct Marketing Management*, Prentice Hall.

Rapp, S., (1989) 'So what is Direct Marketing anyway' *Direct Response* July, p. 27.

Seaton, H., (1988) 'The Data Alliance' *Campaign* 22nd April 1988, pp. 57–59.

Sharp, B., (1989) 'Direct Marketing – the database' *Marketing Intelligence & Planning* vol. 7, ½, pp. 19–21.

Shaw, R. and Stone, M., (1988) Competitive Superiority through Database Marketing, *Long Range Planning*, vol. 21, no. 5, pp. 24–40.

Shaw, R. and Stone, M., (1988) *Database Marketing* Gower.

Stone, M. and Shaw, R., (1987) 'Database Marketing for Competitive Advantage *Long Range Planning* vol. 20, no. 2, pp. 12–20.

Reproduced from Fletcher, Keith, Wheeler, Colin and Wright, Julia (1990). The role and status of UK database marketing. *The Quarterly Review of Marketing*, Autumn, 7–14, by permission of The Chartered Institute of Marketing.

DESIGNING A CUSTOMER RETENTION PLAN
Glenn DeSouza

Glenn DeSouza is President of Strategic Quality Systems Inc., a consulting firm based in Belmount, Massachusetts. He is also a Visiting Assistant Professor at the University of Massachusetts at Boston.

This article emphasizes the need to develop a customer retention plan. It provides a simple four-step process to design a customer retention strategy, suggests a classification for 'type of defector' and emphasizes the need for benchmarking demonstrated best practice to identify ways to build switching costs and develop approaches to yield higher levels of customer retention.

Nothing may seem more obvious than the need to keep customers coming back. Yet, customer retention is either overlooked or devalued when it comes to strategy development. Any marketing manager can provide you with a market share estimate, but ask for the customer retention rate and you may well get a blank stare.

Buck Rodgers, who headed worldwide marketing for IBM as the company's sales grew from $10 billion to $50 billion, speaks forcefully about the importance of customer retention in his book, *The IBM Way*: 'It seems to me,' observes Rodgers, 'that most companies are a lot better at prospecting for new customers than maintaining their customer list. As far as I'm concerned, customer maintenance is imperative to doing business ... Someone once said I behaved as if every IBM customer were on the verge of leaving and that I'd do anything to keep them from bolting.'

It pays to be obsessive about retaining customers. A cost study of service companies by Bain & Co. found that customer retention has a more powerful effect on profits than market share, scale economies, and other variables that are commonly associated with competitive advantage. More specifically, Bain found that companies that reduce customer defections by 5% can boost profits from 25% to 85%.[1]

As customer retention goes up, marketing costs go down. Moreover, loyal customers frequently bring in new business. The role of the customer as salesperson is especially important in the case of complex products. Buying a telecommunications system that will be at the heart of a business is a major risk. Prospects are filled with worries: Will the dealer provide prompt service? Can the system be expanded later? Will the dealer go out of business? To get reliable answers, prospects tend to rely on friends and colleagues rather than on salespersons or brochures.

The true cost of losing a customer is the amount that person could have spent while involved in a business relationship with the company over a life-time. The bitter and enduring memories created by a bad buying experience are illustrated by the problems currently facing Detroit.

In 1980, according to a J.D. Power and Associates survey, the owners of General Motors, Ford, and Chrysler automobiles recorded three times the number of problems with cars 90 days out of the showroom than did owners of Japanese automobiles. By 1990, US manufacturers had trimmed the quality gap to 25%. Yet, during the same decade, the Japanese market share rose eight points.[2]

A plan to foil defectors

Here are four steps that a company should consider in designing a successful customer retention strategy. These steps integrate concepts from marketing and quality management and apply them to the challenge of keeping customers.

Measure customer retention

In sports, even in individual events like the long jump, it is essential to keep score. Without measurement, there is no impetus to do better, no records to break. It's the same in business. Nothing is real unless it gets measured.

If customer retention is not measured, it will not be managed. Fortunately, it is easy to calculate measures of customer retention, since only internal file data is required for the calculations.

The crude retention rate measures the absolute percentage of customers that are retained. If the number of customers drops from 500 to 475, the crude rate is 95%. The crude rate treats every customer loss as equivalent. The weighted retention rate resolves this problem by weighting customers by the amount they buy. If the 25 defecting customers had unit purchases that were double the average, the weighted rate is 90%.

If customers source from multiple vendors, high retention rates can mask a problem. For example, when an airline decided to split an order between Boeing 767s and Airbus Industrie A-300s, Boeing retained a customer, but on a shared basis. To reflect multiple sourcing, a customer penetration index must be calculated by evaluating whether sales to retained customers are growing as fast as market-unit sales. The differences reflect changes in customer penetration.

Interview former customers

Many companies write off customers who are definitely lost; this is a mistake. One can learn a great deal by talking to former customers, either directly or through a consultant. There is no need to guess why customers leave when you can ask them. The information they provide is likely to be more specific and actionable than usual market research.

Customers defect for various reasons, and not all of them are preventable. Some defections result from forces that are external to the business. Other defections can be prevented if corrective actions are taken or new strategies are adopted. Consider these six types of defectors.

- *Price defectors* are customers who switch to a low-priced competitor. For example, low price was the sole attraction of People Express, the discount airline started by Donald Burr in 1981. Passengers could fly between Boston and New York (Newark NJ, actually) for about half the fare charged on the Eastern shuttle. Bargains like this were compellingly attractive to tourists, students, and other discretionary travelers. By 1984, People had become the fastest-growing airline in the history of aviation.
- *Product defectors* are customers who switch to a competitor that offers a superior product. This type of defection can be irreversible. A customer who is lost because of price can be 'bought back', but it is almost impossible to get a customer back who has switched to a competitor that is perceived as offering a better product.
- *Service defectors* are customers who leave because of poor service. For example, within a few years, customers of People Express began to leave because of poor service, which included lost bags, scrambled reservations, overbooking, and delayed flights. The exodus accelerated once the major carriers used their computer systems to selectively match People's low prices (e.g., American Airlines offered an Ultimate Saver Fare).

By 1986, the party was over for People Express. Declining load factors and negative cash flows forced a sellout to Continental Airlines.

In an ironic footnote, Donald Burr was again working for his old boss, Frank Lorenzo, a man he had called Darth Vader.

- *Market defectors* are customers who are lost, but not to a competitor. The customer may go out of business or move out of the market area. During the early 1980s, for example, companies that sold equipment to oil drillers and explorers lost many of their customers when oil prices dropped sharply and customers filed for bankruptcy.
- *Technological defectors* are customers who convert to a product offered by companies from outside the industry. During the 1980s, Wang Lab's customers converted en masse from dedicated word processors to multipurpose personal computers. Wang could have prevented these defections, but only by embracing the new technology. Wang did eventually introduce a personal computer, but never marketed it with any seriousness. It was too little and too late.
- *Organizational defectors* are customers who are lost because of internal or external political considerations. For example, Boeing frequently runs into political problems when selling to state-owned airlines in the developing world. Boeing claims that many of these airlines buy Airbus equipment because they are told that the aid they receive from European governments may be contingent on their willingness to buy from Airbus.

Analyze complaint and service data

It is natural to regard complaints as a nuisance and an irritant – an unpleasant side effect of doing business. However, complaint data can be a gold mine for the analyst who wants to identify problems that cause customer defections. After all, for every customer who complains, there are possibly 10 others who did not voice their complaints. Listening and acting on these grievances can help retain not only the customers who complain, but, more important, those who did not.

The introduction of toll-free complaint lines has increased the amount of complaint data available for analysis. In 1977, Procter & Gamble became the first company to print a toll-free telephone number on all its packages. Doing this did not reduce the volume of mail P&G received, and the net result was an increase in the number of customer contacts. To enable a meaningful statistical analysis, complaints must be classified by problem, product model, product year, and dealer; the product's registration number should also be noted.

Complaint data must be statistically analyzed. The analysis must go beyond the computation of means and variances. Individual elements must be plotted to identify patterns in the data as well as elements that lie outside the normal expected range. Without statistical methods, attempts to improve a process are hit or miss.

As emphasized by W. Edwards Deming, most problems result from systemic factors such as faulty design, poor supervision, and machines out of order. Complaint analysis may reveal that a particular model or factory account for a disproportionate share of complaints. This indicates that the problem is systemic and can be eliminated by management action.

Some systemic problems can be eliminated by product redesign. For example, Polaroid has used complaint information to make its cameras easy to use. On an early model, Polaroid received thousands of calls about torn pictures; customers could not pull the film out without tearing the prints. In the next model, Polaroid built in an automatic ejection feature for the film.

Polaroid also received calls complaining that the camera did not work. When callers were asked if they had checked the battery, most replied that they did not know the camera contained a battery. To handle this problem, Polaroid decided to locate the battery in the film pack so that the battery was changed along with the pack.[3]

The need for complaint analysis has been recognized by the judges of the Malcolm Baldrige National Quality Award. Baldrige Award judges not only examine whether contestants resolve complaints promptly, but also how they analyze complaints and translate the findings into improvements.

Service data can be helpful in trying to understand why customers defect. In particular, if certain service problems keep recurring, this suggests that the cause is systemic. Some products, such as an automobile, need routine and emergency service if they are to operate at peak efficiency. For other products, service may be as simple as teaching customers how to use the product.

For example, software firms have set up pay-for-service lines where registered customers can receive advice on how to resolve a particular problem or perform a particular application. The callers are often sophisticated users of the software who have a problem that their colleagues are unable to answer. By analyzing the calls, a company can identify attractive new features or insert helpful suggestions into its user manual.

Service data differs from complaint data. The complainer is an aggrieved individual, with a problem that may be trivial or extreme. The person who needs service is a customer with a standard, technical problem that demands and gets actual attention. Because service data differs from complaint data, its analysis may offer new insights into systemic problems.

Complaint and service data is inherently useful; if such data is not being used, this suggests poor statistical analysis or reporting. Few companies use statistics effectively, a point made by Deming in his book *Quality, Productivity, and Competitive Position*. To quote him: 'No resource in any company is scarcer than statistical knowledge and ability. No source of knowledge can contribute more to quality, productivity, and competitive position.'

In the context of reporting complaint data, the most common mistake made is to prepare a single, multipurpose report. Senior managers will not read a thick report; they will find most of the information irrelevant.

A series of reports must be prepared and at least one of them should highlight possible, corrective actions.

Identify switching barriers

A company that limits itself to analyzing defections and complaints is backfilling – identifying problems that need to be corrected. But a good retention strategy must move beyond problem resolution. It should identify barriers that will prevent a customer from switching to a competitor, even one who is perceived as offering a better product at a lower price.

Lotus Development Corp., for example, sells against competitors that offer software that is cheaper and in some ways more technically advanced. Yet Lotus still dominates the market. There is a Lotus infrastructure consisting of millions of users, scores of applications and macros, and many special-purpose user groups. Hidden costs associated with a switch from Lotus far exceed the direct savings realized by buying the cheaper software.

To identify switching barriers, look outside your own industry for the best demonstrated practices. If you borrow a practice that is farthest afield from your own industry, your chances of surprising the competition are better. A borrowed practice will, of course, need to be modified to fit your customer's needs.

Electronic data interchange (EDI) is a technological example of a switching barrier. Department stores have traditionally been the most fickle of buyers. In the past, they would readily grant shelf space to a new vendor with a trendy look or a big price discount, but less so today.

Vendors with an EDI link enjoy a protected status. Under EDI, the store and vendor share data. The vendor can look at a terminal, see how many items have sold at the department store, and ship more product. The result is that the department store carries minimal inventory. The reward – a newfound loyalty to the vendor.

Strategic bundling can also create a barrier to defections. A bundle is a group of products or services offered as a single cost-saving and convenient package. A banking bundle, for example, includes checking and savings accounts, a credit card, a preapproved auto loan, and a special cash flow statement. A customer who buys a bundle is less likely to defect if someone offers a better deal on one of the items in the bundle.

Paradoxically, the ultimate barrier to competition may be a new twist on that old standby – account management. Many companies use the Willy Loman approach, where Willy deals with the buyer or some other middle manager. This relationship is placed in jeopardy if Willy moves on to greener pastures or alienates the contact at the account. In the new model, a team approach is used to forge a bond that lasts no matter which person on the sales force is the key contact in the relationship.

The account team may be headed by the CEO.[4] Typically, CEO efforts are limited to talking with fellow CEOs to forge companywide programs. But the involvement can go beyond the ceremonial.

At Xerox, CEO Paul Allaire personally handles six of the copier company's largest accounts. At Bose Corp., founder Amar Bose gets directly involved in opening markets. He visits Japan at least twice a year, which may explain in part why Bose is one of the largest sellers of high-performance loudspeakers in Japan.

Team account management is an all-hands-on proposition. Even the clerical staff should get involved. Nothing can be more frustrating to a customer than a conflict with an anonymous clerk at the billing or shipping department.

I recently surveyed two corporate subsidiaries, both of which were using identical service systems. Yet customers rated one subsidiary higher. The reason was the person who managed customer service at the better subsidiary. She had been with the company for 20 years and was on a first-name basis with customers, many of whom she had met at trade shows.

To companies that are financially strapped, installing a free terminal in a customer's office or sending a clerical supervisor to a trade show may seem like an unwarranted extravagance. However, creating switching barriers requires a willingness to spend, to experiment, and to break with industry tradition. To the extent that customer retention actually improves, the expenditures are a justifiable investment. There are few things that are more closely associated with superior business performance than a high rate of customer retention.

References

1 F.F. Reichheld and W.E. Sasser, Jr., 'Zero Defections: Quality Comes to Services.' *Harvard Business Review* (Sept.-Oct. 1990), p. 106.
2 'A New Era for Auto Quality.' *Business Week* (Oct. 22, (1990), p. 85.
3 J. Goodman, *Summary of White House Complaint Handling Study,* Technical Assistance Research Programs (Washington DC 1981), p. 12.
4 See 'Chief Executives Are Increasingly Chief Salesmen,' *Wall Street Journal* Aug. 6, 1991.

Index